SPSS for Psychologists

SPSS for Psychologists
A Guide to Data Analysis using SPSS for Windows

(Versions 8, 9 and 10)

NICOLA BRACE,
RICHARD KEMP
AND
ROSEMARY SNELGAR

palgrave

SPSS Screen Images © SPSS Inc.

SPSS is a registered trademark and the other product names are trademarks of SPSS Inc.
For information about SPSS contact:
SPSS UK Ltd, St Andrew's House, Woking, Surrey, UK, GU21 1EB
Tel: +44 1483 719200 Fax: +44 1483 719290 http:www.spss.com

Published 2000 by
PALGRAVE
Houndmills, Basingstoke, Hampshire RG21 6XS and
175 Fifth Avenue, New York, N. Y. 10010
Companies and representatives throughout the world

PALGRAVE is the new global academic imprint of
St. Martin's Press LLC Scholarly and Reference Division and
Palgrave Publishers Ltd (formerly Macmillan Press Ltd).

ISBN 0–333–73471–8

This book is printed on paper suitable for recycling and made from fully managed and sustained forest sources.

A catalogue record for this book is available from the British Library.

10   9   8   7   6   5   4
07 06 05 04 03 02 01

Printed and bound in Great Britain by
Antony Rowe Ltd, Chippenham, Wiltshire

Contents

Acknowledgements

We have been using SPSS in our own research for a long time, and have been teaching our students to use SPSS for almost as long. At least one of us can remember programming SPSS jobs using punch cards, and the first teaching materials we produced were for SPSS-PC. With each new group of students and each new version of SPSS we would write new materials and wonder whether we should write a book.

It is inevitable that a book with such a long gestation period will have been influenced by many people. We would like to take this opportunity to thank a few of these. In particular we would like to thank all of our students who have provided us with feedback on the materials we wrote for them. This feedback was invaluable because we could never predict how something would be interpreted. We remember the occasion when (using an old version of SPSS) a student encountered the message "Now Press Any Key to Continue" and asked us "But where is the 'Any' Key?" We would also like to thank those colleagues who used our materials and gave us feedback on them. In particular we would like to thank John Golding for his advice on some of our early materials. We would also like to acknowledge the input of Patrick Tissington. Patrick taught us to make our word processors do things that they really didn't want to do, and made us think carefully about the design of the book. We are also extremely grateful for the support that Graham Pike has given us. Not only was Graham willing to share his expert knowledge of SPSS, but he also allowed us to use his computer! Each of us would also like to acknowledge the influence of our own lecturers, supervisors, and helpful colleagues from our early days as lecturers.

Finally, we would like to thank Frances Arnold, Keith Povey and the rest of the team at the publishers for their extraordinary patience and good humour. We only hope that they think this book was worth the wait!

We hope that you will find this book and SPSS useful tools to support your research, and that they will enable you to become active participants in the discipline of psychology.

January 2000   Nicola Brace, Richard Kemp and Rosemary Snelgar

Chapter One

Introduction

How to use this book
Conducting psychological research
Data analysis
Working with SPSS
Starting SPSS
How to exit from SPSS

Section 1: How to use this book

This book is designed to help you analyse psychological data on your own. With the exception of the first few sections in this first chapter, we recommend that you read the book whilst sitting at a computer that is running SPSS. The book is divided into different chapters and within each chapter there are several sections. Chapters 1, 2 and 5 cover issues related to research design, data entry and data handling, whereas Chapters 3, 4, 6 and 7 explain how to undertake a variety of statistical procedures using SPSS. The order of the statistical tests covered in the book reflects the way in which many Psychology departments teach research methods and statistics. Chapter 8 provides additional information that you will find useful as an experienced user of SPSS.

Like all academic books, it is not necessary to read this book from cover to cover. In particular, if you are confident in your knowledge of statistics and research methods in psychology, then you may be able to skip straight to Section 4 of this chapter. If you have used previous versions of SPSS, then you may wish to proceed straight to the section covering the statistical test you wish to perform.

To provide you with an overview of the structure of this book, a summary of the material covered and the rationale underpinning each chapter is given below. Please note that we include a glossary at the end of the book, which may be of help should you come across a term that you do not understand.

Chapter 1

This first chapter provides a brief overview of the basic concepts and terminology used in psychological research and statistical analysis, and introduces SPSS. We describe some basic methods of data collection and the types of data that are collected in quantitative research. We then consider data analysis and provide you with an introduction to the windows and buttons you will use when analysing your data with SPSS. Finally, we show you how to start and exit SPSS.

Chapters 2 and 5

In Chapter 2, we show you how to create and save a data file and how to obtain some simple descriptive statistics. Chapter 5 also focuses on the data file, showing you how data can be manipulated and modified in SPSS. Although a novice user may not need to use these techniques, they are valuable for more sophisticated analyses and when analysing larger data files, especially those resulting from surveys.

Chapters 3, 4, 6 and 7

In Chapters 3 and 4, we cover inferential statistical tests that can be used to determine whether a difference or a relationship exists between two variables. In Chapters 6 and 7, we look at tests that are appropriate for more complex designs.

In general, each chapter covers a family of related tests, each of which is described in its own section. We introduce each statistical test with a brief description. This description is not intended to replace that which you will find in a statistics text; rather it is intended to act as a reminder of when and how to use the test. We also include an example of a typical or real piece of research that might be analysed using this test to give you a concrete example. We then give very detailed step-by-step instructions on how to perform the test using SPSS. In the earlier chapters, we include screen shots (pictures) and a full description of every step required to perform the test. In later chapters, we assume that you will have become a little more familiar with the workings of SPSS, and therefore summarise some of the more simple operations. Each chapter includes an annotated example of the output produced by SPSS to help you understand the results of your analyses. Finally, we include a note on how you should report the results of your analyses.

Chapter 8

This chapter is a little different. Here, we describe a range of procedures that our students have wanted to undertake, for example how to insert SPSS output into a text document. It is important to note that a full description of what SPSS can do is beyond any one book, but we show you here how to use the on-line help provided by SPSS, so that you can discover for yourself how to do something not covered in this book. For more experienced researchers, we also include some notes on the use of the Syntax Window.

The data we have used to demonstrate the statistical tests can be found in the Appendix of this book, or can be downloaded from the Macmillan Website (www.macmillan-press.co.uk/psychology/brace).

> **TIP**   In this book, in line with the policy of the British Psychological Society, we use the word *participants,* instead of *subjects,* to refer to the people who take part in studies. For statistical terms, however, the word subjects may be required: for example, matched-subjects or between-subjects designs.

Section 2: Conducting psychological research

As a science, much of psychological research is concerned with testing hypotheses as objectively as possible. As this book is about data analysis, the research that we are referring to is quantitative rather than qualitative. In this type of research, we are concerned with something that is observable (for example, reaction time) and that something must be measurable (for example, reaction time is measured in milliseconds). We may collect our data through observation, questionnaires or interviews. Alternatively, we may decide to carry out an experiment. We shall describe this method in more detail as the details of the experimental design affect how the data is entered and analysed using SPSS.

THE EXPERIMENTAL METHOD

A variable is something that may have different values at different times or for different participants: for example, reaction time, height, IQ. In most experiments we are interested in the effect of one variable on another variable: for example, the effect of marijuana on reaction time. The experimenter systematically manipulates the *independent variable*. Each value of the independent variable is called a *level*, and the levels of the independent variable are the experimental conditions. The *dependent variable* is that which is measured (the values of the dependent variable depend on the independent variable).

TIP   SPSS data files can handle much larger numbers of participants and variables than are included in the examples given in this book.

Experimentation is really a special form of observation. In other forms of observation, like the case study or observation in a natural setting, one simply looks at what has happened or is happening, and carefully records behaviour. The basic difference lies in the fact that in experimentation, the scientist is deliberately manipulating one variable (the independent variable), measuring another (the dependent variable) and aims to control all other variables so that they do not affect the outcome. In observation in the natural setting, all variables are free to vary, so we cannot be sure that changes in one particular variable occur as a result of changes in another variable. That is, in natural observation we cannot make statements about causation. In experimentation, by controlling all other variables (or as many as practically possible) we can reach a certain level of certainty that the

---

independent variable is the causative variable. That is, that the manipulation of the independent variable caused any change measured in the dependent variable.

Irrelevant and confounding variables

In an ideal experiment, all variables except the independent variable are held constant. There may be other factors, however, which affect the dependent variable: these are called *irrelevant variables*. It is impossible to hold all variables constant, and problems arise when irrelevant variables change systematically across conditions. In these situations, they are called *confounding variables*.

> **TIP**　SPSS will analyse the data you collect, but you need to evaluate what the results from the SPSS analysis mean and reflect on the possible effect of irrelevant and confounding variables.

Three basic experimental designs

Here we describe the three most commonly used basic experimental designs. Other designs are described in Chapters 4, 6 and 7 of this book.

1. **Repeated measures design**: each participant performs under both conditions of the experiment: thus, each participant acts as his or her own control. This, however, can introduce the confounding variable of *order effects*. To prevent an order effect systematically affecting the dependent variable we *counterbalance;* that is, half the participants perform condition A followed by condition B; and the other half perform condition B followed by condition A. Repeated measures should only be used if order effects are symmetrical.

> **TIP**　If you employ a repeated measures design you will enter at least two different data points for each participant in the SPSS data file.

2. **Matched subjects design**: imitates repeated measures without each participant doing both conditions. We would attempt to match participants on all the variables that might affect the dependent variable. A key problem facing researchers using this design is knowing which variables are important and should form the basis of the matching. Also, it requires a large pool of potential participants, in order to obtain a sample matched on all the important variables. One ideal group of participants for this design is monozygotic ("identical") twins, but, of course, they are rare.

3. **Independent groups design**: each participant takes part in one condition only. Participants should be divided on a strictly random basis, using tables of random numbers or a lottery. Independent groups design should really only be used if there is some reason why you cannot use repeated measures design.

Experimental design is aimed at preventing irrelevant variables from becoming confounding variables. There are two types of irrelevant variable:

1. *Participant variables:* IQ, hearing, age, motivation, etc. The effect of participant variables will depend on the design you employ
2. *Situational variables:* experimenter effect, lack of standardised instructions, testing conditions, etc.

DATA AND SCALES

We collect data when conducting quantitative research. Data are numbers that have some meaning – the numbers might represent age, sex, exam marks, height, volume or indeed almost anything. When we collect data, we use a *scale* of some sort. It is very important that we think very carefully about the types of scales we might use and the data that results from their use.

Nominal data

Nominal data are numbers where the number should not be taken to imply any more than a label (or a name, hence nominal): for example, we might have decided to code sex of participant in our file and have adopted the coding scheme 1 = Male, 0 = Female. Clearly we are not implying that men are **more** than women in any sense. Similarly, it would be a nonsense to calculate the mean sex of our participants.

> **TIP**   SPSS does not know about the level of measurement used to collect your data. It is up to you to make sure that you do not ask SPSS to perform any mathematical calculations on nominal data.

Ordinal data

These are numbers that can be ordered with some justification. For example, suppose your lecturer gave a class a statistics test and then ranked the scores. The student coming top will have a rank of 1, the next best student a rank of 2, and so on. The student receiving the rank of 1 was better than the student who received a rank of 2. Someone else seeing the ranks will not know, however, how much better one student is from another. It is possible that students who differ by one rank may differ by 1% or 30% in terms of their original test scores.

Interval data

Now we are getting on to numbers that are more number-like. With interval data we know that 3 is more than 2, and 4 is more than 3. Furthermore, we know that the interval between all points on the scale is the same; for example, the difference between 23 and 24 is the same as the difference between 102 and 103.

However, with interval data we do not know what zero represents. For example, IQ is meant to be a measure of intelligence, but a score of zero on an IQ test would not mean that the participant had no intelligence at all (but it might mean that they are dead!); rather that they had a very low intelligence. What we have to ask ourselves when deciding if a scale is interval is "does a value of zero mean there is absolutely none of the quantity I am measuring?". If the answer is no, then you probably have an interval scale.

The limitation of an interval scale is that you cannot legitimately calculate the ratios of two values. Suppose we cut the first inch of a tape measure so that the scale no longer had a true zero. If we used this to measure two objects, one 6 inches long and the other 13 inches long, we would record lengths of 7 inches and 14 inches respectively. We would conclude that one object was exactly twice as long as the other; in fact we know this is not the case. To be able to perform such calculations, we need **real** numbers – or what is called a *ratio* scale.

Ratio data

Ratio data are data collected from a ratio scale; that is a scale that has all the qualities of an interval scale with the additional quality of having a true zero.

When trying to decide if data are interval or ratio, students often ask the wrong question. You should **not** ask, "Will I ever observe a score of zero?" Instead, you should ask, "If a score of zero was observed, would it mean there was none of the quantity being measured?"

TIP   SPSS will do exactly what you tell it to. It does not know whether the numbers in the data file you typed in represent nominal, ordinal, interval or ratio data. In other words, if you ask SPSS to do something stupid, it will happily do it and give you a stupid answer. For example, it is quite possible to calculate the mean sex of your population – not a very meaningful thing to do! So it is up to you to ensure that you know what you are asking SPSS to do.

Section 3: Data analysis

WHY DO WE NEED STATISTICS?

Psychology is not like the pure sciences. A chemist, for example, knows that when s/he mixes sulphuric acid with magnesium then the result will be the same every time – every bit of magnesium will react with every bit of sulphuric acid in exactly the same way to give exactly the same result. Human beings, however, are such a complex interaction of emotions, motivations, learned behaviours and genetically determined behaviours, that we cannot even be sure that the same person will always behave in the same way. Psychologists therefore have to work with very "noisy" data to try to identify general principles that seem to be true for most people most of the time. It is for this reason that psychologists rely on statistical methods so heavily.

TWO TYPES OF STATISTICAL ANALYSIS

Frequently, we need to summarise large volumes of data to make them easy to comprehend. When we do this, it is very important that we ensure that the summary is an accurate reflection of the original data. This is one of the jobs of statistics. Secondly, we sometimes want to draw inferences from a large volume of data; for example we might want to learn whether there are differences between elderly and young people's ability to remember appointments. We also use statistical tests to answer this sort of question.

Statistics can be divided into two classes of operation:
1. **Descriptive Statistics:** These are procedures that we use to summarise large volume of data. Some descriptives are used in everyday language, for example, if you talk about "average pay" you are using a descriptive statistic.
2. **Inferential Statistics:** These are procedures that we use to draw inferences from the data we have collected. Inferential statistics allow us to mathematically answer questions of the type "is there a difference …?" or "is there a relationship …?".

CHOOSING THE CORRECT STATISTICAL TESTS

SPSS will not tell you which test you should use to analyse your data. Broadly speaking, you need to consider the design you employed, the number of variables you manipulated and/or measured, the type of data you collected and whether you wish to look for differences or relationships amongst your variables.

Descriptive statistics

Certain descriptive statistics are more appropriate than others for certain data; for example the mean and the standard deviation are calculated when the data are interval or ratio and normally distributed, whereas the median and the range may be more appropriate if the data are ordinal or *skewed*. For example, a few individuals receiving a very high salary can skew data so that the mean is not a good measure of average pay.

Inferential statistical tests

We need to undertake inferential statistics to determine the probability or likelihood that a conclusion based on the data we collect is valid. The problem we face in reaching such conclusions is that any difference or relationship detected might be present purely by chance. We collect data not from the entire population but from a sample that we hope is representative of the population, and we perform inferential tests to determine the confidence we can place in the results from this sample. SPSS will include in the output the p value for the particular analysis that we have undertaken. This p value is the probability that the difference or relationship apparent in the data is due to chance alone and does not reflect a real difference or relationship. Usually, we require this value to be less than 0.05 (5 in 100), for the finding to be considered significant.

> **TIP** To calculate the precise p value, SPSS may ask you to specify whether you are conducting a one-tailed or a two-tailed test; so you will need to think about whether the hypothesis you are testing is one- or two-tailed.

Parametric tests are inferential tests that have the virtue of being statistically powerful and able to handle data collected in complex designs. However, they "assume" first of all, that the data are collected using an interval or ratio scale; secondly that the data are normally distributed; and thirdly that the samples have equal variance. As you will see, SPSS may include in the output information indicating whether you have violated some of these assumptions. It is important to bear in mind that parametric tests involve in their calculation estimates of the mean. If your data are not normally distributed but are skewed, then, as stated above, the mean is not the best estimate of the average. Further, parametric tests involve the variance (or related measures of dispersion), leading to the requirement for equal variances. We advise you to obtain relevant descriptive statistics before analysing your data to get a feel of what your data look like.

There are many occasions in psychology when we collect data that do not satisfy all these requirements. *Nonparametric* tests are inferential tests that make very few assumptions about the data and in particular its distribution. However, they are less *powerful* than their parametric equivalents.

> **TIP** The term *power* has a specific meaning in statistics. A powerful test is one that can detect a small but real difference in the sample while still being able to reject non-real differences that might be apparent. The reduction in power is small (about 5%) but this might be the difference between a significant and non-significant outcome in some cases.

We include in this book the nonparametric equivalents of some of the tests. Strictly speaking, if the data are ordinal then nonparametric tests should be used. Even if data are interval or ratio, however, under circumstances such as extreme outliers going in the "wrong" direction, nonparametric tests are recommended. This is because they are based upon rankings of magnitudes and therefore the contribution of extreme values in terms of interval or ratio measures is greatly reduced compared to their effect in parametric statistical tests. Alternatively, you may consider screening your data and transforming them to remove the effects of outliers.

Finally, if all data are measured on nominal scales then a nonparametric test (such as chi-square) has to be used.

In the remaining sections of this chapter, we shall introduce you to SPSS so that you are ready to enter data in the next chapter.

Section 4: Working with SPSS

SPSS (originally Statistical Package for the Social Sciences) is an enormously powerful programme. Knowing how to use SPSS will allow you to perform a very wide range of statistical operations and, because the computer does all the calculations, you do not have to use formulae or carry out long operations on your calculator. This book is written using Versions 8, 9 and 10. These three versions are very similar, and we indicate any important differences. In addition, you should find this book useful if you are using Version 7 or 7.5. However, you will find that SPSS output is arranged differently in Version 6.

DATA ANALYSIS USING SPSS

There are three basic steps involved in data analysis using SPSS. Firstly, you must enter the raw data and save to a file. Secondly, you must select and specify the analysis you require. Thirdly, you must examine the output produced by SPSS. These steps are illustrated below. The special windows used by SPSS to undertake these steps are described next.

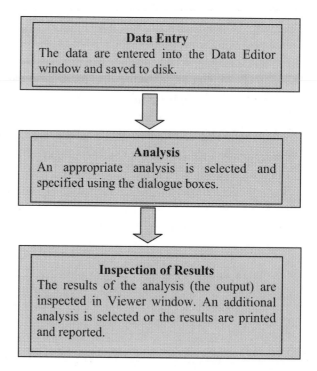

Data Entry
The data are entered into the Data Editor window and saved to disk.

Analysis
An appropriate analysis is selected and specified using the dialogue boxes.

Inspection of Results
The results of the analysis (the output) are inspected in Viewer window. An additional analysis is selected or the results are printed and reported.

THE DIFFERENT TYPES OF WINDOW USED IN SPSS

SPSS utilises several different window types. However, new users of SPSS only need to be familiar with two of these windows, the Data Editor window and the Viewer window. We will be using these two windows in this and the next chapter. The other window types are explained very briefly here and will be covered in more detail elsewhere in the book.

The Data Editor window

The Data Editor window (or data window) is the window you see when you start up SPSS. This spreadsheet-like window is used to enter all the data that is going to be analysed. You can think of this window as containing a table of all your raw data. We will examine this window in more detail when we start up SPSS.

The Viewer window

The Viewer window is used to display the results of your data analysis. For this reason we will sometimes refer to it as the Output window. We will examine this window in more detail when we perform our first simple analysis in the next chapter.

Other windows used in SPSS

1. The Syntax Editor window is used to edit special programme files called syntax files. The use of this window is explained in Chapter 8 and will only be of interest to more advanced users.
2. The Chart Editor window is used to edit standard (not interactive) charts or graphs. The use of this window is explained in Chapter 8.
3. The Pivot Table Editor window is used to edit the tables that SPSS uses to present the results of your analysis. The use of this window is explained in Chapter 8.
4. The Text Output Editor window is used to edit the text elements of the output shown in the Viewer window. The use of this window is described briefly in Chapter 8.
5. The Draft Viewer window is used to display the simple text output. This simple text output can be produced in place of the standard formatted output that is presented in the Viewer window. As it is unlikely that you will want simple text output, we have not described the use of this window.
6. The Script Editor window is used to write special programmes to control the execution of very large SPSS jobs. The use of scripts is not covered in this book.

Section 5: Starting SPSS

It is time to get started. Move the mouse pointer over the SPSS icon and double click on it (that is, press the left-hand mouse button twice in rapid succession). The mouse pointer will change to an hour glass, and then after a brief delay you will see the Data Editor window as shown below.

> **TIP**   If you do not have an SPSS icon on your desktop then click on the Start button at the bottom left hand corner of the screen, then select **Programs** and then either SPSS 8.0 for Windows, SPSS 9.0 for Windows or SPSS 10 for Windows.

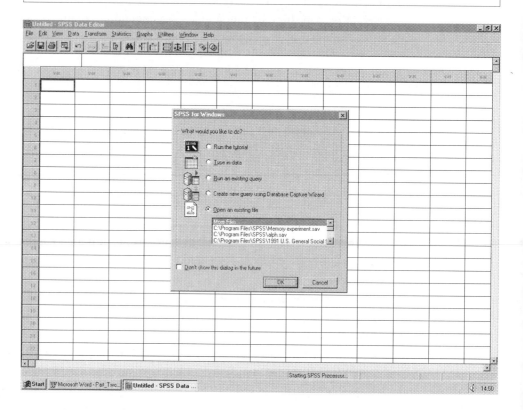

If SPSS opens in a much smaller window than that shown above, then click on the maximise button ▣ in the top right hand corner of the SPSS window. The image shown above is the opening screen for SPSS Version 8. In Versions 9 and 10, the menu item **Statistics** is replaced by **Analyze**. Users of Version 10 will also notice that the very bottom of the Data Editor window looks different from than shown above – this will be explained in Chapter 2.

Unless a previous user has switched it off, the box shown below will appear in the centre of the opening screen. This box is an example of a dialogue box. SPSS makes extensive use of dialogue boxes to allow you to control the programme.

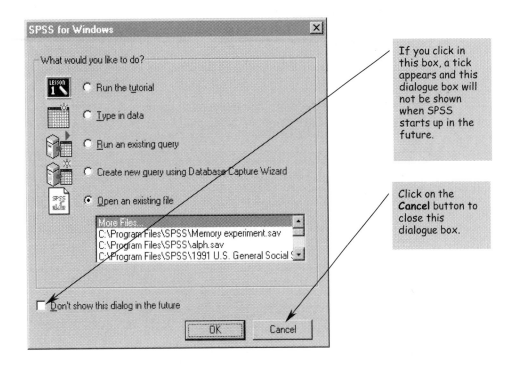

If you click in this box, a tick appears and this dialogue box will not be shown when SPSS starts up in the future.

Click on the **Cancel** button to close this dialogue box.

We are not going to use this dialogue box, so click on the **Cancel** button to close it. We will now examine the Data Editor window.

THE DATA EDITOR WINDOW

You should now be looking at the Data Editor window. The basic components of this window are labelled on the illustration below. The words across the top of the window are the menu items. One of the differences between SPSS Version 8 and SPSS Versions 9 and 10 is that in Versions 9 and 10 the menu item **Analyze** replaces the menu item **Statistics**. Below the menu items is the tool bar. This is a collection of special buttons that perform some of the most common operations. The scroll bars and buttons on the right hand side and bottom edge of the window allow you to move the window over the data table to view all your data. The text areas at the bottom of the window give you information regarding the current status of SPSS.

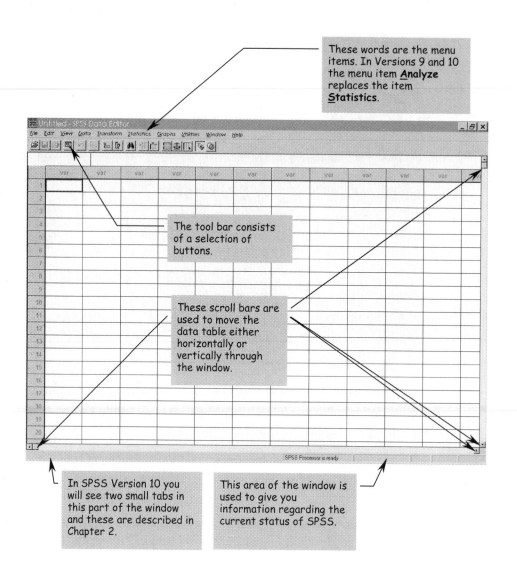

These words are the menu items. In Versions 9 and 10 the menu item **Analyze** replaces the item **Statistics**.

The tool bar consists of a selection of buttons.

These scroll bars are used to move the data table either horizontally or vertically through the window.

In SPSS Version 10 you will see two small tabs in this part of the window and these are described in Chapter 2.

This area of the window is used to give you information regarding the current status of SPSS.

The menu and tool bars from the Data Editor windows

The menu and toolbars from the Data Editor window of SPSS Version 8 and Versions 9 and 10 are shown below. The buttons duplicate functions that are also available from the menus. Some of the more useful buttons are explained below.

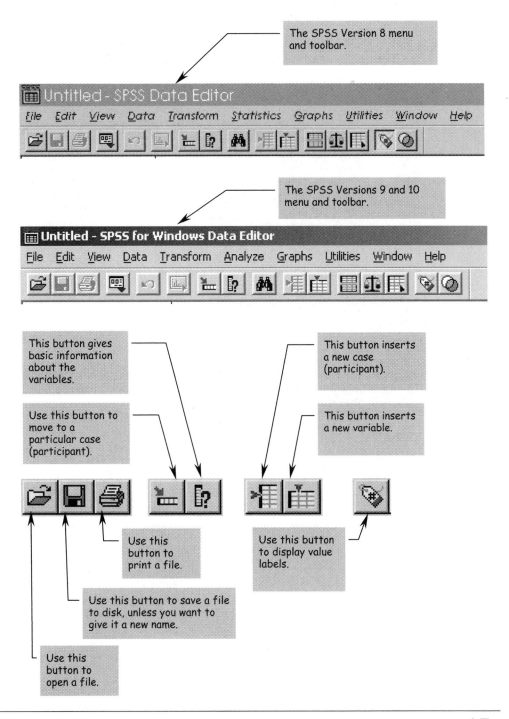

The SPSS Version 8 menu and toolbar.

The SPSS Versions 9 and 10 menu and toolbar.

This button gives basic information about the variables.

This button inserts a new case (participant).

Use this button to move to a particular case (participant).

This button inserts a new variable.

Use this button to print a file.

Use this button to display value labels.

Use this button to save a file to disk, unless you want to give it a new name.

Use this button to open a file.

Section 6: How to exit from SPSS

When you have finished working in SPSS you must exit the programme. Do this in the following way:

1. Click on the word **File** at the top of the screen (see below).
2. Click on the word **Exit** from the pull-down menu (list of options) presented.

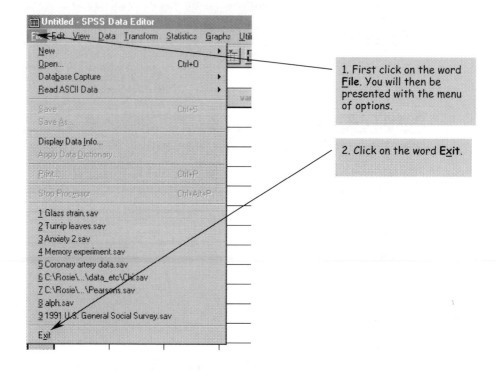

1. First click on the word **File**. You will then be presented with the menu of options.

2. Click on the word **Exit**.

3a. If you have made any changes to either the Data Editor window or the output Viewer window since you last saved these files, then SPSS will display a Dialogue box asking you if you want to save these files before you exit from SPSS (see below). Click on the **Yes** button to resave the file and then exit SPSS.

3b. If you do not want to save your changes, click on the **No** button to exit without saving.

3c. If you want to abort the Exit, perhaps to allow you to save the file under a different name, click on the **Cancel** button.

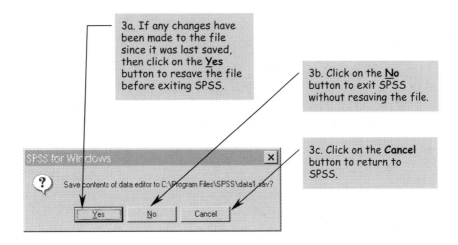

We have now shown you how to get into and out of SPSS. In the next chapter, we show you how to enter your data and obtain descriptive statistics.

Chapter Two

Data entry in SPSS

The Data Editor window
Defining a variable in SPSS Versions 8 and 9
Defining a variable in SPSS Version 10
Entering data
Saving a data file
Opening a data file
Data entry exercises
Answers to data entry exercises
Summary descriptive statistics and the Viewer window

Section 1: The Data Editor window

When you start SPSS, the Data Editor window is the active window. We are going to use this window to record all the data we want to analyse. The window is arranged as a table with a large number of cells in rows and columns. If you have previously used a spreadsheet programme then it should look familiar. In effect this window is a special sort of spreadsheet.

The table can be very large, and only small part of it can be seen through the Data Editor window any one time. You can use the scroll bars on the edges of the window to move round the table. Make sure that you are positioned at the beginning of the table – the top left hand corner

In Psychology, we almost always enter data in the same way. Each *participant* normally occupies a *row* of the table whereas each *variable* (each thing about which we have recorded information from the participants) occupies a *column* of the table. You can think of the row numbers down the left-hand side of the table as the participant numbers (SPSS refers to these as *case numbers*).

> **TIP** Normally each row represents an individual participant and each column represents a variable.

THE ARRANGEMENT OF THE DATA IN THE DATA EDITOR WINDOW

The precise way that the data is entered in the Data Editor window is critical and will depend, in part on the details of your study. If you are entering data from an experiment, then you need to consider the design employed. In an independent groups design, each participant will provide one measure of performance. In addition, you will need to indicate which of your experimental groups each participant was assigned to. Thus, the most basic independent groups design will require that you use one column of your data table to record which group your participant was in, and a second column to record that participant's score. By comparison, in a repeated measures design each participant's performance will be assessed (at least) twice. Thus you will have a measure of performance under one set of conditions and a second measure of performance under different conditions. You will therefore need to use two columns of your data table to record these two performance levels.

> **TIP**   In SPSS, the word "variable" means a column in the data table; it does not have the same meaning as it does in experimental design. For example, in a repeated measures design there is one dependent variable that is recorded across two columns of the data table.

Before you can enter any values you must first set up the Data window. That is, you need to tell SPSS what you are going to call each variable (i.e. you must give a name to each column in the table) and what sort of values you are going to put into that column. One of the changes introduced with Version 10 of SPSS is designed to make this process slightly easier. For this reason, in the following sections of this chapter, we have provided separate instructions for users of Versions 8/9 and Version 10.

Users of SPSS Versions 8 and 9 (or earlier versions) should:
1. Read Section 2
2. Skip Section 3
3. Continue reading from Section 4.

Users of SPSS Version 10 should:
1. Skip Section 2
2. Go straight to Section 3
3. Continue reading from Section 3.

All other sections of this book cover Versions 8, 9 and 10.

Section 2: Defining a variable in SPSS Versions 8 and 9

If you are using SPSS Version 10, skip this section and go straight to Section 3.

Before you can enter your data, the Data Editor window must be set up so that it is ready to receive your data. SPSS needs to know the name of each of your variables so that these names can be inserted at the top of the columns of the data table. In addition, you need to give SPSS other important information about each of your variables. This process of defining the variables is described below

THE DEFINE VARIABLE DIALOGUE BOX

Double-click on the grey header (which will probably be labelled **var**) at the top of the column you wish to define (see below). SPSS will present you with the **Define Variable** dialogue box containing information about this column.

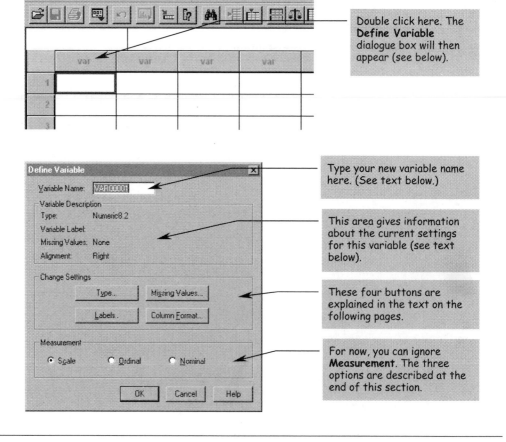

Double click here. The **Define Variable** dialogue box will then appear (see below).

Type your new variable name here. (See text below.)

This area gives information about the current settings for this variable (see text below).

These four buttons are explained in the text on the following pages.

For now, you can ignore **Measurement**. The three options are described at the end of this section.

Variable name

The first thing you need to do is to give the variable a meaningful name. At the moment the box labelled **Variable Name** will probably contain the default variable name VAR00001. If you start typing a new variable name, the default name will disappear and be replaced by your new name. You should choose a variable name that makes sense to you and you are not likely to forget. Students often use the variable name "score". This is not a good choice as it tells us almost nothing about the variable. Examples of more useful variable names might include "memscore" (for participants' scores in a memory experiment), "introver" (a participant's introversion score), "sex" or "famfaces" (the number of famous faces named by a participant). Variable names must not be more than 8 characters long, and must start with a letter of the alphabet (i.e., not a number). Variable names cannot contain spaces or any special characters such as full stops, colons, hyphens or commas (the @, # $ and _ characters are allowed). If you enter an invalid variable name SPSS will warn you later.

> **TIP** The underline character (_) can be used in place of spaces in variable names. For example the name "Q1_1" might be used for the scores from Question 1 Part 1.

CHANGE SETTINGS

In the **Define Variable** dialogue box (shown on the previous page) there are four buttons labelled **Type**, **Labels**, **Missing Values**, and **Column Format**. Clicking on these buttons allows you to change some of the characteristics of the variable. We will now describe each of these buttons in turn.

The type button

From the **Define Variable** dialogue box, click on the **Type** button. You will be presented with a new dialogue box titled **Define Variable Type** (see below). This allows you to select whether your data is in the form of numbers (**Numeric**) or letters (**String**), or one of a number of other formats. We strongly recommend that, until you are an experienced user, you only use numeric variables. It is very easy to use numbers to represent strings and will save you trouble later (e.g., you can use the numbers 1 and 2 rather than "m" and "f" to record the sex of your participants). You are unlikely to need to use any of the other variable types.

> **TIP** If at all possible avoid using string variables in SPSS – if you ignore this advice you will regret it later!

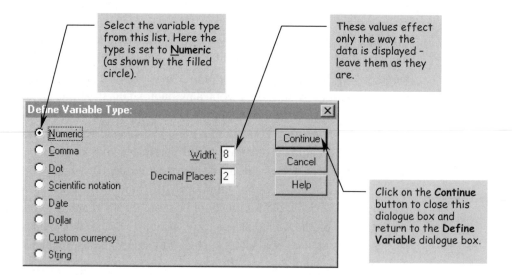

Select the variable type from this list. Here the type is set to **Numeric** (as shown by the filled circle).

These values effect only the way the data is displayed – leave them as they are.

Click on the **Continue** button to close this dialogue box and return to the **Define Variable** dialogue box.

This dialogue box also allows you to set the **Width** of the variable. This is the number of characters before and after the decimal place used to display the variable in the Data Editor and output Viewer windows. This setting does not affect the way the value is stored or the number of decimal places used in statistical calculations. With numeric data the default settings are for a total **Width** of 8 with 2 **Decimal Places** (e.g., 12345.78). If you attempt to input a data value that will not fit into this width, then SPSS will round it in order to display the value. However, the value you entered is stored by SPSS and used in all calculations. One effect of this is that unless you set **Decimal Places** to zero, all values, even integers (whole numbers without decimal places), will be displayed with 2 decimal places. Thus if you enter a value of "2" in the Data Editor window SPSS will display "2.00". This might look a little untidy, but is of no consequence and it is probably not worth altering these settings to stop this happening.

TIP   You can probably leave all the variable type settings at their default values.

You can now click on the **Continue** button on the right hand side of the dialogue box. This will close the **Define Variable Type** dialogue box and return you to the **Define Variable** dialogue box.

The labels button

From the **Define Variable** dialogue box, click on the **Labels** button. You will be presented with the **Define Labels** dialogue box (see below). This dialogue box gives you the opportunity to attach two types of label to a variable: variable labels and value labels.

TIP Both variable labels and value labels are printed on the output produced by SPSS. Although they are not essential, they act as a reminder about the variables and can be very helpful when you are interpreting the output. We recommend you take the time to use them whenever appropriate.

A **Variable Label** is simply a phrase that is associated with the variable name and which helps you to remember what data this variable contains. This label is useful because the variable name itself is limited to 8 characters. If you have called a variable something like "sex", then you probably do not need to be reminded about what it is describing. If, however, you have a large number of variables, then variable labels can be very useful. For example, if you are entering the data from a questionnaire, you might have a variable named "q3relbef". In this case a variable label might be invaluable, as it could remind you that this variable coded the responses to question 3 on your questionnaire which asked about religious belief. You can type in any phrase using any characters that you like, but it is best to keep it fairly short. SPSS will not try to interpret this label; it will simply insert it into the output next to the appropriate variable name when you perform any analysis.

To add a variable label, type it in to the box marked **Variable Label**.

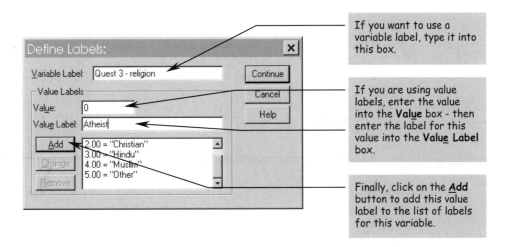

A **Value Label** is a label assigned to a particular value of a variable. You are most likely to use value labels for nominal or categorical variables. For example, we might want to use labels to remind ourselves that, when entering values for the religion of our respondents, we used the codes: 1 = Buddhist; 2 = Christian; 3 = Hindu; 4 = Muslim; 5 = Other; 0 = Atheist.

A second use for value labels is with a grouping or independent variable. For example, you might want to compare the reaction time of participants who were tested under one of several different doses of alcohol. You could use a value label to remind yourself that group 1 received no alcohol, group 2 received 1 unit of alcohol and group 3, 2 units. Value labels will be inserted into the SPSS output to remind you what these values mean.

To add value labels click on the box marked **Value** and enter the first value you have used (for example, 1). Then click on the box marked **Value Label** and enter the phrase that describes what this value means (for example, Buddhist). Now click on the **Add** button. This will add the line 1 = "Buddhist" to the box at the bottom of the **Define Labels** dialogue box. Now enter the second value (e.g. 2) and the appropriate label (e.g. Christian) and again click **Add**. Continue like this until you have added labels for each value of the variable that you are defining.

When you are happy with all your label settings, click on the **Continue** button to return to the **Define Variable** dialogue box.

Do not forget to click the **Add** button after typing the last label. If you do, SPSS will warn that "Any pending add or change operations will be lost" when you click on the **Continue** button.

TIP   It would not be appropriate to add value labels to some variables. For example, you would not want to add a label to every possible value of a continuous variable such as reaction time. A good rule-of-thumb is that you should add value labels to all nominal variables and should consider adding them to ordinal variables. They will probably not be needed for interval or ratio variables.

The missing values button

Sometimes you will not have a complete set of data. For example, some participants might decline to tell you their religion or their age, or you might lose or be unable to collect data from some participants (for example as the result of equipment failure). These gaps in the data table are known as missing values.

When we have a missing value we need to be able to tell SPSS that we do not have valid data for this participant on this variable. We do this by choosing a value that cannot normally occur for this variable. In the religion example above, we might choose to code religion as 9 when the participant does not state their religion. Thus, 9 is the missing value for the variable religion. The missing value can be different for each variable. For age it could be 99 (unless you are testing very old people).

To specify a missing value click on the **Missing Values** button in the **Define Variable** dialogue box. The **Define Missing Values** dialogue box will appear (see below).

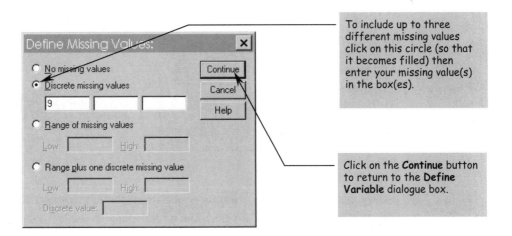

To include up to three different missing values click on this circle (so that it becomes filled) then enter your missing value(s) in the box(es).

Click on the **Continue** button to return to the **Define Variable** dialogue box.

SPSS allows you to specify the missing values in several ways:

1. **No missing values**: This is the default setting for this dialogue box. If this option is selected, SPSS will treat all values for this variable as valid.
2. **Discrete missing values**: This option allows you to enter up to three discrete values. For example, 7, 9 and 11 could all be set as missing values by selecting this option and entering the values in the three boxes. If you have only one missing value enter it into the first of the three boxes.
3. **Range of missing values**: This option allows you to indicate that a range of values is being used as missing values. For example, selecting this option and entering the values 7 and 11 in the **Low** and **High** value boxes would instruct SPSS to treat the values 7, 8, 9, 10 and 11 as missing values.
4. **Range plus one discrete missing value**: This option allows you to set a range of values plus one additional value as missing (for example 7–11 plus 0).

In practice we rarely need more than one missing value for a variable (occasionally you might want more than one – for example you might wish to distinguish between an unanswered question and an illegible answer as both are missing values). You will therefore almost always want to enter your missing value into the first of the **Discrete missing values** boxes. To do this, simply click on the circle next to the words **Discrete missing values** and then enter your missing value into the first of the three boxes. Now click on the **Continue** button to return you to the **Define Variable** dialogue box.

The column format button

From the **Define Variable** dialogue box, click on the **Column Format** button to bring up the **Define Column Format** dialogue box (see below).

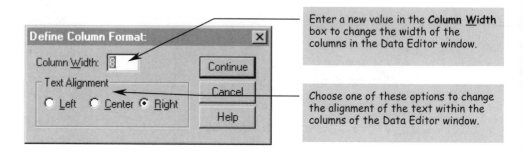

Enter a new value in the **Column Width** box to change the width of the columns in the Data Editor window.

Choose one of these options to change the alignment of the text within the columns of the Data Editor window.

The column format specification does not affect the data values. It only affects the width of the column and the position of the data in the cell in the Data Editor window. You can therefore leave these settings as they are unless you want to change the appearance of the data window. You may, for example, want to fit more columns onto the screen in order to see more variables without having to scroll. In this case you could reduce the width of each column.

When you have finished adjusting the column format settings press the **Continue** button to return to the **Define Variable** dialogue box.

> **TIP**   Be careful when changing column widths – you might think that you only need a column width of 1 for a variable that contains numbers in the range 0–9. However, if the column width is set too small, the variable name that appears at the top of the column will not be legible. A good compromise, if you really need to change column widths, is to set the width equal to no less than the number of characters in the variable name (e.g. a column width of 3 for the variable "sex").

Completing the variable definition

When you have made the changes you require to the variable name, type, labels, missing values and column format, you will notice that the new settings are reflected in the information displayed in the **Define Variable** dialogue box (see below). This acts as a useful note of the settings for each variable.

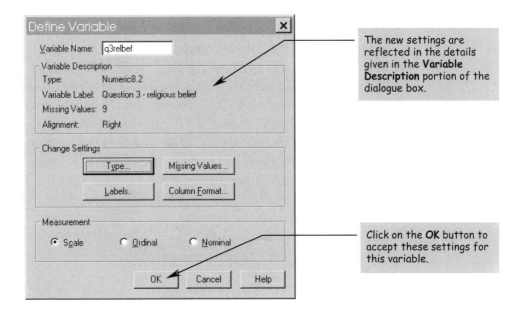

The new settings are reflected in the details given in the **Variable Description** portion of the dialogue box.

Click on the **OK** button to accept these settings for this variable.

Click on the **OK** button to accept this variable definition. After a short delay you will see the name of your new variable appear at the top of the appropriate column of the Data Editor window (see below). If you have made an error or if you want to change anything, simply double click on the variable name and adjust the setting.

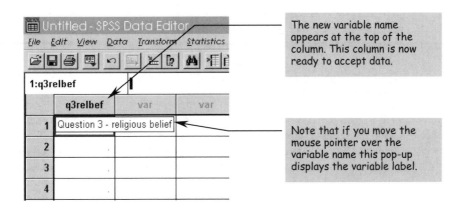

The new variable name appears at the top of the column. This column is now ready to accept data.

Note that if you move the mouse pointer over the variable name this pop-up displays the variable label.

You must now repeat this process for each of the variables in your data files. Once all the variables are defined you are ready to enter your data.

> **TIP**   Remember, for most variables you can accept the default settings. In practice all you need to do is to enter a variable name and, if appropriate, add variable and value labels.

A NOTE ON THE DEFINE VARIABLE DIALOGUE BOX

At the bottom of the **Define Variable** dialogue box there is a box titled **Measurement** that contains three options, **Scale**, **Ordinal** and **Nominal**. These options are used to indicate the level of measurement of the variable. Psychologists usually distinguish four levels of measurement, Nominal, Ordinal, Interval and Ratio (see Chapter 1). SPSS does not distinguish between Interval and Ratio data and uses the term **Scale** to cover a variable measured using either of these levels of measurement. It is not essential to set the measurement option as it is only used in the creation of Interactive Charts (see Chapter 8).

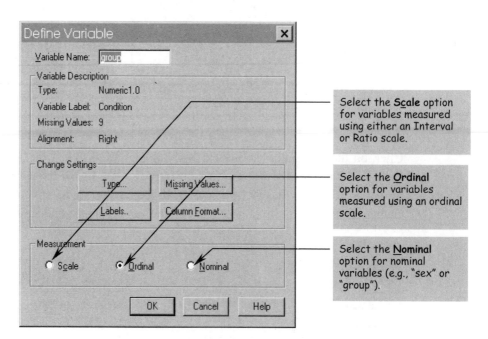

Select the **Scale** option for variables measured using either an Interval or Ratio scale.

Select the **Ordinal** option for variables measured using an ordinal scale.

Select the **Nominal** option for nominal variables (e.g., "sex" or "group").

> **TIP**   You can usually leave the measurement option at its default setting. If you open a data file created using an earlier version of SPSS, the option will be set for you – variables with value labels will be set as **Nominal**, while variables with only a small number of values will be set as **Ordinal**. All other variables will be set as **Scale**.

Section 3: Defining a variable in SPSS Version 10

If you are using SPSS Version 8 or 9 (or an earlier version) this section is not relevant to you. Skip this section and go straight to Section 4.

THE DATA VIEW AND VARIABLE VIEW

If you look at the bottom left hand corner of the Data Editor window you will notice two "tabs". One tab is labelled "Data View" and the other is labelled "Variable View". You can think of these as the index tabs for two different pages of information. When you first enter the Data Editor window the Data View tab will be selected and you will be looking at the empty data table. If you click on the Variable View tab the second screen of information will be displayed. These two different views are illustrated on the next page.

The Data View is the screen you will use when entering your data into SPSS. At present this view shows an empty data table in which each of the variables (columns) is labelled "var". Before you can type your data into this data table you must set it up so that it is ready to receive your data. SPSS needs to know the name of each of your variables so that these names can be inserted at the top of the columns of the data table. In addition, you need to give SPSS other important information about each of your variables. This process of defining the variables is undertaken in the Variable View. If you click on the Variable View tab you will notice that in this view the columns are headed **Name**, **Type**, **Width**, **Decimals** etc. In the Variable View of the data table the Variables are arranged down the side of the table and each column gives information about a variable. For example, in the column headed **Name** we are going to type the name of each variable, in the **Type** column we are going to going to tell SPSS what type of variable this is, and so on.

> **TIP** As explained earlier, in SPSS each row of the data table represents data from one case and each column contains data from one variable. However, in the Variable View of the Data Editor window, the columns and rows are used differently. In this view each row gives information about one variable. Don't let this confuse you – remember once you have set up all your variables and are ready to enter your data, you will return to the Data View where a row is a case (usually a participant) and a column is a variable.

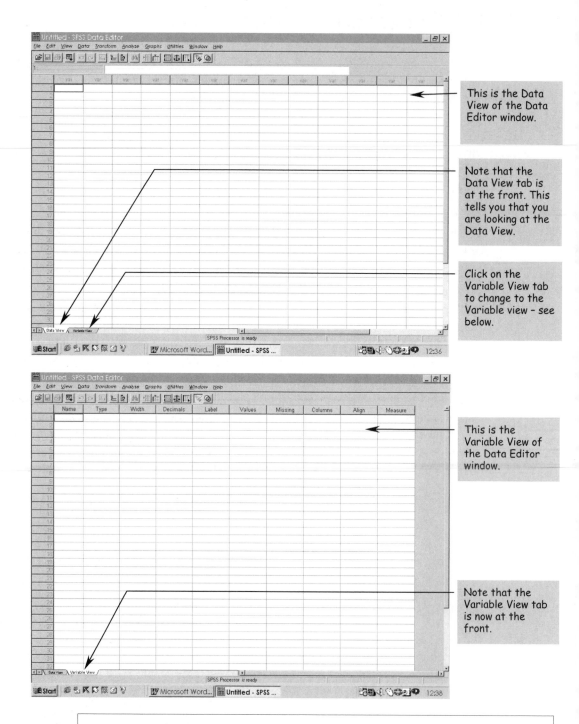

This is the Data View of the Data Editor window.

Note that the Data View tab is at the front. This tells you that you are looking at the Data View.

Click on the Variable View tab to change to the Variable view – see below.

This is the Variable View of the Data Editor window.

Note that the Variable View tab is now at the front.

TIP   Henceforth, when we refer to "the Data Editor window" without specifying which view, we will be referring to the Data View.

SETTING UP YOUR VARIABLES

If you are not already in the Variable View of the Data Editor, click on the Variable View tab to switch to that view. We will now use this view to set up each of the variables we need.

> **TIP**   An alternative way to switch from the Data View to the Variable View is to double click on the grey header (which will probably be labelled **var**) at the top of the column you wish to define. This will take you to the appropriate row of the Variable View.

Variable name

The first thing we need to do is to give the variable a meaningful name. Type the name of your first variable into the first row of the **Name** column. You should choose a variable name that makes sense to you and you are not likely to forget. Students often use the variable name "score". This is not a good choice as it tells us almost nothing about the variable. Examples of more useful variable names might include "memscore" (for participants' scores in a memory experiment), "introver" (a participant's introversion score), "sex" or "famfaces" (the number of famous faces named by a participant). Variable names must not be more than 8 characters long, and must start with a letter of the alphabet (i.e. not a number). Variable names cannot contain spaces or any special characters such as full stops, colons, hyphens or commas (the @, # $ and _ characters are allowed). If you enter an invalid variable name SPSS will warn you when you try to move from the **Name** column.

> **TIP**   The underline character (_) can be used in place of spaces in variable names. For example the name "Q1_1" might be used for the scores from Question 1 Part 1.

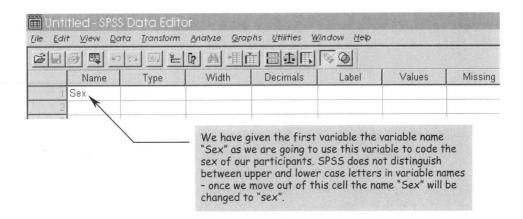

We have given the first variable the variable name "Sex" as we are going to use this variable to code the sex of our participants. SPSS does not distinguish between upper and lower case letters in variable names – once we move out of this cell the name "Sex" will be changed to "sex".

Once you have entered the variable name, use either the mouse (point and click) or the tab key to move to the next column of the table. As you move the cursor, several of the other columns of the table will be filled with either words or numbers. These are the default settings for the variable "sex". You can leave these settings as they are, or you can change some or all of them before moving on to define your next variable. Below we explain each of the settings and how to adjust them.

Variable type

The second column in the Variable View table is headed **Type**. SPSS can have handle variables of several different types. For example, variables can be numeric (containing numbers) or string (containing letters) or even dates. The **Type** column is used to indicate what type each variable is. The **Type** will now be set to **Numeric** (unless the default settings have been changed on your copy of SPSS). If you want to change the variable type, move to the **Type** column and click on the button that appears next to the default setting This will call up the **Define Variable Type** dialogue box (see below).

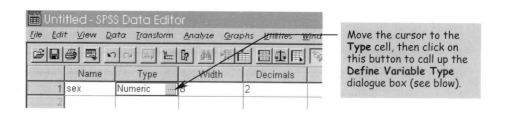

Move the cursor to the **Type** cell, then click on this button to call up the **Define Variable Type** dialogue box (see blow).

Select the variable type from this list. Here the type is set to **Numeric** (as shown by the filled circle).

These values effect only the way the data is displayed – leave them as they are.

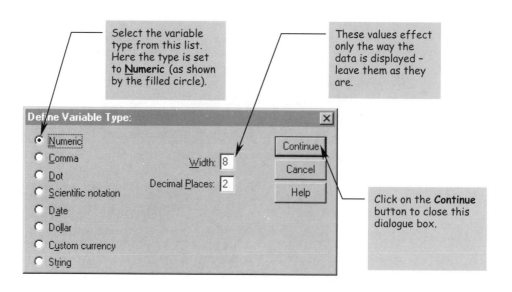

Click on the **Continue** button to close this dialogue box.

We strongly recommend that, until you are an experienced user, you only use numeric variables. It is very easy to use numbers to represent strings and this will save you trouble later (e.g., you can use the numbers 1 and 2 rather than "m" and "f" to record the sex of your participants). You are unlikely to need to use any of the other variable types.

| TIP | If at all possible avoid using string variables in SPSS – if you ignore this advice you will regret it later! |

Variable width and decimal places

The **Define Variable Type** dialogue box also allows you to set the **Width** and **Decimal Places** of the variable (see above). Alternatively, these settings can be changed in the third and fourth columns of the Variable View (see below).

These settings adjust the number of characters before and after the decimal place used to display the variable in the Data Editor and Output Viewer windows. These settings do not affect the way the value is stored or the number of decimal places used in statistical calculations. With numeric data the default settings are for a total **Width** of 8 with 2 **Decimal Places** (e.g. 12345.78). If you attempt to input a data value that will not fit into this width, then SPSS will round it in order to display the value. However, the value you entered is stored by SPSS and used in all calculations. One effect of this is that unless you set **Decimal Places** to zero, all values, even integers (whole numbers without decimal places) will be displayed with 2 decimal places. Thus if you enter a value of "2" in the Data Editor window, SPSS will display "2.00". This might look a little untidy, but is of no consequence and it is probably not worth altering these settings to stop this happening.

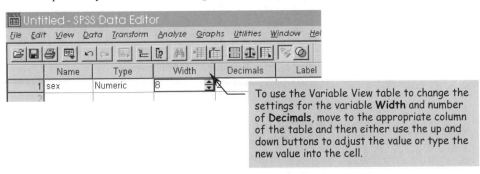

To use the Variable View table to change the settings for the variable **Width** and number of **Decimals**, move to the appropriate column of the table and then either use the up and down buttons to adjust the value or type the new value into the cell.

| TIP | You can probably leave the variable **Type**, **Width** and **Decimals** settings at their default values. |

Variable label

The fifth column in the Variable View table is headed **Label**. This column is used to enter a variable label.

A variable label is simply a phrase that is associated with the variable name and which helps you to remember what data this variable contains. This label is useful because the variable name itself is limited to 8 characters. If you have called a variable something like "sex", then you probably do not need to be reminded about what it is describing. If, however, you have a large number of variables, then variable labels can be very useful. For example, if you are entering the data from a questionnaire, you might have a variable named "q3relbef". In this case a variable label might be invaluable, as it could remind you that this variable coded the responses to question 3 on your questionnaire which asked about religious belief. You can type in any phrase using any characters that you like, but it is best to keep it fairly short. SPSS will not try to interpret this label; it will simply insert it into the output next to the appropriate variable name when you perform any analysis.

To add a variable label, type it in to the column **Label**.

> **TIP**   Variable labels are printed on the output produced by SPSS. Although they are not essential, they act as a reminder about the variables and can be very helpful when you are interpreting the output. We recommend you take the time to use them whenever appropriate.

Value labels

A value label is a label assigned to a particular value of a variable. You are most likely to use value labels for nominal or categorical variables. For example, we might want to use labels to remind ourselves that, when entering values for the religion of our respondents, we used the codes: 1 = Buddhist; 2 = Christian; 3 = Hindu; 4 = Muslim; 5 = Other; 0 = Atheist.

A second use for value labels is with a grouping or independent variable. For example, you might want to compare the reaction time of participants who were tested under one of several different doses of alcohol. You could use a value label to remind yourself that group 1 received no alcohol, group 2 received 1 unit of alcohol and group 3, 2 units. Value labels will be inserted into the SPSS output to remind you what these values mean.

Value labels are entered using the **Values** column of the Variable View table. At present this column will probably contain the word **None**. Click the mouse on this cell, or use the tab key to move to this cell. As you do so a button will appear at the right hand side of the cell. Click on this button to call up the **Value Labels** dialogue box (see below).

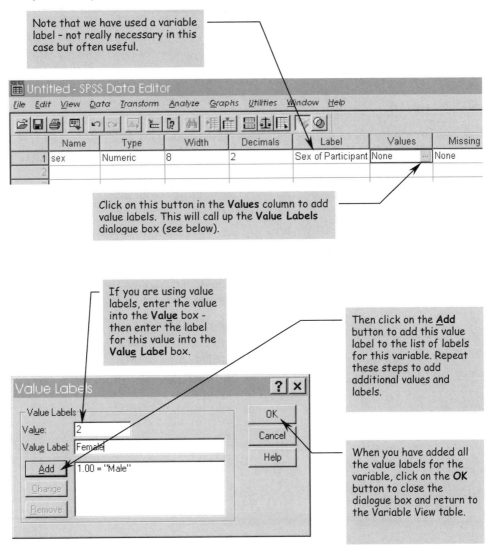

Note that we have used a variable label – not really necessary in this case but often useful.

Click on this button in the **Values** column to add value labels. This will call up the **Value Labels** dialogue box (see below).

If you are using value labels, enter the value into the **Value** box - then enter the label for this value into the **Value Label** box.

Then click on the **Add** button to add this value label to the list of labels for this variable. Repeat these steps to add additional values and labels.

When you have added all the value labels for the variable, click on the **OK** button to close the dialogue box and return to the Variable View table.

Do not forget to click the **Add** button after typing the last label. If you do, SPSS will warn that "Any pending add or change operations will be lost" when you click on the **OK** button. When you return to the Variables View table, the first of your labels will be visible in the **Values** cell.

Missing values

Sometimes you will not have a complete set of data. For example, some participants might decline to tell you their religion or their age, or you might lose or be unable to collect data from some participants (for example as the result of equipment failure). These gaps in the data table are known as missing values.

When we have a missing value we need to be able to tell SPSS that we do not have valid data for this participant on this variable. We do this by choosing a value that cannot normally occur for this variable. In the religion example above, we might choose to code religion as 9 when the participant does not state their religion. Thus, 9 is the missing value for the variable religion. The missing value can be different for each variable. For age it could be 99 (unless you are testing very old people).

Before you specify any missing values, the cell in the **Missing** column of the Variable View table will contain the word **None**. To specify a missing value click in the **Missing** column of the Variable View table. A button will appear at the right hand end of the cell. Click on this button to call up the **Missing Values** dialogue box (see below).

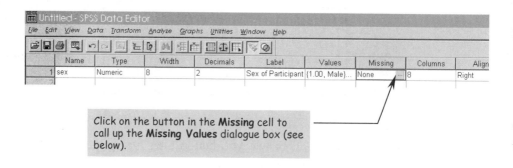

Click on the button in the **Missing** cell to call up the **Missing Values** dialogue box (see below).

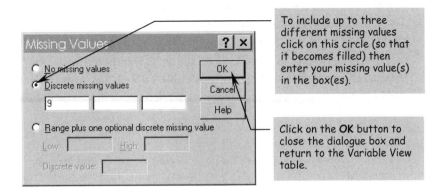

To include up to three different missing values click on this circle (so that it becomes filled) then enter your missing value(s) in the box(es).

Click on the **OK** button to close the dialogue box and return to the *Variable View* table.

SPSS allows you to specify the missing values in several ways:

1. **No missing values**: This is the default setting for this dialogue box. If this option is selected, SPSS will treat all values for this variable as valid.

2. **Discrete missing values**: This option allows you to enter up to three discrete values. For example, 7, 9 and 11 could all be set as missing values by selecting this option and entering the values in the three boxes. If you have only one missing value enter it into the first of the three boxes.

3. **Range plus one optional discrete missing value**: This option allows you to indicate that a range of values is being used as missing values. For example, selecting this option and entering the values 7 and 11 in the **Low** and **High** value boxes would instruct SPSS to treat the values 7, 8, 9, 10 and 11 as missing values. If, in addition to this range of values, the value 0 were typed into in the **Discrete value** box, then SPSS would treat the values 7, 8, 9, 10, 11 and 0 as missing.

In practice we rarely need more than one missing value for a variable (occasionally you might want more than one – for example you might wish to distinguish between an unanswered question and an illegible answer as both are missing values). You will therefore almost always want to enter your missing value into the first of the **Discrete missing values** boxes. To do this, simply click on the circle next to the words **Discrete missing values** and then enter your missing value into the first of the three boxes. Now click on the **OK** button to return to the Variable View table.

Column format

The next column of the Variable View table is labelled **Columns**. This entry in the table is used to specify the width of the column that the variable occupies in the Data View table of the Data Editor window. You can leave this value at its default setting unless you want to change the appearance of the Data View table. You may, for example, want to fit more columns onto the screen in order to see more variables without having to scroll. In this case you could reduce the width of each column. To adjust the settings, click on the cell and then use the up and down buttons that will appear at the right hand end of the cell to adjust the value. You can look at the effect of the change you have made by switching to the Data View.

> **TIP**   Be careful when changing column widths – you might think that you only need a column width of 1 for a variable that contains numbers in the range 0–9. However, if the column width is set too small, the variable name that appears at the top of the column will not be legible. A good compromise, if you really need to change column widths, is to set the width equal to no less than the number of characters in the variable name (e.g. a column width of 3 for the variable "sex").

Column alignment

The column of the Variable View labelled **Align** allows you to specify the alignment of the text within the cells of the Data View of the Data Editor Window. This setting has no effect on the operation of SPSS and only changes the appearance of the Data View table. The default setting is right alignment in which the decimal points of the values in the column are lined up. In left alignment the values are flush to the left-hand end of the cell. In centre alignment the values are centred in the cell (and thus the decimal points will not necessarily line up).

If you wish to change the Column Alignment, click in the **Align** cell and then click on the menu button that will appear in the cell and select the required alignment from the drop-down list (see below).

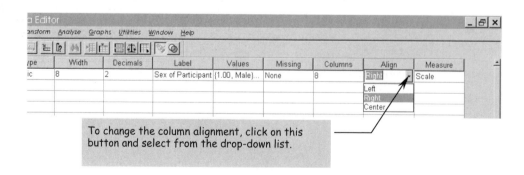

To change the column alignment, click on this button and select from the drop-down list.

> **TIP**   If you alter either the column width or alignment, remember you will have to switch to the Data View to see the effect of your changes. An alternative way of adjusting the column width is to click and drag the line dividing the columns in the Data View. The change you make will be reflected in the **Columns** value in the Variable View.

Measurement

The final column of the Variable View table is labelled **Measure.** This column is used to specify the level of measurement for the variable. SPSS offers three options, **Nominal**, **Ordinal**, and **Scale.**

Psychologists usually distinguish four levels of measurement, Nominal, Ordinal, Interval and Ratio (see Chapter 1). SPSS does not distinguish between Interval and Ratio data and uses the term **Scale** to cover a variable measured using either of these levels of measurement.

It is not essential to set the measurement option as it is only used in the creation of Interactive Charts (see Chapter 8). However, if you wish to set it, click in the **Measure** cell of the Variable View table and then click on the button that appears in the cell and select from the drop-down list (see below).

> **TIP**   You can usually leave the measurement option at its default setting. If you open a data file created using an earlier version of SPSS, the option will be set for you – variables with value labels will be set as **Nominal**, while variables with only a small number of values will be set as **Ordinal**. All other variables will be set as **Scale**.

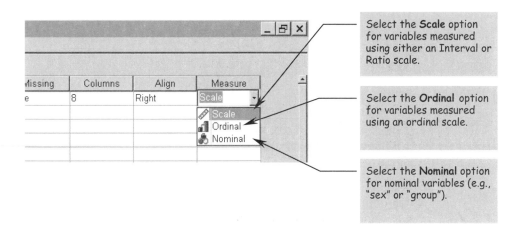

Select the **Scale** option for variables measured using either an Interval or Ratio scale.

Select the **Ordinal** option for variables measured using an ordinal scale.

Select the **Nominal** option for nominal variables (e.g., "sex" or "group").

Once you have completed the definition of your first variable, switch to the Data View (click on the Data View tab at the bottom right-hand corner of the table). You will now see the name of your new variable appear at the top of the appropriate column of the Data Editor window (see below). If you changed the column width and/or alignment you will see the effect of these changes.

Now switch back to the Variable View of the Data Editor Window and repeat this process for each of the variables required for your data file.

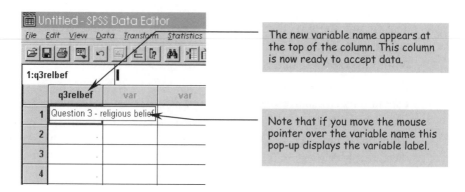

The new variable name appears at the top of the column. This column is now ready to accept data.

Note that if you move the mouse pointer over the variable name this pop-up displays the variable label.

> **TIP**   Remember, for most variables you can accept the default settings. In practice all you need to do is to enter a variable name and, if appropriate, add variable and value labels.

COPYING VARIABLE SETTINGS

In SPSS Version 10 it is easy to copy the settings from one variable and "paste" these on to one or more new variables. This is one of the major advantages of the Variable View table that was introduced in Version 10 (in earlier versions of SPSS it was possible to copy variable settings, but this was a rather complex process).

Suppose, for example, that you have administered a questionnaire that contains 20 items. Each item consists of a printed statement to which the participant is asked to respond by choosing from one of several options such as "Strongly Disagree", "Disagree", "Neither Agree or Disagree", "Agree", and "Strongly Agree". In our SPSS data table, each question will be represented by a variable, which we might call Q1, Q2 etc. For each of these variables it would be useful to enter the value labels 1 = "Strongly Disagree", 2 = "Disagree" etc. This would be rather time consuming. However, if we enter these value labels for the first variable, we can then move the cursor to the **Values** cell of the Variable View table and select **Copy** from the **Edit** menu. If we now click in the cell (or select the range of cells) we want to copy these labels to, and select **Paste** from the **Edit** menu, the value labels will be copied to all the selected cells.

Section 4: Entering data

A FIRST DATA ENTRY EXERCISE

As a data entry exercise, we will enter the data from a very simple study in which we have recorded the sex (coded as 1 = male, 2 = female), the age and the memory score (number of words recalled from a list of 20) for each of five participants.

Before we can enter this data, we need to define the three variables to be used (see the previous section for details of how to define a variable). Remember that as sex is a nominal variable, we should use value labels to remind ourselves what the values 1 and 2 represent.

Once the three variables have been defined we can begin entering the data. You can copy the data from the screen-shot shown below.

Click on the top left-hand cell of the table (ensure that you are at the top left hand corner of the window by checking the scroll bars). This cell will become highlighted (it will have a bold border). Any number you now type will appear in the bar above the variable names at the top of the window. If you press the Enter key or the Tab key, or use the mouse or cursor keys (up, down, left, and right arrows) to move to another cell, this number will be inserted into the cell.

Moving around the Data Editor window

> **TIP**   If using Version 10, check that you are in Data View table before entering data.

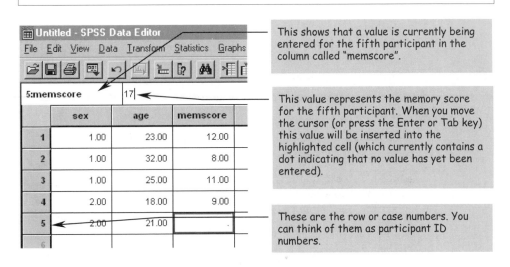

This shows that a value is currently being entered for the fifth participant in the column called "memscore".

This value represents the memory score for the fifth participant. When you move the cursor (or press the Enter or Tab key) this value will be inserted into the highlighted cell (which currently contains a dot indicating that no value has yet been entered).

These are the row or case numbers. You can think of them as participant ID numbers.

You will probably find it easier to use the cursor keys rather than the mouse to move round the data table. Alternatively, you can press the Enter key to move down to the next participant for the current variable, or the Tab key to move across to the next variable for the current participant.

It is best to enter the data one participant at a time, working across the data table. For example, you should enter the sex, age and memory score for the first participant in row one, then for the second participant in row two, and so on. If you enter the data a column at a time working down the columns (e.g. the sex of all the participants first, then their ages etc.), it is more likely that you will make a mistake. Such an error is likely to result in the data from one participant being assigned to another participant.

Once you have entered all your data into the data table, you should carefully check that you have entered it correctly. Cross-checking the data file against the original record of the data is a very important stage in the process of analysis. Either cross check the original records against the data on the screen, or against a printout of the data (see Chapter 8, Section 4 for details of how to print a copy of your data).

> **TIP**   It is very easy to accidentally enter an extra row of data. This will appear as a row of cells filled with dots. If this has happened it is worth taking the time to remove the blank line(s) as SPSS will interpret each blank line as a participant for whom you have no data. Thus SPSS will tell you it has more cases than you expect. This "phantom participant" can affect some statistical calculations. To delete the blank case, click on the case number associated with the extra row; the case will become highlighted. Now click on the **Edit** menu and choose **Cut**. The blank case will now be deleted from the table.

Sometimes new SPSS users panic that they have "lost" their data because they cannot see it on the screen. This is often because the data has scrolled out of the window. Check that the scroll bars are set to the top left-hand corner of the window.

The value labels button

If you have assigned value labels to one or more of your variables, you can choose whether you want SPSS to display the values you enter, or whether it should translate these values into the appropriate labels and display these labels. For example, in this file, we have assigned the value labels "Male" and "Female" to the values 1 and 2 of the variable "Sex". SPSS can either display the values (i.e. the numerals "1" or "2") or the labels "Male" or "Female". Clicking on the **Value Labels** button on the toolbar of the Data Editor window will toggle between these two display states (see below). Note, regardless of whether you choose to display values or labels, you must enter the data in the form of values (i.e. you must enter "1" or "2" and not "Male" or "Female"). This option affects only the way the data is displayed in the Data Editor window, and not the way it is entered or analysed.

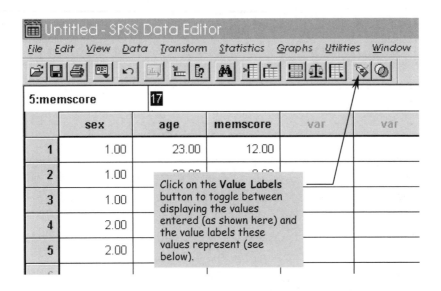

Click on the **Value Labels** button to toggle between displaying the values entered (as shown here) and the value labels these values represent (see below).

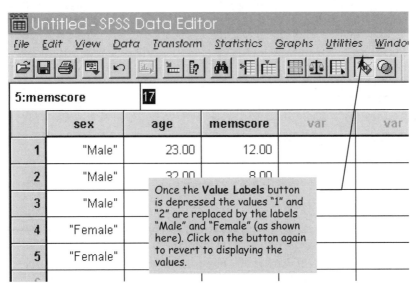

Once the **Value Labels** button is depressed the values "1" and "2" are replaced by the labels "Male" and "Female" (as shown here). Click on the button again to revert to displaying the values.

When your data is entered, checked and if necessary corrected, it should be saved to disk. We describe how to save the data file in the next section.

Section 5: Saving a data file

You will have spent a lot of time entering your data, so remember to save the data file as soon as you have checked it carefully. If you are entering a large amount of data it is a good idea to save the file every few minutes.

TO SAVE THE DATA TO A FILE

Click on the menu item (word) **File** at the top of the screen. Now click on either **Save** or **Save As**.

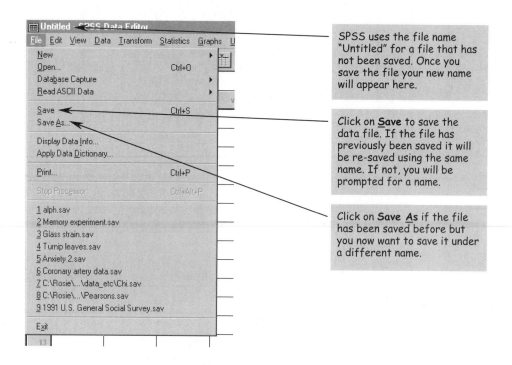

SPSS uses the file name "Untitled" for a file that has not been saved. Once you save the file your new name will appear here.

Click on **Save** to save the data file. If the file has previously been saved it will be re-saved using the same name. If not, you will be prompted for a name.

Click on **Save As** if the file has been saved before but you now want to save it under a different name.

Select **Save** to resave the file using the existing name. The resaved file will replace the old version. If the file has not previously been saved, or if you click on **Save As**, you will be presented with the **Save Data As** dialogue box (see below).

Type the name for the file into the **File name** box. The file name you choose should be reminiscent of the study from which the data originated (for example, "memorystudy"). You should not use a full stop in the file name and should not attach a suffix to the file name. By default SPSS will attach the suffix ".sav" to any name you enter. Do not change this suffix, or SPSS might not recognise the file as a data file. Check which disk and which directory the file is going to be saved to, before you click the **Save** button. You may want to save the file to your floppy disk in drive A. To do this follow the instructions given below ("Changing the drive or directory"). Alternatively you can put the drive letter at the start of the file name (e.g. "a:\mnemonic experiment").

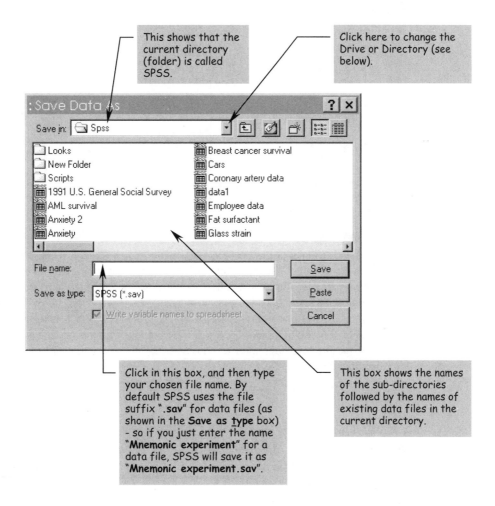

Changing the drive or directory

To change the current drive or directory before saving a file, click on the button at the end of the **Save in** box, and select the drive or directory you require from the drop-down list that appears (see below).

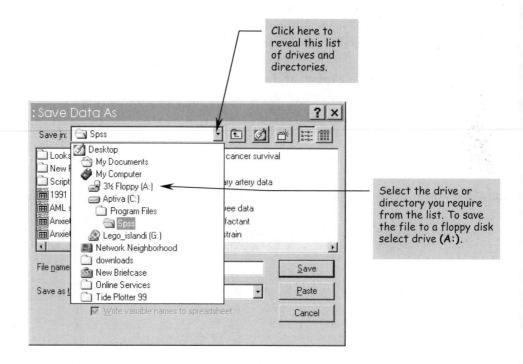

Click here to reveal this list of drives and directories.

Select the drive or directory you require from the list. To save the file to a floppy disk select drive (A:).

TIP   Avoid using a dot in an SPSS file name. If you do use a dot, and if you include three characters after the dot, then SPSS will treat the characters after the dot as the suffix. For example, if you call the file "file name with a .dot" SPSS will treat the ".dot" part of the name as the suffix, and will not add the standard ".**sav**" suffix. This is important because when you come to reopen the file, SPSS will not list it as a data file. Students often tell us that the computer has "lost" their data file and this is usually the explanation. If you think this has happened to you, see the tip box at the end of the next section ("Opening a data file").

You can now enter and save data in SPSS. To practice your new skills enter the data from the experiments described in Section 7. We will be using this data later to undertake some statistical procedures. First, though, we will tell you how to open a file that has been saved previously.

Section 6: Opening a data file

To open a data file follow the instructions below.

1. Ensure that the Data Editor window is the active window. If this is not the case, click on the **Goto Data** button on the toolbar at the top of the window (alternatively, select the Data Editor window from the list available under the **Window** menu).

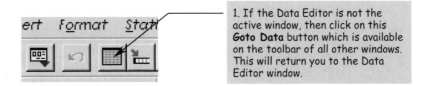

1. If the Data Editor is not the active window, then click on this **Goto Data** button which is available on the toolbar of all other windows. This will return you to the Data Editor window.

2. Click on the **File** menu.
3. Select **Open** from the drop-down menu.

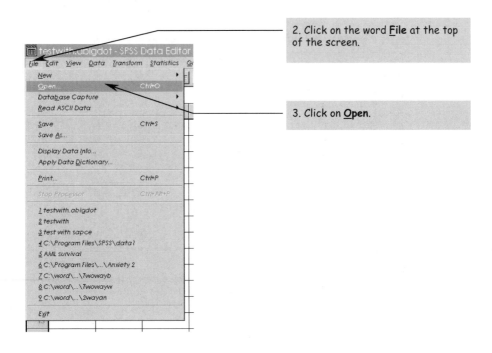

2. Click on the word **File** at the top of the screen.

3. Click on **Open**.

The Open File dialogue box will now appear (see below).

4. The current directory is indicated in the box labeled **Look in**. To change the directory or to select a different drive (such as drive **A:**), then click on the button at the right hand end of this box, and select the drive or directory you require (as explained at the end of Section 5).

5. Examine the list of data files shown in the box, and click on the name of the file you want to open.

6. The name of the file you have selected will appear in the **File name** box. Alternatively, if you are sure you know it, you can type the name of the file directly into this box.

7. Finally, click on the **Open** button to open the file and load the data into the Data Editor window.

TIP   If you double-click on the name of the file it will be opened immediately without the need to click on the **Open** button.

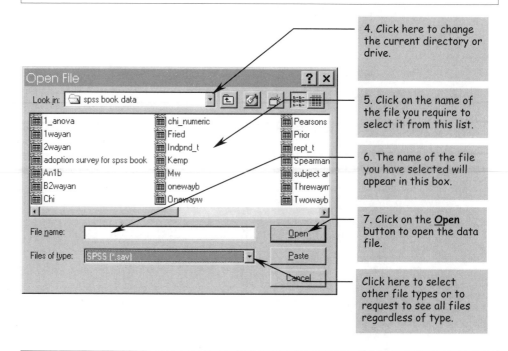

4. Click here to change the current directory or drive.

5. Click on the name of the file you require to select it from this list.

6. The name of the file you have selected will appear in this box.

7. Click on the **Open** button to open the data file.

Click here to select other file types or to request to see all files regardless of type.

TIP   If the file you are looking for has a suffix other than "**.sav**", SPSS will not recognise it as a data file and will not display it in the dialogue box. If you can't find the file you are looking for, and think that it may have been saved with some other file name suffix, click on the button at the right hand end of the **Files of type** box and select "**All files *.***" from the list of file types offered. All the files in the current directory, regardless of type or suffix name will now be displayed in the dialogue box. If you find that your data file was saved with some other suffix, load it and then immediately resave it with the "**.sav**" suffix.

Section 7: Data entry exercises

In this section, we are going to practice entering data from two different types of experimental design. Later in this chapter and in subsequent chapters we will use these data files to demonstrate other procedures. Take the time to complete these exercises, as they will help you to appreciate the way that the design employed in a study influences the shape of the data file. When you have completed these two data files, compare them to the ones shown in the next section.

DATA FROM AN INDEPENDENT GROUPS (OR BETWEEN SUBJECTS) DESIGN

As we saw in Chapter 1, in the independent groups design we are comparing the performance of two or more groups of different participants. In the example below, we have used this design to investigate the effect of a mnemonic instruction given to a group of participants before they were asked to learn a total of 20 words.

RODENTS IN SPACE: A SIMPLE MEMORY EXPERIMENT

Twenty-one first year undergraduates participated in a simple memory experiment designed to investigate the effect of a mnemonic strategy upon memory for paired words. The participants were randomly divided into two groups. All participants were given 2 minutes to memorize a list of 20 words presented in pairs. All the participants were told to memorise the words, but those in one group, the mnemonic instruction group, were advised to try to form a mental image to link the two words in a pair (for example, for the word pair ROCKET – HAMSTER a participant might imagine a small furry rodent being fired off into outer space). The participants in the other group, the non-mnemonic group, were not given this instruction. After learning the words for 2 minutes the participants were then required to complete some simple mental arithmetic problems for 2 minutes. Finally they were required to recall any of the words that they could remember. The number of words correctly recalled was recorded. The data are summarised below.

Memory scores (out of 20) for the mnemonic instruction group:

    20, 18, 14, 18, 17, 11, 20, 18, 20, 19, 20

Memory scores (out of 20) for the non-mnemonic group:

    10, 20, 12, 9, 14, 15, 16, 14, 19, 12

Using this data attempt to do the following:

1. Set up a data file to record this data. Give appropriate names to the variables you are using.
2. Apply value and variable labels where appropriate
3. Enter and check the data, then save the file to floppy disk using an appropriate file name.
4. Ensure that you can re-open the file.

Now compare the data file you have constructed to the one illustrated in the next section of this chapter.

DATA FROM A REPEATED MEASURES (OR WITHIN-SUBJECTS) DESIGN

As you will remember, in the repeated measures design, every participant is exposed to each condition and thus contributes a data point from each level of the independent variable. This will be reflected in the structure of the data file, which will have a column for each level of the independent variable. In the example below we have used this design to investigate mental representation.

COMPARING MENTAL IMAGES

If you ask someone the question "how many windows are there in the front of your home?" most people will report that they attempt to answer the question by "inspecting" a mental image of their house. There has been a great deal of debate about the use of mental images, with some psychologists claiming that information is actually stored in a more abstract form and that the mental images that we feel we are inspecting are illusory (that is they are an "epiphenomenon"). However, several lines of evidence do support the idea that we are able to manipulate information utilising a form of representation that shares many qualities with mental images. This experiment is modelled on one such line of evidence.

Continued overleaf.

Imagine you were asked to decide whether or not a Lion was bigger than a Wolf. You could make your decision by recalling information about size that was represented in some abstract form. Alternatively, you could form a mental image of these two animals standing side-by-side and decide which was the taller. If you adopted the mental imagery approach, then you might expect the decision to take longer when the two animals were of a similar size than when they were of very different sizes. If the decision were based on a more abstract form of representation, then you would expect the relative size of the animals to have no effect on the speed of the decision. Thus, psychologists have argued that if it takes longer to compare the size of two similar sized animals than two dissimilar sized animals, this offers some support for the idea that these decisions are based on the manipulation of image-like forms of mental representation.

In our experiment each of 16 participants undertook 20 trials. In each trial the participant was presented with a pair of animal names and had to decide as quickly as possible which of the animals was the largest. The time taken to make this decision was recorded (in milliseconds). For half of the trials the difference in size between the two animals was large (e.g. Mosquito – Elephant) and for the other half of the trials the difference in size was small (e.g. Horse – Zebra). In the data table below we have recorded the mean decision time (in milliseconds) for the large size difference trials and for the small size difference trials.

DATA

Participant	Large diff.	Small diff.
1	936	878
2	923	1005
3	896	1010
4	1241	1365
5	1278	1422
6	871	1198
7	1360	1576
8	733	896
9	941	1573
10	1077	1261
11	1438	2237
12	1099	1325
13	1253	1591
14	1930	2742
15	1260	1357
16	1271	1963

Using the above data, attempt to do the following:

1. Set up an SPSS data file to record this data. Give appropriate names to the variables you are using.
2. Apply value and variable labels where appropriate.
3. Enter and check the data, then save the file to floppy disk using an appropriate file name.
4. Ensure that you can re-open the file.

Now compare your data file to the one shown in the next section of this chapter.

Section 8: Answers to data entry exercises

RODENTS IN SPACE: AN EXAMPLE OF THE DATA FILE FROM AN INDEPENDENT GROUPS DESIGN

Below is a screen-shot of the data file we constructed for this simple memory experiment. Your data table might not look identical, but should have the same basic characteristics. Note that there are two variables. The first is a nominal variable (or *grouping variable)* that we have used to record whether the participant was in the mnemonic or the non-mnemonic group. The second variable is a ratio variable and has been used to record the number of words each participant recalled. If you have the **Value Labels** button (on the tool bar) depressed, then the first column will display the value labels rather than the values (i.e. mnemonic or non-mnemonic rather than 1 or 2 as shown here).

> **TIP** Remember, the data file constructed for an experiment that employed an independent groups design will always require a nominal variable that is used to indicate the condition under which each participant was tested.

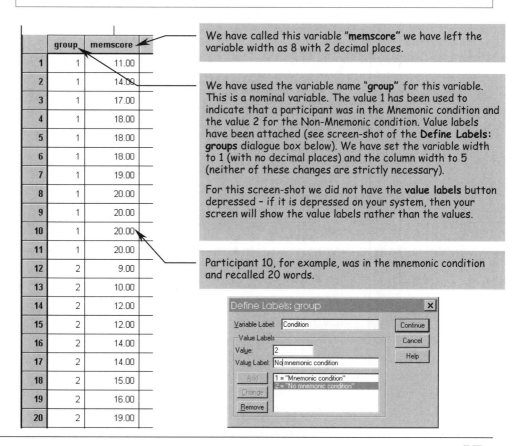

We have called this variable **"memscore"** we have left the variable width as 8 with 2 decimal places.

We have used the variable name **"group"** for this variable. This is a nominal variable. The value 1 has been used to indicate that a participant was in the Mnemonic condition and the value 2 for the Non-Mnemonic condition. Value labels have been attached (see screen-shot of the **Define Labels: groups** dialogue box below). We have set the variable width to 1 (with no decimal places) and the column width to 5 (neither of these changes are strictly necessary).

For this screen-shot we did not have the **value labels** button depressed – if it is depressed on your system, then your screen will show the value labels rather than the values.

Participant 10, for example, was in the mnemonic condition and recalled 20 words.

COMPARING MENTAL IMAGES: AN EXAMPLE OF THE DATA FILE FROM A REPEATED MEASURES DESIGN

Below is a screen-shot of the data file we constructed to record the data from our mental imagery experiment. Your data table might not look identical, but should have the same basic characteristics.

There are two variables in the file, but in contrast to the data table for the independent groups design, here each of the variables is used to record the performance of the participants. As this is a repeated measures design each participant was tested under both conditions. There is therefore no need for a nominal variable.

Compare this data file to the one on the previous page. Make sure that you understand why these two files have a different structure.

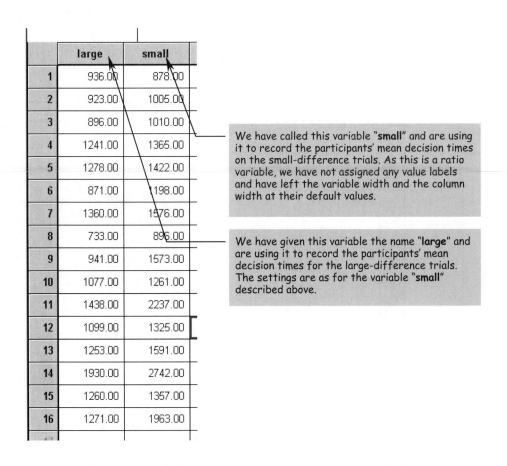

	large	small
1	936.00	878.00
2	923.00	1005.00
3	896.00	1010.00
4	1241.00	1365.00
5	1278.00	1422.00
6	871.00	1198.00
7	1360.00	1576.00
8	733.00	896.00
9	941.00	1573.00
10	1077.00	1261.00
11	1438.00	2237.00
12	1099.00	1325.00
13	1253.00	1591.00
14	1930.00	2742.00
15	1260.00	1357.00
16	1271.00	1963.00

We have called this variable "**small**" and are using it to record the participants' mean decision times on the small-difference trials. As this is a ratio variable, we have not assigned any value labels and have left the variable width and the column width at their default values.

We have given this variable the name "**large**" and are using it to record the participants' mean decision times for the large-difference trials. The settings are as for the variable "**small**" described above.

Section 9: Summary descriptive statistics and the Viewer window

DESCRIPTIVE STATISTICS

Descriptive statistics are a set of statistical tools that allow us to accurately describe a large volume of data with just a few values. Common descriptives include measures of central tendency (for example, mean, median and mode) and measures of dispersion (for example, range, minimum & maximum, interquartile range, standard deviation and variance). A research report should always include descriptive statistics. You should use them to provide the reader with some information about the sample, and to describe the data before performing an inferential statistical test.

There are several ways of obtaining descriptive statistics from SPSS. Descriptive statistics are often available as an optional output from the inferential statistics, but there are also several SPSS commands designed specifically to produce descriptives. Two of the most useful of these procedures are **Frequencies** and **Tables**.

The **Frequencies** command is very useful when you want to obtain descriptive statistics on all participants – for example if you want to find out the mean age of your participants. The major limitation of the **Frequencies** command is that unless you also use some other procedure (see Chapter 5), you cannot obtain descriptive statistics broken down by a grouping variable. For example, using the **Frequencies** command alone you cannot find easily the mean age for the male and for the female participants, or, in the case of an independent groups design, the mean memory score for participants in groups 1 and 2. In these situations, the **Tables** command should be used to produce descriptives broken down by one or more variable.

THE FREQUENCIES COMMAND

The **Frequencies** command produces frequency distribution tables showing the number of cases (participants) who have a particular score on each variable. For example, a frequency distribution table of the variable age would tell you how many of your participants were 20 year olds, how many 21 and so on for each of the ages represented in the group of participants. In addition to this important function, the **Frequencies** command will also produce a range of descriptives including measures of central tendency and measures of dispersion.

To obtain a Frequencies output in SPSS Version 8:

1. Once your data is entered, checked and saved, click on the word **Statistics** at the top of the screen (see below).
2. Select (click on) **Summarize**.
3. Select **Frequencies**.

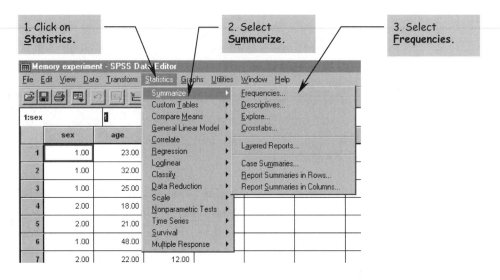

To obtain a Frequencies output in SPSS Versions 9 and 10:

1. Once your data is entered, checked and saved, click on the word **Analyze** at the top of the screen (see below).
2. Select (click on) **Descriptive Statistics**.
3. Select **Frequencies**.

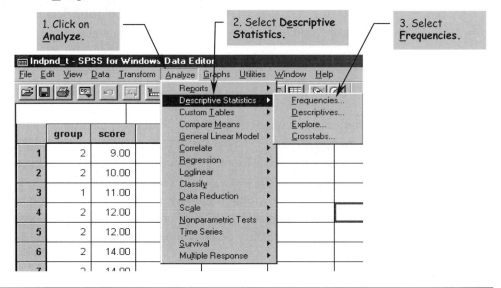

Regardless of whether you are using Version 8, 9 or 10, SPSS will now present you with the Frequencies dialogue box shown below. This dialogue box contains two boxes. The left-hand box lists all the variables in the data file. The right-hand box (which will be empty when you first use the command) lists the names of the variables which will be analysed (i.e. for which a frequencies printout will be produced).

4. Select the first variable you want included in the frequency analysis by clicking on the variable name in the left-hand box.

5. The arrow button between the two boxes will now be highlighted and will be pointing to the right-hand box. Click on this arrow button. The selected variable will be moved to the right-hand box. Repeat this procedure until the right-hand box contains the names of all the variables you want included in the Frequencies analysis.

TIP   You can select more than one variable by holding down the either the <shift> key or the <cntrl> while clicking on the names of the variables. If you <shift> click the first and last variables in a list, all the variables in the list will be selected. By contrast, holding down the <cntr> key while clicking on the names of variables will either select or deselect just that variable. By using <cntrl>click and <shift>click in combination you can quickly select just those variable you require. You can then click on the arrow key to move all the selected variables into the right-hand box.

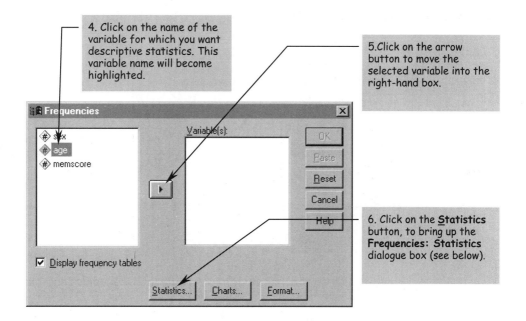

4. Click on the name of the variable for which you want descriptive statistics. This variable name will become highlighted.

5.Click on the arrow button to move the selected variable into the right-hand box.

6. Click on the **Statistics** button, to bring up the **Frequencies: Statistics** dialogue box (see below).

6. When you have selected all the variables you are interested in, click on the statistics button – Statistics.. (**not** the word **Statistics** on the menu bar in Version 8). This will reveal the **Frequencies: Statistics** dialogue box (shown below) which lists all the descriptive statistics available in the **Frequencies** command.

7. In the **Frequencies: Statistics** dialogue box (see below) select all the descriptive statistics you require by clicking in the boxes so that a tick appears.

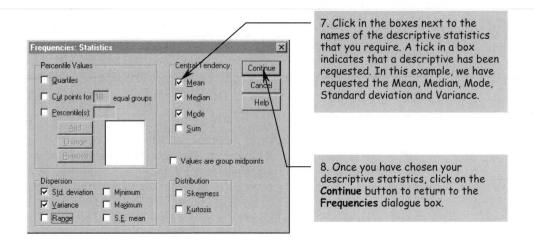

7. Click in the boxes next to the names of the descriptive statistics that you require. A tick in a box indicates that a descriptive has been requested. In this example, we have requested the Mean, Median, Mode, Standard deviation and Variance.

8. Once you have chosen your descriptive statistics, click on the **Continue** button to return to the **Frequencies** dialogue box.

8. When you have selected all the statistics you require, click on Continue (the Continue button) to return you to the Frequencies dialogue box (see below).

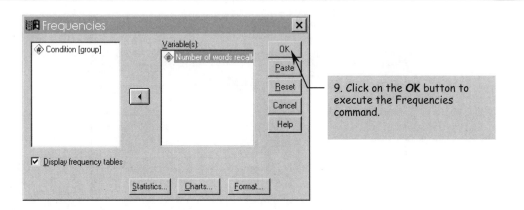

9. Click on the **OK** button to execute the Frequencies command.

9. Finally, click on the OK button to execute the frequencies command.

The Viewer window will now become the active window. The results of the frequencies analysis will be presented in this window.

> **TIP**   Clicking on the <u>F</u>ormat button in the Frequencies dialogue box will allow you to adjust the way the output appears on the page. Experiment with these settings to discover the different ways of organising the output.

On page 66 we have annotated the Frequencies output. This output was produced using the data file for the mental imagery experiment that we entered earlier in this chapter. We requested the mean, mode, median, standard deviation and variance for both of the variables in this file. However, before we examine this output we need to learn a little about the Viewer window.

THE VIEWER WINDOW

The Viewer window is composed of two distinct parts or "panes". The left-hand pane acts as a "navigator" or "outline". This is a bit like a table of contents that lists all of the components of the output that are shown in the larger pane. Clicking on an icon in the navigator pane moves you to that part of the output in the main or "display" pane.

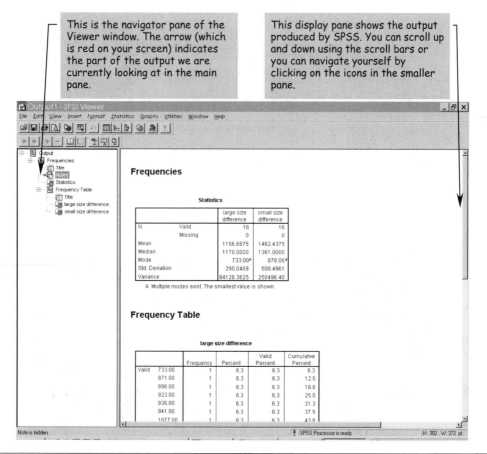

Points to note about the two panes of the Viewer window

1. Output can be hidden or displayed. A closed book icon represents a hidden section of output and an open book represents a section of output that is being displayed. Double click on a book icon to either open or close it and either display or hide the associated section of output.

2. Click on one of the minus signs to collapse and hide all of the output from a command. Click on a plus sign to expand and display all of the output from a command.

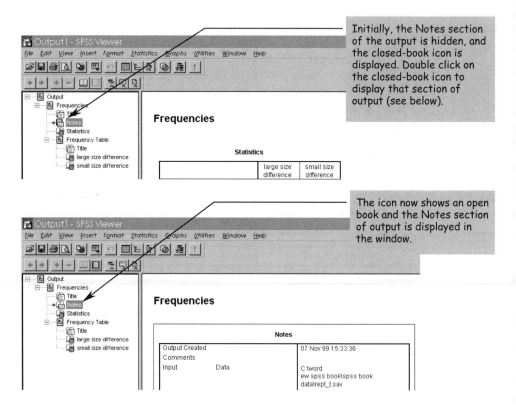

Initially, the Notes section of the output is hidden, and the closed-book icon is displayed. Double click on the closed-book icon to display that section of output (see below).

The icon now shows an open book and the Notes section of output is displayed in the window.

3. Most of the output produced by the SPSS commands is in the form of tables known as Pivot Tables. The "Statistics" table shown above is an example of a Pivot Table. Pivot Tables can be edited in various ways – see Chapter 8 for full details.

4. Some parts of the output are in the form of plain text. The title "Frequencies" is an example of text output.

5. You can select output either by dragging the mouse over the section in the main pane or by clicking on the appropriate icons in the navigator window. Click on the name of a command to select all the output from that command. You can select all of the output by clicking on the highest level "Output" icon. Lower level icons (e.g. "Statistics") select only that particular part of the output.

6. Selected output can be cut, copied and pasted using the relevant options on the Edit menu or can be printed using the Print command available under the File menu (see Chapter 8 for details of printing output).

> **TIP**   Sometimes you will want to delete all the output in the Viewer window. The easiest way to do this is to click on the "Output" icon in the navigator pane and then press the Delete key on your keyboard. You can now start your new analyses with a blank output window.

7. You can change the relative width of the two panes by clicking on and dragging the line that separates the two panes

> **TIP**   If you find the icons in the navigator pane too small you can enlarge them by selecting **Outline Si<u>z</u>e** from the **<u>V</u>iew** menu. Now select **<u>S</u>mall**, **<u>M</u>edium** or **<u>L</u>arge**.

Now that we can navigate our way around the output in the Viewer window, we can look in more detail at the output produced by the Frequencies command.

THE OUTPUT PRODUCED BY THE FREQUENCIES COMMAND

Frequencies

This is the title for the output produced by the Frequencies command.

Statistics

This table lists all the descriptive statistics we requested. One column gives these figures for the "large size difference" variable, the other for the "small size difference" variable. We can see that the mean decision time was longer when the size difference was small.

		large size difference	small size difference
N	Valid	16	16
	Missing	0	0
Mean		1156.6875	1462.4375
Median		1170.0000	1361.0000
Mode		733.00[a]	878.00[a]
Std. Deviation		290.0489	500.4961
Variance		84128.3625	250496.40

a. Multiple modes exist. The smallest value is shown

Frequency Table

This is the Frequencies Table for the "large size difference" variable (the table for the other variable is not shown here).

large size difference

		Frequency	Percent	Valid Percent	Cumulative Percent
Valid	733.00	1	6.3	6.3	6.3
	871.00	1	6.3	6.3	12.5
	896.00	1	6.3	6.3	18.8
	923.00	1	6.3	6.3	25.0
	936.00	1	6.3	6.3	31.3
	941.00	1	6.3	6.3	37.5
	1077.00	1	6.3	6.3	43.8
	1099.00	1	6.3	6.3	50.0
	1241.00	1	6.3	6.3	56.3
	1253.00	1	6.3	6.3	62.5
	1260.00	1	6.3	6.3	68.8
	1271.00	1	6.3	6.3	75.0
	1278.00	1	6.3	6.3	81.3
	1360.00	1	6.3	6.3	87.5
	1438.00	1	6.3	6.3	93.8
	1930.00	1	6.3	6.3	100.0
	Total	16	100.0	100.0	

The Frequency Column tells you how many participants recorded each decision time (1 in each case here).

The Percent column tells us what percentage of participants recorded a particular time.

The Valid Percent column is the percentage adjusted for any missing cases – there are none here so the values are the same as in the Percent column.

We can see from the Cumulative Percent column that 56.3% of our participants made a decision in 1241 m.secs or less.

TIP When reporting summary descriptive statistics, you should think about how many decimal places to use. A rule-of-thumb is to round to one more decimal place than you measured.

THE TABLES COMMAND

The Tables command allows you easily to obtain descriptive statistics for separate groups of participants. For example, we can use it to display the mean and standard deviation of the memory scores separately for the participants in the Mnemonic and Non-Mnemonic groups of our simple memory experiment.

To obtain a Tables output:

1. On the menu bar, click on the word **Statistics** (Version 8) or **Analyze** (Versions 9 and 10).
2. Click on **Custom Tables**.

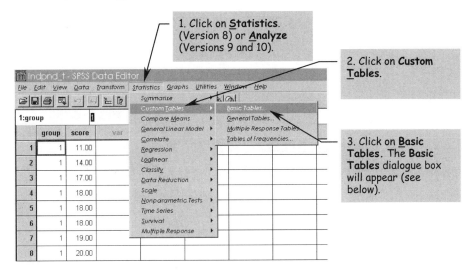

3. Click on **Basic Tables**. This will display the **Basic Tables** dialogue box (see below).

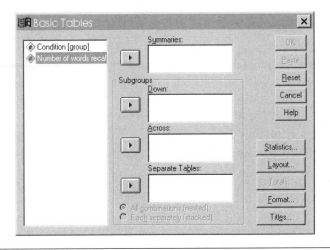

4. Click on the name of the variable for which you require summary descriptive statistics ("memscore" in this example) then click on the arrow button next to the **Summaries** box to move the variable into the **Summaries** box.

5. Next click on the name of the grouping variable. The grouping variable will be used to create the two or more groups for which the descriptive statistics will be calculated. In this example, we want descriptive statistics for each of our two experimental groups, so the variable "Group" is the grouping variable. Click on the variable name "Group".

6. Now click on the arrow next to either the **Down**, the **Across** or the **Separate Tables** boxes. Which of these you choose determines how the table will appear in the output. The **Down** option produces a separate row for each level of the grouping variable, whereas the **Across** options produces a separate column for each level of the grouping variable. The **Separate Tables** option produces a separate table for each level of the grouping variable. Experiment with these settings to see which suits you best.

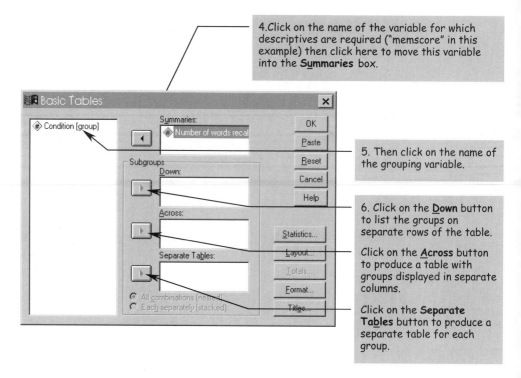

4. Click on the name of the variable for which descriptives are required ("memscore" in this example) then click here to move this variable into the **Summaries** box.

5. Then click on the name of the grouping variable.

6. Click on the **Down** button to list the groups on separate rows of the table.

Click on the **Across** button to produce a table with groups displayed in separate columns.

Click on the **Separate Tables** button to produce a separate table for each group.

7. Now click on the **Statistics** button (**not** the word **Statistics** on the menu bar in Version 8). The **Basic Tables: Statistics** dialogue box will appear (see below).

8. Select the descriptive statistics you require by picking them from the list in the left of the dialogue box. Click on the **Add** button. To add the selected statistics to the box marked **Cell Statistics**. You may need to scroll down through the list of statistics available to find all of those you require.

9. Once the required statistics have been selected, click on the Continue button. This will return you to the Basic Tables dialogue box. Now click on the OK button. The table of statistics requested will now appear in the Viewer window.

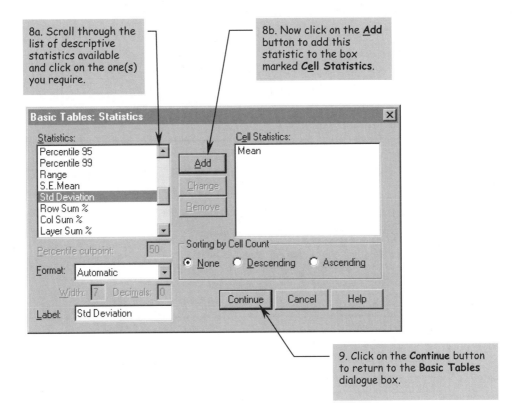

8a. Scroll through the list of descriptive statistics available and click on the one(s) you require.

8b. Now click on the **Add** button to add this statistic to the box marked **Cell Statistics**.

9. Click on the **Continue** button to return to the **Basic Tables** dialogue box.

Typical output from the Tables command is illustrated on the following page.

TIP   There are several other buttons and options on these dialogue boxes that control the appearance of the table and the way that the figures are presented. Experiment with these settings and/or use the help button to discover how the various options work.

OUTPUT FROM THE TABLES COMMAND

These tables were created using the data file from the memory experiment that we entered earlier in this chapter. We have requested three descriptive statistics, the Mean, the Standard Deviation and the Count (the number of cases).

The first table was produced using the **Down** button to request that the statistics for each level of the independent variable were arranged in separate rows of the table.

The second table was produced by using the **Across** button to request a table in which the statistics were arranged in two separate columns.

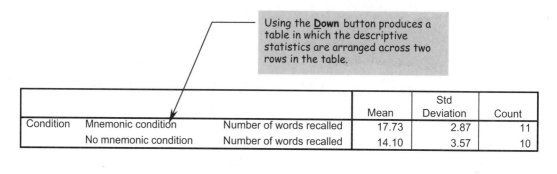

Using the **Down** button produces a table in which the descriptive statistics are arranged across two rows in the table.

			Mean	Std Deviation	Count
Condition	Mnemonic condition	Number of words recalled	17.73	2.87	11
	No mnemonic condition	Number of words recalled	14.10	3.57	10

Using the **Across** button produces a table in which the descriptive statistics are arranged in two columns.

	Condition					
	Mnemonic condition			No mnemonic condition		
	Count	Mean	Std Deviation	Count	Mean	Std Deviation
Number of words recalled	11	17.73	2.87	10	14.10	3.57

> **TIP**   We used an independent groups design to illustrate how the Tables command can be used to give summary statistics for each group separately. It can also be used, however, to give summary descriptive statistics for all the data in one or more columns. Thus you could use it for a repeated measures design in the following way: at step 4 above click on the two variable names and move them both into the **Summaries** box; omit steps 5 and 6 (as there is no grouping variable); then carry out steps 7, 8 and 9.

Chapter Three

Tests of difference for two sample designs

An introduction to the t-tests
The independent t-test
The paired t-test
An introduction to the nonparametric
   equivalents of the t-test
The Mann–Whitney test
The Wilcoxon test

Section 1: An introduction to the *t*-tests

DIFFERENT TYPES OF *t*-TESTS

The *t*-test is a parametric test used to determine whether two means are significantly different from one another. There are three types of *t*-test:

1. The single sample *t*-test
2. The independent *t*-test
3. The paired *t*-test (sometimes called the repeated, the dependent or the correlated *t*-test).

The single sample *t*-test, which is the most simple, determines whether the observed mean is different from a set value. This form of the test will not be dealt with here. The independent *t*-test is used when comparing means from two independent groups of individuals. The paired *t*-test is used when comparing the means of two sets of observations from the same individuals or from pairs of individuals (e.g. when using a matched-subjects design).

The *t*-test requires that the data are of at least interval level of measurement, are normally distributed, and have equal variances.

In some textbooks you might find this test referred to as the Student's *t*-test. This is because William Gossett who devised the test, worked for the Guinness Brewing Company who did not permit him to publish under his own name. For this reason he wrote under the pseudonym of "Student".

Section 2: The independent *t*-test

This test compares the performance of the participants in group A with the performance of the participants in group B. This test should be used when the data are parametric and obtained using an independent groups design. These two groups could constitute a male and a female group because we wish to examine sex differences, or they could constitute two groups of participants who undergo different drug conditions, one a low dose drug condition and one a high dose drug condition. This type of *t*-test is often also called an *unrelated t*-test. In the example shown next, we use the data from the memory experiment used in the data entry exercise in Chapter 2. It was hypothesised that the group receiving mnemonic instructions would remember more than the group who did not receive any specific mnemonic instructions. If you use this data and follow the instructions given next, then you will be able to compare the output you produce with the annotated output that we give at the end of this section.

TO PERFORM AN INDEPENDENT *t*-TEST

1. Click on the menu item **Analyze** (Versions 9 and 10) or **Statistics** (Version 8).
2. Click on the words **Compare Means**.
3. Now click on the words **Independent Samples T test**.

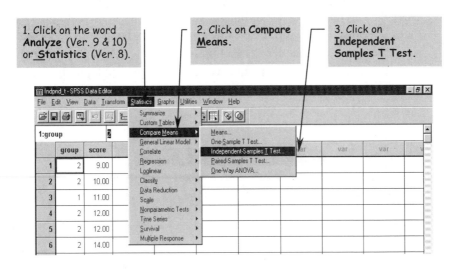

4. You will now be presented with the **Independent-Samples T Test** dialogue box (see below). As is typical in SPSS, the box on the left lists all of the variables in your data file. Click on the name of the dependent variable in your analysis and

then click on the arrow button to move this variable name into the box marked **Test Variable(s)**.

5. Now click on the name of the independent variable and then click on the arrow button to move this into the box marked **Grouping Variable**.

Once you have entered the dependent and independent variables into their appropriate boxes, the dialogue box will look like this:

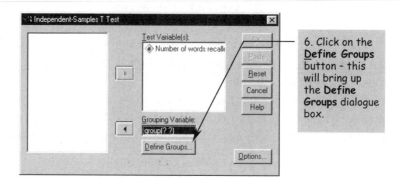

6. Click on the **Define Groups** button to bring up the **Define Groups** dialogue box (see below). This dialogue box is used to specify which two groups you are comparing. For example, if your independent variable is SEX which you have coded as 1 = Male, 2 = Female, then you need to enter the values 1 and 2 into the boxes marked Group 1 and Group 2 respectively. This might seem rather pointless, but you might not always be comparing groups that you had coded as 1 and 2. For example you might want to compare two groups who were defined on the basis of their religious belief (Atheists and Christians who could be coded as 0 and 2 respectively – see Chapter 2, Section 3 on Value Labels). In this case we would enter the values 0 and 2 into the two boxes in this dialogue box. (We will not be describing the use of the **Cut point** option here.)

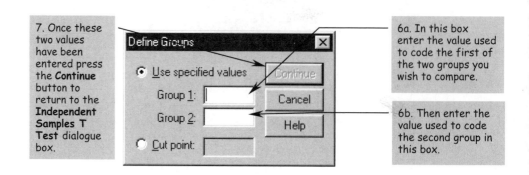

SPSS for Psychologists – Chapter Three

7. Clicking on the **Continue** button in the **Define Groups** dialogue box will return you to the **Independent-Samples T Test** dialogue box. You will see that your two values have been entered into the brackets following the name of your independent variable (you may have noticed that previously there were question marks inside these brackets).

8. Finally, click on ⬜ OK ⬜ in the **Independent-Samples T Test** dialogue box. The output of the *t*-test will appear in the Output window.

The output from this independent *t*-test is shown, with annotations, on the following page.

Obtained Using Menu Items: Compare <u>Means</u> > Independent-Samples <u>T</u> Test

t-Test

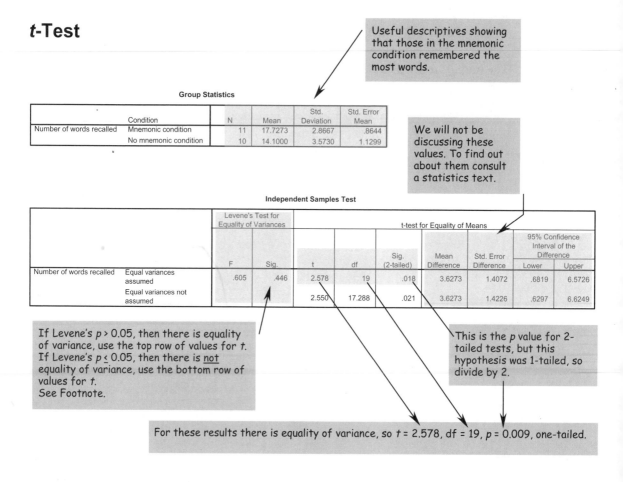

Useful descriptives showing that those in the mnemonic condition remembered the most words.

Group Statistics

	Condition	N	Mean	Std. Deviation	Std. Error Mean
Number of words recalled	Mnemonic condition	11	17.7273	2.8667	.8644
	No mnemonic condition	10	14.1000	3.5730	1.1299

We will not be discussing these values. To find out about them consult a statistics text.

Independent Samples Test

		Levene's Test for Equality of Variances		t-test for Equality of Means					95% Confidence Interval of the Difference	
		F	Sig.	t	df	Sig. (2-tailed)	Mean Difference	Std. Error Difference	Lower	Upper
Number of words recalled	Equal variances assumed	.605	.446	2.578	19	.018	3.6273	1.4072	.6819	6.5726
	Equal variances not assumed			2.550	17.288	.021	3.6273	1.4226	.6297	6.6249

If Levene's *p* > 0.05, then there is equality of variance, use the top row of values for *t*.
If Levene's *p* ≤ 0.05, then there is <u>not</u> equality of variance, use the bottom row of values for *t*.
See Footnote.

This is the *p* value for 2-tailed tests, but this hypothesis was 1-tailed, so divide by 2.

For these results there is equality of variance, so *t* = 2.578, df = 19, *p* = 0.009, one-tailed.

In a report you would write: There was a significant difference between the conditions (*t* = 2.578, df = 19, *p* = 0.009, one-tailed). More words were recalled in the mnemonic condition (mean = 17.7 words) than in the no mnemonic condition (mean = 14.1 words).

Footnote

Equality (or at least similarity) of variance is one of the requirements for using parametric statistical tests. SPSS, however, carries out two versions of the independent groups *t*-test: the top row for when there is equality of variance and the bottom row for when the variances are unequal. If you use the latter in a report, you must note that fact.

Section 3: The paired *t*-test

In the repeated measures design, data is collected from each participant in all levels of the independent variable. For example, we might compare participant 1's memory performance under noisy conditions with participant 1's memory performance under quiet conditions. In this situation it is likely that the data from participants will be correlated, for example if participant A has a good memory then his/her scores on a memory test will be high regardless of condition. It is for this reason that a repeated measures *t*-test is often called a *correlated t*-test. With a repeated measures design, it is essential that the data is kept in the correct order, so that participant 1's data on variable A is indeed compared with participant 1's data on variable B. The test itself considers pairs of data together, and for this reason this test is also known as a *paired t*-test.

To demonstrate the use of the paired *t*-test we are going to analyse the data from the mental imagery experiment, shown in the second data entry exercise in Chapter 2. It was hypothesised that, as participants would compare their mental images of the two animals to determine which was the larger, their decision times for the small size difference trials would be longer than for the large size difference trials. A paired *t*-test is conducted to test this hypothesis.

TO PERFORM A PAIRED *t*-TEST

1. Click on the menu item **<u>A</u>nalyze** (Versions 9 and 10) or **<u>S</u>tatistics** (Version 8).
2. Click on the words **Compare <u>M</u>eans**.
3. Click on the words **Paired-Samples T Test**.

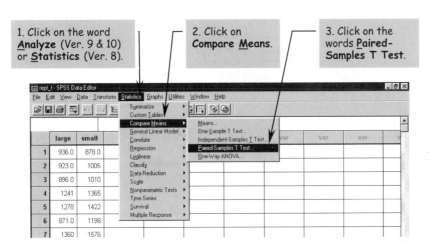

4a. You will now see the **Paired-Samples T Test** dialogue box (see below). You need to choose the names of the two variables that you want to compare. As before, all of the variables in your data file are listed in the left-hand box. Click on each of the **two** variables that you want to compare. These variable names will now be highlighted.

4b. Note that the names of the two variables you have highlighted will appear in the box marked **Current Selections.** This is useful when you have a large number of variables in your data file, as you may not be able to see both of the selected variables at the same time.

5. Now click on the rightwards-pointing arrow. This will move the two variables into the box marked **Paired Variables**.

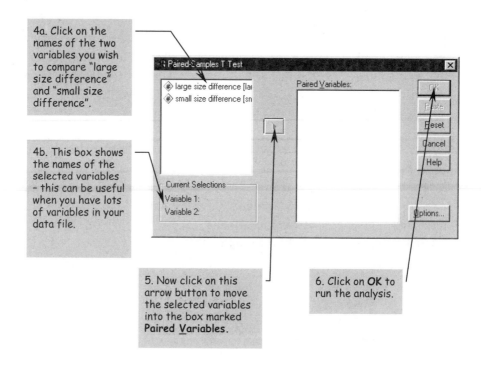

4a. Click on the names of the two variables you wish to compare "large size difference" and "small size difference".

4b. This box shows the names of the selected variables – this can be useful when you have lots of variables in your data file.

5. Now click on this arrow button to move the selected variables into the box marked **Paired Variables**.

6. Click on **OK** to run the analysis.

6. Now click on [OK] and SPSS will perform the paired *t*-test. The annotated output is shown on the following page.

Obtained Using Menu Items: > Compare Means > Paired-Samples T Test

t-Test

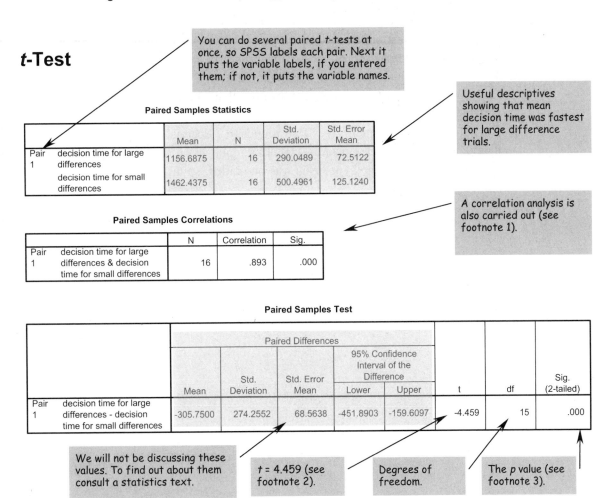

You can do several paired *t*-tests at once, so SPSS labels each pair. Next it puts the variable labels, if you entered them; if not, it puts the variable names.

Paired Samples Statistics

		Mean	N	Std. Deviation	Std. Error Mean
Pair 1	decision time for large differences	1156.6875	16	290.0489	72.5122
	decision time for small differences	1462.4375	16	500.4961	125.1240

Useful descriptives showing that mean decision time was fastest for large difference trials.

Paired Samples Correlations

		N	Correlation	Sig.
Pair 1	decision time for large differences & decision time for small differences	16	.893	.000

A correlation analysis is also carried out (see footnote 1).

Paired Samples Test

		Paired Differences							
					95% Confidence Interval of the Difference				Sig.
		Mean	Std. Deviation	Std. Error Mean	Lower	Upper	t	df	(2-tailed)
Pair 1	decision time for large differences - decision time for small differences	-305.7500	274.2552	68.5638	-451.8903	-159.6097	-4.459	15	.000

We will not be discussing these values. To find out about them consult a statistics text.

t = 4.459 (see footnote 2).

Degrees of freedom.

The *p* value (see footnote 3).

In a report you would write: The time to decide which of the pair of animals was larger, was significantly longer for small size difference trials than for large size difference trials ($t = 4.459$, df = 15, $p < 0.00025$, two-tailed).

Footnotes

1. SPSS performs a Pearson's correlation (see Chapter 4, Section 2) to see if the two variables are correlated. Ignore this, if you only want a t-test. A significant correlation would tell you that participants who were fast on large size difference trials were also fast on small size difference trials. A significant result on this test does not mean that the scores are significantly different.

2. The minus sign just means that the mean value for the first variable name in the **Paired Variables** box is lower on average than the mean value for the second variable name.

3. A p value can never equal zero. SPSS rounds to 3 decimal places, so p must be less than 0.0005 or it would appear as .001. In a report put $p < 0.0005$ if the hypothesis was two-tailed. Here the hypothesis was one-tailed, so divide by 2 which gives $p < 0.00025$, one-tailed.

Section 4: An introduction to the nonparametric equivalents of the *t*-test 非参数の

MANN–WHITNEY TEST AND WILCOXON MATCHED-PAIRS SIGNED-RANKS TEST

The Mann–Whitney test and the Wilcoxon matched-pairs signed-ranks test are nonparametric tests of whether two samples are different. In both of these tests ranking takes place, and the calculations are carried out on the ranks. In the annotated output pages for these tests, there is a brief explanation of how each test is performed. When reporting descriptive statistics to accompany the results of a nonparametric test of difference, such as the Mann–Whitney or Wilcoxon test, you should normally give the median and range (not the mean and standard deviation) as the measures of central tendency and dispersion. The median and range are more appropriate descriptives for nonparametric tests because these are distribution-free tests and do not assume normal distribution.

The Wilcoxon test is the nonparametric equivalent of the paired *t*-test, and is used for data from repeated measures and matched pairs designs. The Mann–Whitney test is the nonparametric equivalent of the independent *t*-test, and is used to compare data collected in an independent groups design. It is worth pointing out that there is an independent groups version of the Wilcoxon test. When you request a Mann–Whitney U test, SPSS also gives the statistic for this version of the Wilcoxon test.

These nonparametric tests should be used in preference to the equivalent *t*-tests under the following circumstances:
1. When data are only of ordinal level of measurement;
2. If the data are interval or ratio, but are abnormally distributed (for example are severely skewed);
3. If the data are interval or ratio, but the variances of the two samples do not meet an equality of variance test.

Section 5: The Mann–Whitney test

EXAMPLE STUDY: SEX DIFFERENCES AND EMPHASIS ON PHYSICAL ATTRACTIVENESS

To demonstrate how to perform the Mann–Whitney, we shall use the data from an experiment which was designed to determine whether males and females differ in the emphasis they place on the importance of the physical attractiveness of their partner. Previous research has reported that men are more concerned than women about the physical attractiveness of their heterosexual partner. However, current advertising trends and societal pressure may have altered the emphasis placed on physical attractiveness, and more specifically the importance they attach to "body" or physique compared with other characteristics of their ideal partner.

The hypothesis tested is two tailed: that men and women will differ in the importance they attach to physique. The design employed was an independent groups design. The independent variable was whether the participant was male or female, operationalised by asking equal numbers of males and females to take part in the experiment (only one partner from a relationship participated). The dependent variable was the importance attached to body shape, operationalised by asking participants to rank order 10 characteristics of an ideal partner, one of these being body shape. (These data are available in the Appendix.)

HOW TO DO IT

1. Click on the menu item **Analyze** (Versions 9 and 10) or **Statistics** (Version 8).
2. Click on the words **Nonparametric Tests**.
3. Click on the words **2 Independent Samples**.

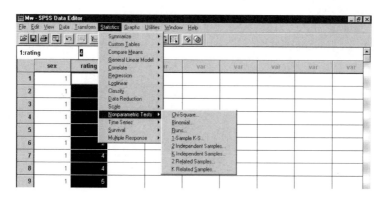

The data has been entered with the variable names "sex" and "rating". Follow steps 4 to 10, shown in the shaded boxes below, then click on [OK]. The SPSS output, which will appear after a short delay, is shown on the following page with explanatory comments.

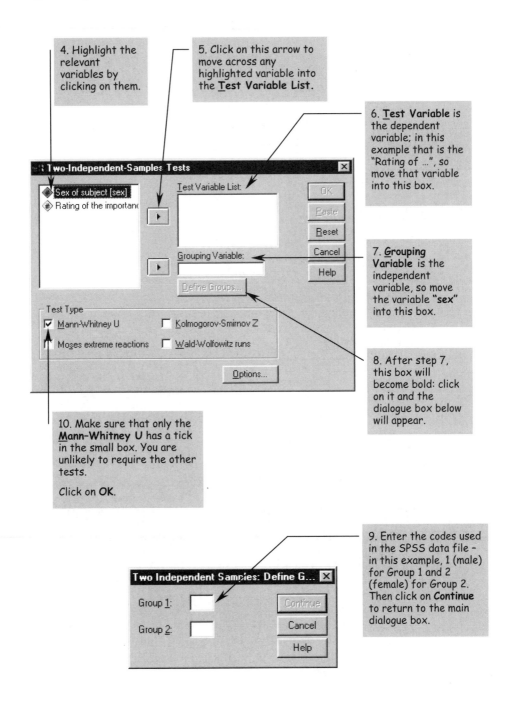

4. Highlight the relevant variables by clicking on them.

5. Click on this arrow to move across any highlighted variable into the **Test Variable List.**

6. **Test Variable** is the dependent variable; in this example that is the "Rating of ...", so move that variable into this box.

7. **Grouping Variable** is the independent variable, so move the variable **"sex"** into this box.

8. After step 7, this box will become bold: click on it and the dialogue box below will appear.

10. Make sure that only the **Mann-Whitney U** has a tick in the small box. You are unlikely to require the other tests.

Click on **OK.**

9. Enter the codes used in the SPSS data file – in this example, 1 (male) for Group 1 and 2 (female) for Group 2. Then click on **Continue** to return to the main dialogue box.

Obtained Using Menu Items: <u>N</u>onparametric Tests > <u>2</u> Independent Samples

NPar Tests

Mann–Whitney Test

Ranks

	Sex of subject	N	Mean Rank	Sum of Ranks
Rating of the importance of body as characteristic in a partner	Male	20	17.88	357.50
	Female	20	23.13	462.50
	Total	40		

You do not need to use this part of the output, which gives you some information about the calculations for the Mann–Whitney U test: first all the data from both groups combined are assigned ranks from the lowest to the highest; then the ranks given to one group are compared with the ranks given to the other group; the mean ranks shown here indicate whether there are more high ranks in one group than in the other.

Test Statistics[b]

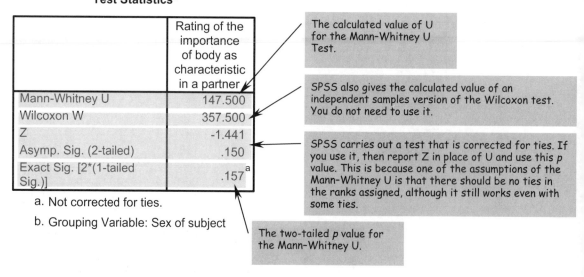

	Rating of the importance of body as characteristic in a partner
Mann-Whitney U	147.500
Wilcoxon W	357.500
Z	-1.441
Asymp. Sig. (2-tailed)	.150
Exact Sig. [2*(1-tailed Sig.)]	.157[a]

a. Not corrected for ties.

b. Grouping Variable: Sex of subject

The calculated value of U for the Mann–Whitney U Test.

SPSS also gives the calculated value of an independent samples version of the Wilcoxon test. You do not need to use it.

SPSS carries out a test that is corrected for ties. If you use it, then report Z in place of U and use this p value. This is because one of the assumptions of the Mann–Whitney U is that there should be no ties in the ranks assigned, although it still works even with some ties.

The two-tailed p value for the Mann–Whitney U.

In a report you would write: There was no significant difference between men and women in the importance they attached to body shape in a partner (U = 147.500, N_1 = 20, N_2 = 20, p = 0.157, two-tailed).

Section 6: The Wilcoxon test

EXAMPLE STUDY: QUALITY OF E-FIT IMAGES

The police frequently use a computerised facial composite system to help eyewitnesses recall the face of a perpetrator. One such system is E-FIT (the Electronic Facial Identification Technique). In a study by Newlands (1997), participants were shown a short video clip of a mock crime scenario depicting an instance of petty theft. Participants were then asked to generate an E-FIT composite of the perpetrator. On completion, they were asked to rate the likeness of their E-FIT image to the person they remember seeing in the video. They were then shown a photograph of the perpetrator and again asked to rate the likeness of their E-FIT to that person.

The hypothesis tested was one-tailed: that the likeness ratings of the E-FIT to the perpetrator would be more favourable when recalling the perpetrator from memory than when seeing a photograph of the perpetrator. The design employed was a repeated measures design. The independent variable was the presence or absence of a photograph of the perpetrator, operationalised by asking participants to rate the likeness of their E-FIT, first to their recall of perpetrator and then to a photograph of the perpetrator. The dependent variable was measured on an ordinal scale and was the likeness rating, operationalised by the response on a 7-point scale where point 1 was "very good likeness" and point 7 "no likeness".

For the purposes of this book, we have created a data file that will reproduce some of the findings of this study. (These data are available in the Appendix.)

HOW TO DO IT

1. Click on the menu item **<u>A</u>nalyze** (Versions 9 and 10) or **<u>S</u>tatistics** (Version 8).
2. Click on the words **<u>N</u>onparametric Tests**.
3. Click on the words **2 Re<u>l</u>ated Samples**.

The dialogue box shown on the next page will appear. The variable labels, and the variable names (mem and photo), used in the data file appear in the box on the left-hand side. Follow steps 4 to 8, shown in the shaded boxes, then click on ☐ OK ☐. The SPSS output, which will appear after a short delay, is shown on the following page with explanatory comments.

4a. The list of variable labels from the data file. Highlight the two variables that you want to enter into the analysis by clicking on them.

5. This arrow will not become active unless you have highlighted two variable labels in the box to the left.

6. When you click on the arrow, the two variable labels that you highlighted will appear in this box.

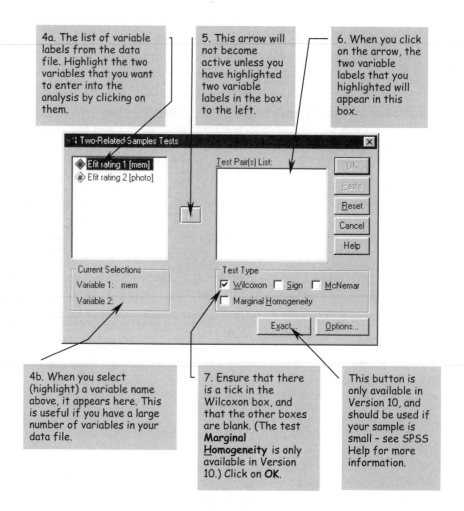

4b. When you select (highlight) a variable name above, it appears here. This is useful if you have a large number of variables in your data file.

7. Ensure that there is a tick in the Wilcoxon box, and that the other boxes are blank. (The test **Marginal Homogeneity** is only available in Version 10.) Click on **OK**.

This button is only available in Version 10, and should be used if your sample is small – see SPSS Help for more information.

Obtained Using Menu Items: <u>N</u>onparametric Tests > 2 Re<u>l</u>ated Samples

NPar Tests

Wilcoxon Signed Ranks Test

Ranks

		N	Mean Rank	Sum of Ranks
Efit rating 2 - Efit rating 1	Negative Ranks	19[a]	20.26	385.00
	Positive Ranks	20[b]	19.75	395.00
	Ties	9[c]		
	Total	48		

a. Efit rating 2 < Efit rating 1

b. Efit rating 2 > Efit rating 1

c. Efit rating 1 = Efit rating 2

These are the variable labels. If you did not enter variable labels, then the variable names will appear here.

This section gives you some information about the calculations for the Wilcoxon test. You don't need it, but: first, for each subject the score for one level of the independent variable is subtracted from the score for the other level; then those differences are ranked, ignoring the sign (whether negative or positive) and omitting ties. Once ranking is completed, the signs are reattached. The mean ranks indicate whether there are more high ranks for the positive differences, or for the negative differences, or whether there is a fairly equal spread of ranks as in this example.

Test Statistics[b]

	Efit rating 2 - Efit rating 1
Z	-.072[a]
Asymp. Sig. (2-tailed)	.943

a. Based on negative ranks.

b. Wilcoxon Signed Ranks Test

This row shows the p value. The hypothesis for this example was one-tailed, so divide the p value by 2 to give p = 0.4715. (That is still much greater than 0.05.)

SPSS gives the **z** value, shown in this row, not the T or W value shown in most textbooks. As Howell (1997) explains, **z** should always be used for large samples but it involves extra calculations. SPSS does that automatically. The negative sign can be ignored (as for the *t*-test).

In a report you would write:

There was no significant difference between the conditions ($z = 0.072$, N-ties = 39, $p = 0.4715$, one-tailed).

Note: if you were performing this test by calculator, the N used to look up the critical value in the statistics table for Wilcoxon is the number of subjects minus the ties (those who got the same score in both conditions).

Chapter Four

Tests of association

The chi-square test
Tests of correlation

Section 1: The chi-square test

The chi-square test is used to explore frequency data – that is data that indicate how often a particular event occurs (nominal data). The chi-square statistic allows us to compare the distribution of frequency data that we have collected in a study with the distribution that we would expect to occur by chance. That is it allows us to compare the observed frequencies with the expected frequencies.

TWO DIFFERENT FORMS OF THE CHI-SQUARE TEST

The goodness-of-fit-test

In the first of these – often referred to as either a 1-dimensional chi or a goodness-of-fit-test – we are testing whether the observed pattern of events differs significantly from what we might have expected by chance alone. For example we might ask whether a group of smokers choose brand A cigarettes more often than brand B. Here we are effectively asking the question "do significantly more than 50% of our smokers choose one brand over the other brand". In practice this form of the chi-square test is not often used in psychology. The example of cigarette brands given above actually relates to one of the few times the authors have ever used this form of the test. An undergraduate student recently undertook a project examining the effect of cigarette advertising on cigarette choice. As part of this project she listed a series of personality characteristics that were implied by cigarette adverts. For example some cigarette advertisements might imply a sophisticated personality. These personality statements were then presented to smokers who were asked to indicate to which of 5 brands of cigarettes they thought the statement best applied. The responses for each statement were analysed using the chi goodness-of-fit-test to test the observed distribution against that predicted by the null-hypothesis (that the 5 brands would be equally often selected). This is an interesting, but rare example of the use of this form of the chi-square test in psychology. Much more common is the second form of this test that allows us to consider whether two variables are independent of one another.

The multi-dimensional chi-square

The multi-dimensional chi allows us to test whether two variables are independent of each other. For example, let us modify our cigarette example and say that 50 Smokers and 50 Non-Smokers were asked to choose which of two cigarette adverts they preferred. This form of the chi-square test would allow us to ask the question:

"Is the pattern of brand choice independent of whether the participant was a smoker or not?" Another example would be to determine whether receiving or not receiving a particular treatment was associated with living or dying. Yet another might be to see whether a person's sex was independent of their choice of favourite colour. In psychology we often need to test whether variables such as these are truly independent of each other. Often we are hypothesising that the 2 variables are not independent of each other – for example we could hypothesise that people receiving a particular treatment are less likely to die than those not receiving the treatment.

In order to use chi-square our data must satisfy the following criteria:

1. The data must be frequency data – which are number counts. In other words, our data must tell us the number of times some event has occurred. We can of course convert other types of data into frequency data. For example, suppose we have IQ scores – we could recode this data, scoring each participant as either "High IQ" or "Low IQ" depending on their score. We would now have frequency data – the *number* of high and low IQ participants we have observed. (See Chapter 5, Section 5 for information on how to recode in this way.)

2. We must have collected data of this sort on at least two variables. For example, in addition to the high/low IQ data above, we might also know whether each of these participants is a smoker or not.

3. The categorisations of each of the variables must be mutually exclusive. In other words, each participant must be **either** a smoker **or** a non-smoker, and **either** high IQ **or** low IQ. Another way of thinking about this is to say that each participant must fall into one and only one of the cells of the table (see below).

4. Every observation must be independent of every other observation. This will not be the case if you have more than one observation per participant.

The N * N contingency table

When we have frequency data of this form we can best display it in what is called a contingency table. If we have two variables, each with two levels (as in the example above) then we draw what is called a 2*2 (pronounced two by two) contingency table. So if we had 100 participants in our example data set the contingency table might look like the one below:

Table 4.1: An illustration of a 2*2 contingency table

	High IQ	Low IQ	Row Totals
Smokers	10	20	30
Non-Smokers	35	35	70
Column Totals	45	55	100 (Grand Total)

The numbers in this table represent the numbers of participants who fall into each cell of the table (and remember that each participant can be in only one cell). So we can see that of the 30 smokers in our study 10 are high IQ and 20 are low IQ. Similarly we can see that of the Low IQ group, 20 are smokers and 35 are non-smokers.

If there were no association between smoking and IQ then we would expect the proportion of smokers in the high IQ group to be the same as the proportion in the total population. That is we would expect 45/100 or 45% of the smokers to be high IQ. As there were 30 smokers in total we would thus expect (45% of 30) = 13.5% of the smokers to be in the high IQ group. In this way we can work out the expected frequencies for each cell. The general formula is:

$$\text{expected frequency} = \frac{\text{row total} * \text{column total}}{\text{grand total}}$$

What chi-square does is to calculate the expected frequency for each cell and then compare the expected frequencies with the observed frequencies. If the observed and expected frequencies are significantly different then it would appear that the distribution of observations across the cells is not random and we can conclude that there is a significant association between the two variables. In this case we would say that IQ and smoking behaviour are not independent for our sample of (fictitious) participants.

Chi-square will actually allow us to calculate whether more than 2 variables are independent of each other. However, it is very difficult to interpret the results of such an analysis, so we would recommend that you resist the temptation to add extra variables unless you are sure you know what you are doing. It is, however, perfectly reasonable to have more than 2 categories of each variable – for example a 3*3 chi-square is quite acceptable.

EXAMPLE STUDY: INVESTIGATING TENDENCY TOWARDS ANOREXIA

To illustrate the use of chi-square we will use some fictitious data based on research conducted by one of our past students. Eighty young women completed an eating questionnaire which allowed them to be classified as either High or Low "Anorexia" (participants with high scores are more likely to develop anorexia). In addition, the questionnaire asked for the employment status of the women's mother (either full-time, part-time or unemployed) and their cultural background (Caucasian, Asian or Other) and type of school they attended (Private or State Comprehensive). Previous research has suggested that the incidence of anorexia is higher among girls attending private schools than state schools, and higher among girls whose mother's are not in full-time employment. In addition the incidence seems to be higher in Caucasian girls than non-Caucasian girls. We therefore hypothesised that there would be an association between these factors and the classification on the eating questionnaire. To test this hypothesis we conducted a series of chi-square analyses. (These data are available in the Appendix.)

TO PERFORM THE CHI-SQUARE TEST

The goodness-of-fit chi-square is accessed via the chi-square command that can be found under **Nonparametric tests** in the **Analyze** menu in Versions 9 and 10 and in the **Statistics** menu in Version 8. However, as this form of the test is used infrequently in psychology we will not be demonstrating it here.

The multi-dimensional chi-square is accessed under the **Crosstabs** command. Crosstabs draws up contingency tables and chi-square is an optional statistic within this command.

1. Click on the menu item **Analyze** (Versions 9 and 10) or **Statistics** (Version 8).
2. Click on the words **Descriptive Statistics**.
3. Now click on the words **Crosstabs**.

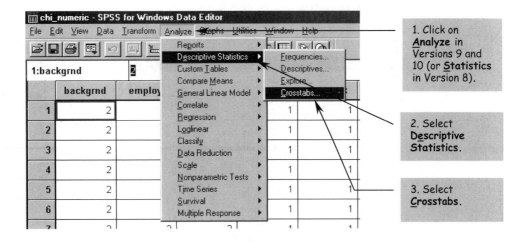

1. Click on **Analyze** in Versions 9 and 10 (or **Statistics** in Version 8).

2. Select **Descriptive Statistics**.

3. Select **Crosstabs**.

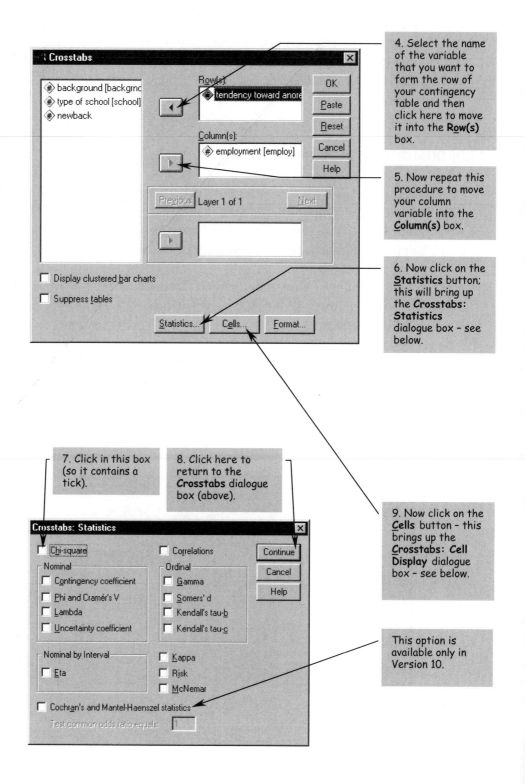

4. Select the name of the variable that you want to form the row of your contingency table and then click here to move it into the **Row(s)** box.

5. Now repeat this procedure to move your column variable into the **Column(s)** box.

6. Now click on the **Statistics** button; this will bring up the **Crosstabs: Statistics** dialogue box – see below.

7. Click in this box (so it contains a tick).

8. Click here to return to the **Crosstabs** dialogue box (above).

9. Now click on the **Cells** button – this brings up the **Crosstabs: Cell Display** dialogue box – see below.

This option is available only in Version 10.

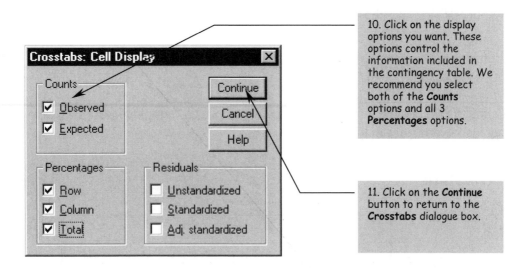

10. Click on the display options you want. These options control the information included in the contingency table. We recommend you select both of the **Counts** options and all 3 **Percentages** options.

11. Click on the **Continue** button to return to the **Crosstabs** dialogue box.

Finally, click on the ⌐ok⌐ button in the **Crosstabs** dialogue box. SPSS will now switch to the output window and display the contingency table and the chi-square results. Two sets of annotated output are given on the next four pages. The first is from the 2*3 chi-square exploring the association between the incidence of tendency towards anorexia and mother's employment status. The second is from the 2*2 chi-square exploring the association between tendency towards anorexia and type of school attended.

Obtained Using Menu Items: Summarize (Version 8) or Descriptive Statistics (Versions 9 and 10) > Crosstabs

Output for first chi-square: tendency toward anorexia * employment (a variable with two levels against a variable with three levels)

Crosstabs

> In this table, SPSS reminds you of the variables entered into the analysis and gives you some summary information about the cases in your data file.

Case Processing Summary

	Cases					
	Valid		Missing		Total	
	N	Percent	N	Percent	N	Percent
tendency toward anorexia * employment	80	100.0%	0	.0%	80	100.0%

> This is the variable put into the rows of the table, and these are its two levels.

> This table gives you some simple descriptive statistics: counts and percentages for the crosstabulation of the two variables.

> This is the variable put into the columns, and these are its three levels.

tendency toward anorexia * employment Crosstabulation

			employment			
			f/t	none	p/t	Total
tendency toward anorexia	high	Count	14	13	11	38
		Expected Count	14.7	11.9	11.4	38.0
		% within tendency toward anorexia	36.8%	34.2%	28.9%	100.0%
		% within employment	45.2%	52.0%	45.8%	47.5%
		% of Total	17.5%	16.3%	13.8%	47.5%
	low	Count	17	12	13	42
		Expected Count	16.3	13.1	12.6	42.0
		% within tendency toward anorexia	40.5%	28.6%	31.0%	100.0%
		% within employment	54.8%	48.0%	54.2%	52.5%
		% of Total	21.3%	15.0%	16.3%	52.5%
Total		Count	31	25	24	80
		Expected Count	31.0	25.0	24.0	80.0
		% within tendency toward anorexia	38.8%	31.3%	30.0%	100.0%
		% within employment	100.0%	100.0%	100.0%	100.0%
		% of Total	38.8%	31.3%	30.0%	100.0%

> If you clicked on all the Counts and Percentages that we suggested in the **Crosstabs: Cell Display** dialogue box, then all these descriptives are given for each cell. The meaning of the cells are described on the crosstabulations table for the second chi-square (see page 98).

Chi-Square Tests

	Value	df	Asymp. Sig. (2-sided)
Pearson Chi-Square	.298[a]	2	.862
Likelihood Ratio	.298	2	.862
Linear-by-Linear Association	.008	1	.930
N of Valid Cases	80		

a. 0 cells (.0%) have expected count less than 5. The minimum expected count is 11.40.

This table contains the results of chi-square tests: if either variable has more than two levels (as here), then SPSS reports these three chi-squares.

Pearson's chi-square is used most often, so report this row. (Whichever chi-square test you use, you should give its name when describing the statistical test used.)

In a report you would write:

There was no relationship between tendency towards anorexia and the employment status of the mother ($\chi^2 = 0.298$, df = 2, $p = 0.862$).

Output for second chi-square: tendency toward anorexia * education (two variables each with two levels)

A row gives information about each level of the column variable; e.g. this row gives information for girls in the "high" group. It shows the figures for those in comprehensive education separately from those in private education. The total is for all girls in the "high" group. Here we can see that of the total of 38 "high" girls, 4 were in comprehensive education and 34 were in private education.

tendency toward anorexia * type of school Crosstabulation

			type of school comp	type of school private	Total
tendency toward anorexia	high	Count	4	34	38
		Expected Count	15.7	22.3	38.0
		% within tendency toward anorexia	10.5%	89.5%	100.0%
		% within type of school	12.1%	72.3%	47.5%
		% of Total	5.0%	42.5%	47.5%
	low	Count	29	13	42
		Expected Count	17.3	24.7	42.0
		% within tendency toward anorexia	69.0%	31.0%	100.0%
		% within type of school	87.9%	27.7%	52.5%
		% of Total	36.3%	16.3%	52.5%
Total		Count	33	47	80
		Expected Count	33.0	47.0	80.0
		% within tendency toward anorexia	41.3%	58.8%	100.0%
		% within type of school	100.0%	100.0%	100.0%
		% of Total	41.3%	58.8%	100.0%

Within each cell we are given:

Count = the number of participants falling into the cell; i.e. the number of girls who are "low" and attended comprehensive education (the observed frequency)

Expected count: the number expected for this cell assuming no association (see text)

% within tendency toward anorexia: the cases in this cell as a % of row total; i.e. % of "low" girls who attend comprehensive school

% within type of school: the cases in this cell as a % of the column total; i.e. the % of girls who attend comprehensive school who are "low".

% of total: the cases in this cell as a % of the total number of participants.

A column gives information about each level of the row variable. This column shows figures for girls in private schools. Figures are given separately for those in the "high" and "low" groups and for the total for all girls in private education.

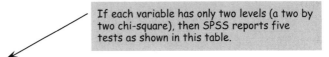

If each variable has only two levels (a two by two chi-square), then SPSS reports five tests as shown in this table.

Chi-Square Tests

	Value	df	Asymp. Sig. (2-sided)	Exact Sig. (2-sided)	Exact Sig. (1-sided)
Pearson Chi-Square	28.193[b]	1	.000		
Continuity Correction[a]	25.830	1	.000		
Likelihood Ratio	30.895	1	.000		
Fisher's Exact Test				.000	.000
Linear-by-Linear Association	27.840	1	.000		
N of Valid Cases	80				

a. Computed only for a 2x2 table

b. 0 cells (.0%) have expected count less than 5. The minimum expected count is 15.68.

Continuity correction is the Yates's corrected chi-square. See text below.

You can ignore Fisher's Exact Test, unless any of the cells have an expected count of less than five (see output for fourth chi-square on page 101).

If you used Pearson's chi-square, then in a report you would write:
There was a relationship between tendency towards anorexia and the type of school attended ($\chi^2 = 28.193$, df $= 1$, $p < 0.0005$).

Reporting and interpreting results from chi-square

SPSS reports several different measures of p. It is probably best to use Pearson's (the chi-square test was developed by Karl Pearson). If your table was a 2*2 table, SPSS will also calculate the result with and without what is usually called "Yates's correction". This is a statistical correction used in cases with relatively few participants or in which you have reason to believe that your sample is not a very good approximation to the total population. A good rule of thumb is, if SPSS provides chi-square with Yates's correction, then report this value.

It is important to understand that the chi-square result on its own cannot tell you about the pattern of your results. For that you have to look at the contingency table. For example, when reporting the results of the second chi-square result shown above, you might write: "within the comprehensive school a minority (only 12%) of pupils scored high on the scale, whereas in the private school the majority (72%) scored high on the scale."

If you made a specific one-tailed prediction about the direction of the relationship between the two variables (here we predicted that there will be a higher tendency towards anorexia in the private school pupils) and the pattern of results revealed by the contingency is compatible with this prediction (as here), then you can use the chi-square results to assess whether this association is significant.

A problem with chi-square

You should not use the chi-square statistic if any of the cells in your contingency table have an expected frequency of less than 5. You will see on the output above, that SPSS prints a note at the bottom of the table of statistics (note b). This note informs you of the number of cells with expected frequencies (what SPSS calls expected counts) of less than 5. It is very important that you always check this note. In both the cases above there are no cells with this problem. However, if you do perform a chi-square analysis and SPSS reports that there are 1 or more cells with an expected frequency of less than 5 then you must take some action. If you are performing a 2*2 chi-square, then SPSS reports an additional statistic called Fisher's Exact test. This test can be used when cells have low expected frequencies (see Siegel and Castellan, 1988, pp. 103–111). However, this test is only available for 2*2 tables. If you are performing something other than a 2*2 chi-square and encounter this problem you will have to use the Recode command to collapse some of your cells.

To demonstrate this for you, we have undertaken two further chi-square analyses, exploring a possible association between cultural background and tendency towards anorexia.

The third SPSS output shown on page 101 reports that 2 cells have an expected frequency of less than 5. As this was a 2*3 chi-square we cannot report the result as it stands. Our solution is to use the Recode command (see Chapter 5, Section 5) to combine the "Asian" and "Other" groups into one "Non-Caucasian" group. This turns our 2*3 into a 2*2 analysis and ensures that Fisher's Exact test is reported. This final chi-square is reproduced in the fourth SPSS output on page 101.

Output for third chi-square: tendency toward anorexia * cultural background (here with three levels)

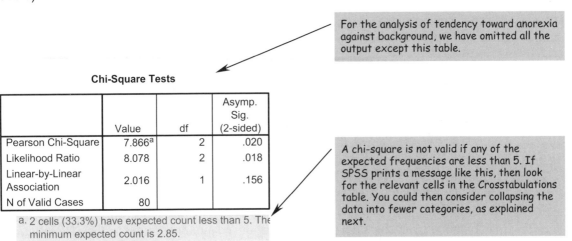

For the analysis of tendency toward anorexia against background, we have omitted all the output except this table.

Chi-Square Tests

	Value	df	Asymp. Sig. (2-sided)
Pearson Chi-Square	7.866[a]	2	.020
Likelihood Ratio	8.078	2	.018
Linear-by-Linear Association	2.016	1	.156
N of Valid Cases	80		

a. 2 cells (33.3%) have expected count less than 5. The minimum expected count is 2.85.

A chi-square is not valid if any of the expected frequencies are less than 5. If SPSS prints a message like this, then look for the relevant cells in the Crosstabulations table. You could then consider collapsing the data into fewer categories, as explained next.

You cannot report this result as some cells have an expected frequency of less than 5. The solution to this problem involves using the Recode command (see Chapter 5, Section 5). The output produced following this recode is reproduced below, where "Asian" and "Other" have been combined into a "Non-Caucasian" group.

Output for fourth chi-square: tendency toward anorexia * cultural background (here with two levels)

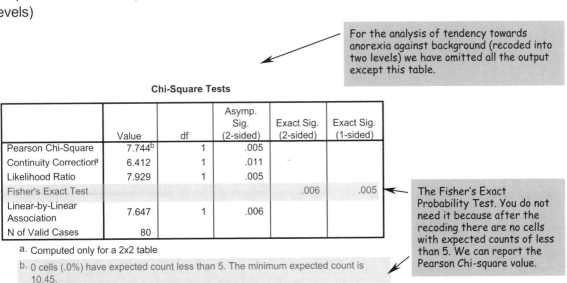

For the analysis of tendency towards anorexia against background (recoded into two levels) we have omitted all the output except this table.

Chi-Square Tests

	Value	df	Asymp. Sig. (2-sided)	Exact Sig. (2-sided)	Exact Sig. (1-sided)
Pearson Chi-Square	7.744[b]	1	.005		
Continuity Correction[a]	6.412	1	.011		
Likelihood Ratio	7.929	1	.005		
Fisher's Exact Test				.006	.005
Linear-by-Linear Association	7.647	1	.006		
N of Valid Cases	80				

a. Computed only for a 2x2 table

b. 0 cells (.0%) have expected count less than 5. The minimum expected count is 10.45.

The Fisher's Exact Probability Test. You do not need it because after the recoding there are no cells with expected counts of less than 5. We can report the Pearson Chi-square value.

In a report you would write:

There was a relationship between tendency towards anorexia and cultural background ($\chi^2 = 7.744$, df = 1, $p = 0.005$).

Section 2: Tests of correlation

INTRODUCTION TO CORRELATION

Researchers often wish to measure the degree of relationship between two variables. For example, there is likely to be a relationship between age and reading ability in children. Such an investigation is not a true experiment, for the same reason that a natural independent groups design (for example, when age or sex is selected as the grouping variable) is not a true experiment. In both, the experimenter does not manipulate the independent variable, and no statement about causation can be made. In a natural independent groups design, the experimenter chooses the levels of the independent variable from "natural" characteristics. In a correlation there is no independent variable: you simply measure two variables. So, if someone wished to investigate the effect of smoking on respiratory function, then, in a natural independent groups design, you could choose to measure and then compare respiratory function in smokers with that in non-smokers. A more common design, however, would be for researchers to measure both how many cigarettes people smoke and their respiratory function, and then test for a correlation.

An important point to remember is that correlation does not imply causation. In any correlation, there could be a third variable which explains the association between the two variables that you measured. For example, there may be a correlation between the number of ice creams sold and the number of people who drown. Here temperature is the third variable, which could explain the relationship between the measured variables. Even when there seems to be a clear cause and effect relationship, you cannot prove it by means of a correlation.

Francis Galton carried out early work on correlation, and one of his colleagues, Pearson, developed a method of calculating correlation coefficients for parametric data: Pearson's Product Moment Correlation Coefficient (Pearson's r). When one or both of the scales is **not** either interval or ratio, or if the data do not meet the other two assumptions for using parametric statistical tests, then a nonparametric test of correlation such as Spearman's ρ should be used. (ρ is the Greek letter called rho; some textbooks refer to Spearman's rho, and others to Spearman's r_s – the $_s$ is to distinguish it from Pearson's r.)

One of the easiest ways to tell if two items are related and to spot trends is to plot scattergrams or scatterplots. Figure 4.1 shows a hypothetical example. Each point on the scattergram represents the age and the reading ability of one child. The line running through the data points is called a regression line. It represents the "best fit" of a straight line to the data points. The line in Figure 4.1 slopes upwards from left to right: as one variable increases in value, the other variable also increases in value and this is called a positive correlation. The closer the points are to being on the line itself, the stronger the correlation. If all the points fall along the straight line, then it is said to be a perfect correlation.

Figure 4.1 Scattergram illustrating a positive correlation: hypothetical data for the relationship between age and reading ability in children

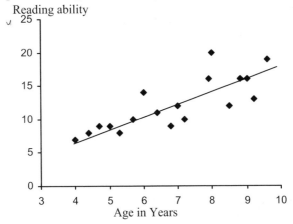

In the scattergram shown in Figure 4.2, the dots are scattered randomly, all over the graph. It is not possible to draw any meaningful best fit line at all, and the correlation would be close to zero: that is, there is no relationship between the two variables.

Figure 4.2 Scattergram showing two variables with zero relationship

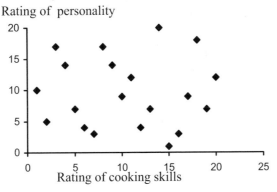

It is often the case that as one variable increases in value, the other variable decreases in value: this is called a negative correlation. In the following example of how to produce a scattergram, we are going to use data which give a negative correlation.

EXAMPLE STUDY: RELATIONSHIP BETWEEN AGE AND CFF

A paper by Mason, Snelgar, Foster, Heron and Jones (1982) described an investigation of (among other things) whether the negative correlation between CFF (explained below) and age is different for people with Multiple Sclerosis than for control participants. For this example, we have created a data file that will reproduce some of the findings for the control participants. CFF can be described briefly and somewhat simplistically as follows. If a light is flickering on and off at a low frequency, then most people can detect the flicker. If the frequency of flicker is increased then eventually it looks like a steady light. The frequency at which someone can no longer perceive flicker is called his or her critical flicker frequency (CFF). (These data are available in the Appendix.)

How to obtain a scattergram with regression line

Click on **Graphs** on the menu bar, and then from the menu select **Scatter**. In the **Scatterplot** dialogue box, shown below, click on the **Simple** display, then click on the **Define** button.

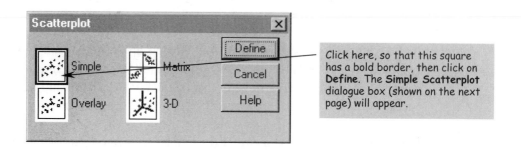

The other options in the **Scatterplot** dialogue box produce more complex graphs, which you can explore in the future. We will only be describing the **Simple** command. After you have clicked on the **Define** button, the **Simple Scatterplot** dialogue box will appear. It is shown below.

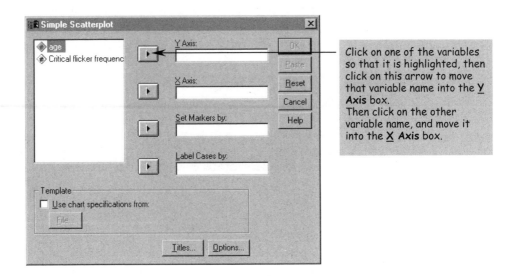

Click on one of the variables so that it is highlighted, then click on this arrow to move that variable name into the **Y Axis** box.
Then click on the other variable name, and move it into the **X Axis** box.

In the **Simple Scatterplot** dialogue box, shown above, move the variable names, one into the box labelled **X Axis**, and one into the **Y Axis** box. You can use the **Titles** button and the **Options** button if you wish. When you have finished, click on **OK**. The Output Window will open, containing the scattergram: a part of that window is shown below. To add the regression line, you have to edit the graph: start by double clicking in the scattergram, and the SPSS Chart Editor Window, shown on the next page, will appear.

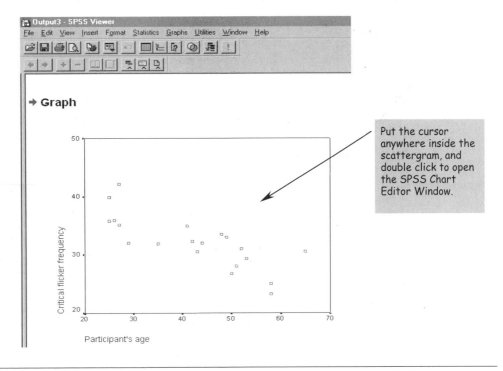

Put the cursor anywhere inside the scattergram, and double click to open the SPSS Chart Editor Window.

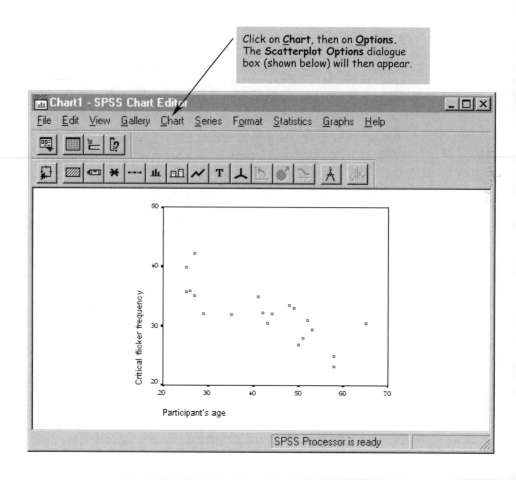

Click on **Chart**, then on **Options**.
The **Scatterplot Options** dialogue box (shown below) will then appear.

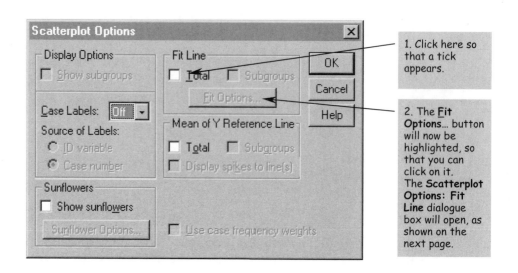

1. Click here so that a tick appears.

2. The **Fit Options...** button will now be highlighted, so that you can click on it. The **Scatterplot Options: Fit Line** dialogue box will open, as shown on the next page.

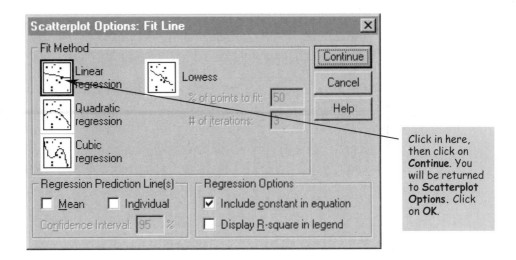

When you have clicked on **OK** in the **Scatterplot Options** dialogue box, the SPSS Chart Editor Window will display the regression line in the scattergram, as shown below. To use the scattergram in other packages, click on **Edit**, **Copy Chart**: the scattergram will be placed on the Clipboard, and may be pasted into word processing documents. You can then add a figure legend as shown below. See Chapter 8 for more information on how to paste SPSS output into other documents.

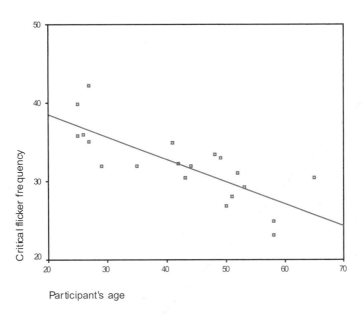

Figure 4.3 Scattergram produced by SPSS, showing critical flicker frequency (in Hz) plotted against the age (in years) of the participants.

Note that a scattergram is only a descriptive statistic. To demonstrate whether or not there is a correlation, an inferential statistical test of correlation has to be carried out. A test of correlation will give both the significance level and the strength of the correlation.

The strength of correlation is indicated by the value of the correlation coefficient which varies between 1 and 0. A perfect negative correlation would have a coefficient of -1, and a perfect positive correlation would have a coefficient of +1. In psychology perfect correlations (in which all the points fall exactly on the regression line) are extremely rare and rather suspect.

PEARSON'S R: PARAMETRIC TEST OF CORRELATION

To illustrate how to carry out this parametric test of correlation, we will use the same data as we used to obtain the scattergram and regression line.

The hypothesis tested was that there would be a negative correlation between CFF and age.

The study employed a correlational design. Two variables were measured. The first was age, operationalised by asking participants who ranged in age from 25 to 66 to participate. The second variable was CFF, operationalised by using a flicker generator to measure CFF for each participant: six measures were made, and the mean taken to give a single CFF score for each participant.

How to perform a Pearson's r

Click on **Analyze** (Versions 9 and 10) or **Statistics** (Version 8). From the sub-menu choose **Correlate**, and from the next sub-menu choose **Bivariate**. The **Bivariate Correlations** dialogue box shown on the next page will then appear. Follow the instructions in the shaded boxes. The SPSS output for Pearson's r is shown on page 110.

> **TIP**   SPSS will produce a complete correlation matrix. This means that it will correlate each variable with every other variable. Thus, if you included three variables A, B and C, it will calculate the correlation coefficient for A * B, A * C and B * C.

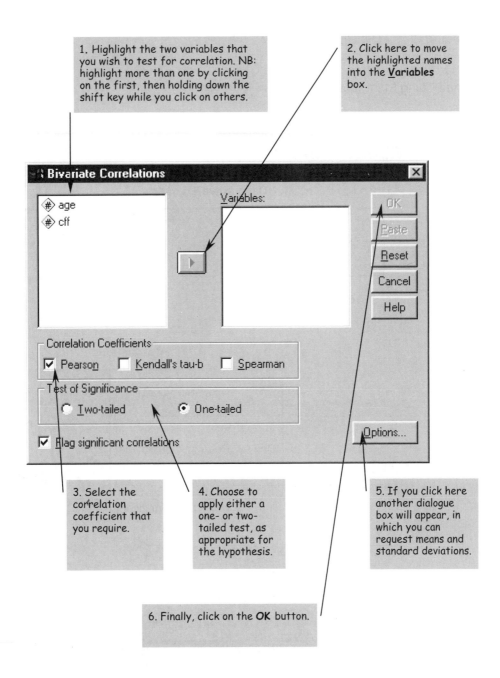

1. Highlight the two variables that you wish to test for correlation. NB: highlight more than one by clicking on the first, then holding down the shift key while you click on others.

2. Click here to move the highlighted names into the **Variables** box.

3. Select the correlation coefficient that you require.

4. Choose to apply either a one- or two-tailed test, as appropriate for the hypothesis.

5. If you click here another dialogue box will appear, in which you can request means and standard deviations.

6. Finally, click on the **OK** button.

TIP   In the **Bivariate Correlations** dialogue box, you have the option of choosing either a one- or two-tailed test, and SPSS will then print the appropriate value of p. In the statistical tests that we have covered previously, SPSS prints the two-tailed p value, and if you have a one-tailed hypothesis you halve that value to give the one-tailed p value.

Obtained Using Menu Item: <u>C</u>orrelate > <u>B</u>ivariate

Correlations

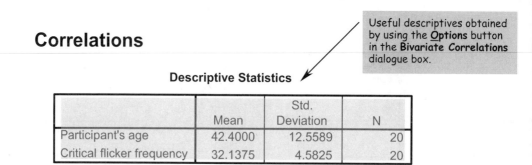

Useful descriptives obtained by using the **Options** button in the **Bivariate Correlations** dialogue box.

Descriptive Statistics

	Mean	Std. Deviation	N
Participant's age	42.4000	12.5589	20
Critical flicker frequency	32.1375	4.5825	20

Correlations

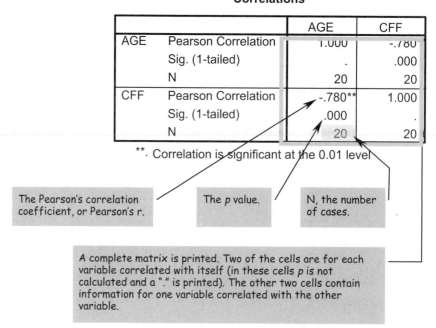

		AGE	CFF
AGE	Pearson Correlation	1.000	-.780
	Sig. (1-tailed)	.	.000
	N	20	20
CFF	Pearson Correlation	-.780**	1.000
	Sig. (1-tailed)	.000	.
	N	20	20

**. Correlation is significant at the 0.01 level

The Pearson's correlation coefficient, or Pearson's r.

The *p* value.

N, the number of cases.

A complete matrix is printed. Two of the cells are for each variable correlated with itself (in these cells *p* is not calculated and a "." is printed). The other two cells contain information for one variable correlated with the other variable.

In a report you would write: There was a significant negative correlation between age and CFF (r = -0.780, n = 20, *p* < 0.0005, one-tailed).

TIP For correlations, the sign of the coefficient indicates whether the correlation is positive or negative, so you must report it (unlike the sign in a *t*-test analysis).

SPEARMAN'S RHO: NONPARAMETRIC TEST OF CORRELATION

If either (or both) of the two variables involved in a correlational design are nonparametic (e.g. because they have not been measured on an interval or ratio scale), then we cannot use a parametric test such as Pearson's to assess the correlation. In such cases we must use a nonparametric measure of correlation. Here, we describe two such tests, Spearman's rho and Kendall's tau B.

Example study: the relationships between attractiveness, believability, and confidence

Previous research using mock juries has shown that attractive defendants are less likely to be found guilty than unattractive defendants, and that attractive individuals are frequently rated more highly on other desirable traits, such as intelligence. In a study undertaken by one of our students, participants saw the testimony of a woman in a real case of alleged rape. They were asked to rate her, on a scale of one to seven, in terms of how much confidence they placed in her testimony, how believable she was and how attractive she was. (These data are available in the Appendix.)

The design employed was a correlation; with three variables each measured on a 7 point scale yielding ordinal data. The hypotheses tested were that:
1. There would be a positive relationship between attractiveness and confidence placed in testimony
2. There would be a positive relationship between attractiveness and believability
3. There would be a positive relationship between confidence placed in testimony and believability.

How to perform Spearman's rho

The steps in SPSS for Spearman's rho are exactly the same as for the Pearson's r (see page 109) except that at step 3 you select **Spearman** instead of **Pearson**.

This example also illustrates the fact that you can carry out more than one correlation at once. There are three variables, and we want to investigate the relationship between each variable with each of the other two. To do this you simply highlight all three variable names and move them all into the **Variables** box.

The SPSS output for Spearman's rho is shown below.

Obtained Using Menu Item: Correlate Bivariate

Nonparametric Correlations

Correlations

			CONFDT	BELIEV	ATTRCT
Spearman's rho	CONFDT	Correlation Coefficient	1.000	.372**	.157
		Sig. (2-tailed)	.	.000	.143
		N	89	89	89
	BELIEV	Correlation Coefficient	.372**	1.000	.359**
		Sig. (2-tailed)	.000	.	.001
		N	89	89	89
	ATTRCT	Correlation Coefficient	.157	.359**	1.000
		Sig. (2-tailed)	.143	.001	.
		N	89	89	89

**. Correlation is significant at the .01 level (2-tailed).

This cell contains the values for the correlation
between variables CONFDT and BELIEV:
.372   is rho
.000   is p
89   is number of cases.
These values would be reported as in the first
statement below.

As in the Pearson's
output a complete
matrix is printed.

When reporting the outcome for each correlation, you would write at the appropriate points:

There was a significant positive correlation between confidence in testimony and believability (rho = 0.372, N = 89, $p < 0.0005$, two-tailed).

There was no significant correlation between confidence in testimony and attractiveness (rho = 0.157, N = 89, $p = 0.143$, two-tailed).

There was a significant positive correlation between attractiveness and believability (rho = 0.359, N = 89, $p = 0.001$, two-tailed).

How to perform Kendall's tau b:

Some researchers prefer to use Kendall's tau to assess the correlation between two variables, at least one of which is nonparametric. To undertake a Kendall's tau, follow the same steps as for Pearson's r, but at step 3 select **Kendall's tau-b**. The output takes the same form as that for Spearman's rho. Kendall's tau b takes ties into account. Kendall's tau c, which ignores ties, is available in **Crosstabs** (see Chapter 4, Section 1).

Chapter Five

Data handling

An introduction to data handling
Sorting a file
Splitting a file
Selecting cases
Recoding values
Computing new variables
Counting values
Ranking cases
Other useful functions

Section 1: An introduction to data handling

In this chapter we describe some commands which can be used to modify, manipulate, transform and correct your data file. We are describing these commands at this stage so that you can get a feel of what is possible in SPSS. However, it is quite likely that you will not need to use some of these commands in earnest until you are more familiar with SPSS.

These commands are most useful when working with complex and large data files where you have a large number of variables for each participant. Files such as these often arise from survey or questionnaire research. Large questionnaires often contain items (questions) which can be grouped into a number of sub-scores. One decision you have to make when entering data from such a research programme is whether to set up a variable for every item in the questionnaire or to score the paper version of the questionnaire and enter only these scores into your data file. The advantage of this second approach is that it can be a lot quicker – especially if you have relatively few participants. However, if you adopt the approach of putting all the raw data into SPSS you gain a considerable degree of flexibility. By using the commands described in this section, you can get SPSS to calculate any sub-scale scores for you, and you can also look at, check and analyse the original data.

These commands are also very useful when you want to clean up your data. This topic is covered in great depth by Tabachnick and Fidell (1996), who describe procedures to check the accuracy of the data and to pre-process the data before engaging in further analysis. An example of this pre-processing of the data would be transforming a variable to reduce distortions such as skewness, which might otherwise invalidate some analyses. All of these techniques will require you to be familiar with the use of the commands described in this chapter.

EXAMPLE DATA

To illustrate the use of these commands, we have created a fictitious data file describing the results of a survey of people's attitudes to cross-racial adoption. The data file contains participant number, and demographic data such as the participant's age, sex, ethnic origin, religious belief and experience of adoption, together with their responses to 10 statements concerning aspects of adoption. These responses were made using a 5 point scale ranging from "Strongly Agree"(1) to "Strongly Disagree"(5). The response to each of these items has been recorded in variables Q1 to Q10.

Section 2: Sorting a file

Students who are new to SPSS often worry about the order in which participants' data are entered into the SPSS data file. For example, do you have to enter all the data from the subjects in one condition before entering all the data from the subjects in another condition? Normally order does not matter. However, there are occasions when you might want to sort a data file so that the data are in some meaningful order. This might be because you are just fussy about neatness and want it this way, or it might be for a more important reason. One such reason involves "splitting" the file – we will cover this topic later. For the moment let us just see how to sort a file into some sensible order.

Suppose that when we were entering the data from our questionnaire, we did not worry about any kind of order – we just entered the data in the order in which we received the questionnaires from our participants. Now, we might decide that we would like our data file sorted so that all the male participants come first followed by all the female participants. Furthermore, within this order we might decide that we would like the participants sorted by ethnicity. Finally, we might decide that within each of these categories we want the participants sorted by whether or not they were adopted. This is easy to achieve using the **Sort Cases** command.

THE SORT CASES COMMAND

While looking at your data in the Data Editor window, follow the steps outlined below.

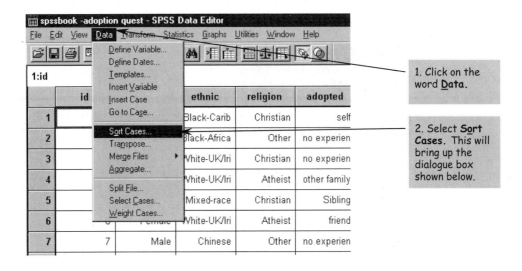

1. Click on the word **Data**.

2. Select **Sort Cases**. This will bring up the dialogue box shown below.

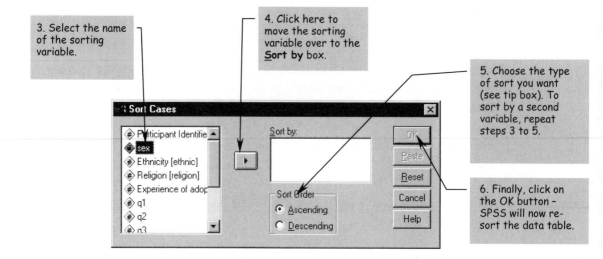

3. Select the name of the sorting variable.

4. Click here to move the sorting variable over to the **Sort by** box.

5. Choose the type of sort you want (see tip box). To sort by a second variable, repeat steps 3 to 5.

6. Finally, click on the OK button – SPSS will now re-sort the data table.

> **TIP**   You can sort in either ascending or descending order. **Ascending** order puts participants with a low value on the sort variable before participants with a higher value (e.g. Male before Female if we used the code Male = 1, Female = 2). **Descending** would sort in the reverse order. You will probably want **Ascending** order. If, after having made the sort, you decide you have sorted in the wrong order you will need to click on the variable name in the **Sort by** box and then click on the appropriate sort order.
>
> You can sort by string variables (variables that contain letters rather than numbers) – but we recommend that you avoid using string variables anyway.

You may have been wondering why we bothered to include a variable called "id" (participant identifier). The answer will be clear when you look at the section of the data table below, which has been sorted (Ascending) on Sex. Once the file has been sorted, the data from participant 1 is not necessarily in the first row of the data table, so the "id" variable provides the only easy way of cross-referencing between the data table and the original questionnaires.

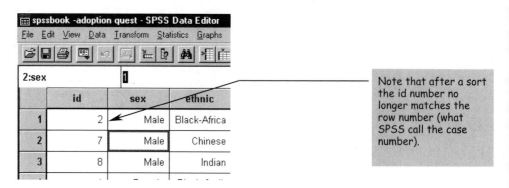

Note that after a sort the id number no longer matches the row number (what SPSS call the case number).

Section 3: Splitting a file

The **Split File** function is a recent and very useful addition to SPSS. **Split File** semi-permanently splits a data file into groups. In subsequent analysis the output is organised according to these groups. For example, you can request SPSS to organise all subsequent output so that statistics are presented separately for male and female participants. To split a file follow the steps shown below.

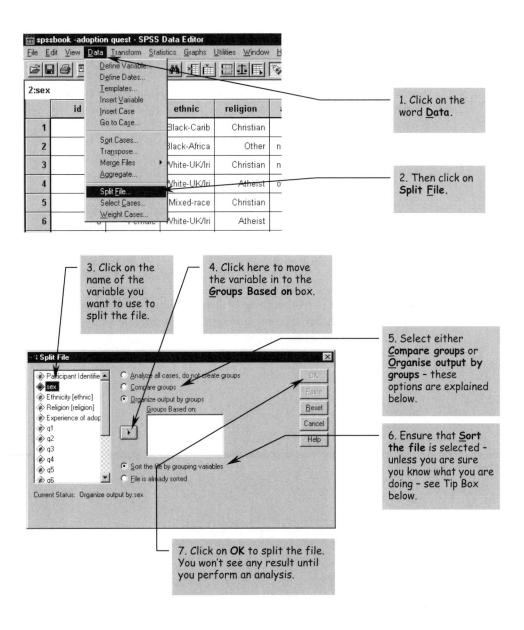

1. Click on the word **Data**.

2. Then click on **Split File**.

3. Click on the name of the variable you want to use to split the file.

4. Click here to move the variable in to the **Groups Based on** box.

5. Select either **Compare groups** or **Organise output by groups** – these options are explained below.

6. Ensure that **Sort the file** is selected – unless you are sure you know what you are doing – see Tip Box below.

7. Click on **OK** to split the file. You won't see any result until you perform an analysis.

OPTIONS

The difference between the options **<u>C</u>ompare groups** and **<u>O</u>rganize output by groups** is worth exploring. The former contrasts the two groups within one section of output whereas the latter produces two different sections of output. Try the two options to see which you prefer.

UN-SPLITTING A FILE

Remember that split file is a semi-permanent change. All the output will be broken down by the selected variable until you reverse the process. To do this, first repeat steps 1 and 2 above and then select the option **<u>A</u>nalyze all cases, do not create groups**. Then click the [OK] button. From this point onwards, all the output will return to the normal format.

TIP   SPSS has to sort a file before it can split it. If you want the file split by Sex and Ethnic Origin, then you would have to first sort the file by these two variables. Failure to do this will result in SPSS producing inappropriate groups. However, you can tell SPSS to sort the file for you before it does the split, by selecting the **<u>S</u>ort file by grouping variables** option. Selecting this option will ensure that the split will work correctly, but it does slow things down a little. If the file is already sorted by these variables then you can save time by selecting the **File is already sorted** option – but this is only worth doing if you have a big file and you are certain you know that your file is sorted correctly. If in doubt do not select this option.

Section 4: Selecting cases

An alternative to splitting a file, is to select certain cases (rows of the data file, each of which is normally one participant's data) and use only these in subsequent analyses. For example, we might be particularly interested in the responses made by our Atheist respondents. **Select Cases** will allow us to look at just these subjects' data. By selecting just those cases where religion = atheist, all subsequent analyses will be performed only on the atheist respondents' data. All other data will be temporarily suppressed.

COMPARING THE SELECT CASES AND SPLIT FILE COMMANDS

Select Cases is different from **Split File**. **Select Cases** suppresses analysis of non-selected cases, whereas **Split File** analyses all cases but arranges output by the sorting variable. Use **Select Cases** when you want to consider only some of your data. Use **Split File** when you want to carry out an analysis separately for each of two or more groups of subjects.

THE SELECT CASES COMMAND

To **Select Cases**, perform the following steps.

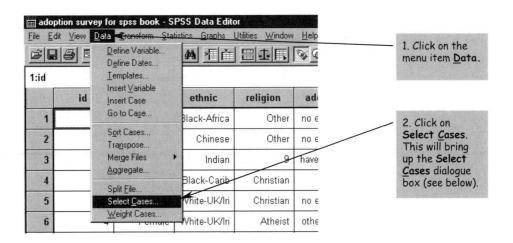

1. Click on the menu item **Data**.

2. Click on **Select Cases**. This will bring up the **Select Cases** dialogue box (see below).

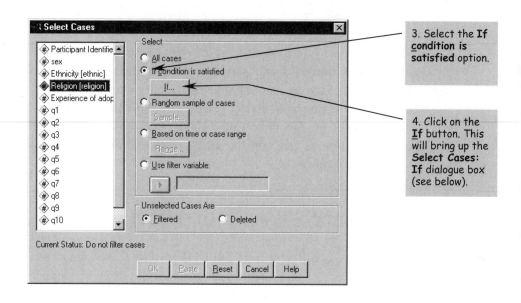

3. Select the **If condition is satisfied** option.

4. Click on the **If** button. This will bring up the **Select Cases: If** dialogue box (see below).

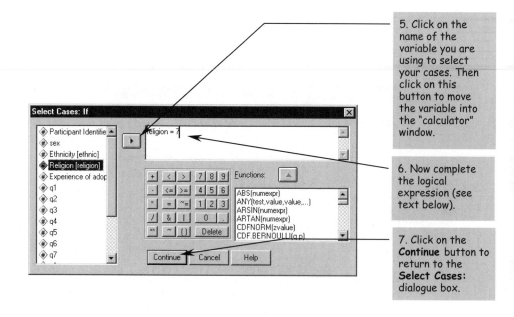

5. Click on the name of the variable you are using to select your cases. Then click on this button to move the variable into the "calculator" window.

6. Now complete the logical expression (see text below).

7. Click on the **Continue** button to return to the **Select Cases:** dialogue box.

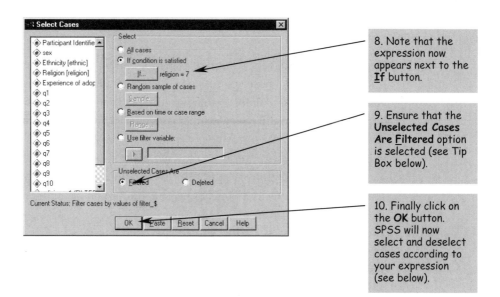

8. Note that the expression now appears next to the **If** button.

9. Ensure that the **Unselected Cases Are Filtered** option is selected (see Tip Box below).

10. Finally click on the **OK** button. SPSS will now select and deselect cases according to your expression (see below).

TIP   In step 9 above, you are asked to check that the **Unselected Cases Are Filtered** option was selected. The alternative is that unselected cases are deleted. This alternative is dangerous – if it is selected then the unselected cases are permanently removed from the data file – if you inadvertently save the file, then the deleted cases cannot be recovered unless you have a back-up copy of your data file. Use this option with extreme caution and always keep a separate copy of your original file.

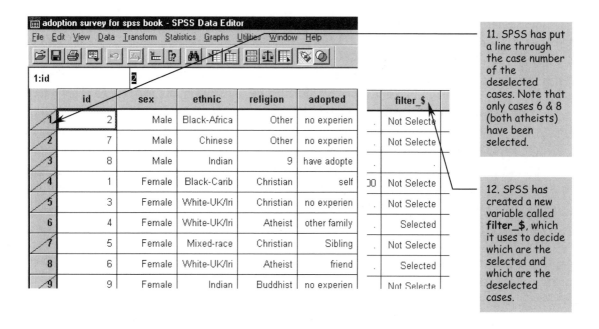

11. SPSS has put a line through the case number of the deselected cases. Note that only cases 6 & 8 (both atheists) have been selected.

12. SPSS has created a new variable called **filter_$**, which it uses to decide which are the selected and which are the deselected cases.

Selection rules

You can construct very complex selection rules by using the logical expressions AND, OR, NOT. These expressions can either be typed in from the keyboard or you can use the calculator keypad that appears in the window. Right click on the keypad buttons to discover which is which. If we wanted to select only those participants who were Atheists and non-Caucasian, but were not adopted themselves, we could enter the following expression:

religion = 7 and ethnic<10 and not adopted = 1

This is not the only way to make this selection – you might like to try others.

The **Select Cases: If** dialogue box also contains a list of functions that you can include in your selection rule. Right-click on the functions to obtain a brief description of each.

De-selecting cases

The **Select Cases** function can be very useful, but it is important to remember that it is semi-permanent. **Select Cases** will stay in force until you either make some other selection or choose the **All cases** option in the **Select Cases** dialogue box (see step 3 above).

Selection methods

The **Select Cases** dialogue box offers a total of four methods of selecting cases (see step 3 above). The **If Condition is satisfied** method is the one we use most frequently. The **Random sample of cases** method allows you to sample your cases in a random way. SPSS offers the options of either selecting an approximate percentage of your cases or of selecting an exact number of cases. The **Based on time or case range** method allows you to select cases, which fall in a particular range of cases (as defined by the SPSS case number on the extreme left of the data table), or to select cases on the basis of a time or date range (this option is outside the scope of this book). In the **Use filter variable** method, a case is selected if the value of the chosen variable is not zero (and is not missing) – this option can be useful especially if you have a yes/no variable coded as 1/0. Using this method you could easily select only the "yes" responses.

It is useful to note that a line of text at the bottom of the **Select Cases** dialogue box indicates the current selection rule.

Finally, remember to re-select **All cases** after you have completed your analysis of the selected cases.

Section 5: Recoding values

There are many occasions when you need to recode some of your data. This might be because you made an error when entering the data, but it is more likely that you will want to recode your data in light of some preliminary data analysis or in order to allow you to undertake an additional analysis.

For example, early analysis of our adoption survey might show that there are very few respondents who have described themselves as agnostic. We might therefore decide that the most sensible course of action is to combine the Agnostic and Atheist categories into one Non-religious category. We could do this manually, but it would be very time consuming. SPSS provides the **Recode** command for this purpose.

SPSS offers two options. We can either change the values in the existing Religion variable, or we can create a new variable in which the Agnostic and Atheist categories are combined. These two options are called **Recode Into Same Variables** and **Recode Into Different Variables**. It is usually safer to recode into a different (new) variable rather than overwriting the original data – that way if you make a mistake you will be able to go back to the original values and try again. To recode a variable, follow the steps outlined below.

RECODE INTO DIFFERENT VARIABLES

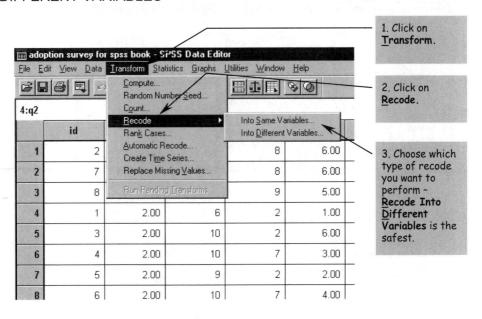

1. Click on **Transform**.

2. Click on **Recode**.

3. Choose which type of recode you want to perform – **Recode Into Different Variables** is the safest.

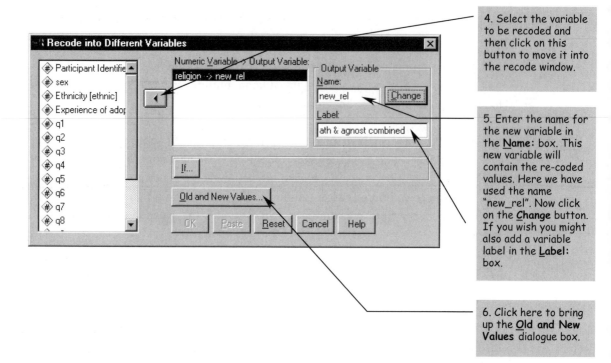

4. Select the variable to be recoded and then click on this button to move it into the recode window.

5. Enter the name for the new variable in the **Name:** box. This new variable will contain the re-coded values. Here we have used the name "new_rel". Now click on the **Change** button. If you wish you might also add a variable label in the **Label:** box.

6. Click here to bring up the **Old and New Values** dialogue box.

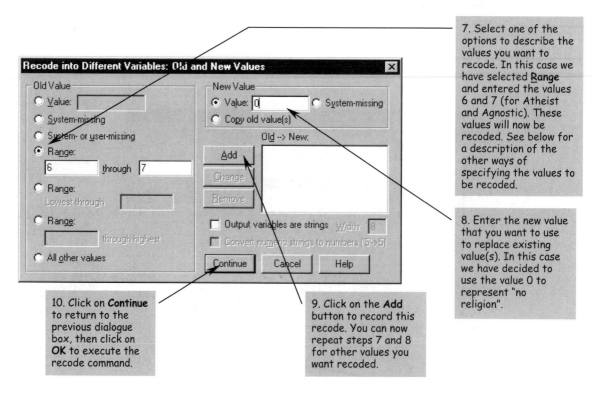

7. Select one of the options to describe the values you want to recode. In this case we have selected **Range** and entered the values 6 and 7 (for Atheist and Agnostic). These values will now be recoded. See below for a description of the other ways of specifying the values to be recoded.

8. Enter the new value that you want to use to replace existing value(s). In this case we have decided to use the value 0 to represent "no religion".

10. Click on **Continue** to return to the previous dialogue box, then click on **OK** to execute the recode command.

9. Click on the **Add** button to record this recode. You can now repeat steps 7 and 8 for other values you want recoded.

In the **Recode Into <u>D</u>ifferent Variables: Old and New Values** dialogue box (see step 7 above), you are offered a total of seven different methods of specifying the values you want to recode, and you can use a combination of these methods if required. The **Ra<u>n</u>ge: Lowest through** and the **Range: through highest** are often very useful – for example if you want to recode all categories 6 and above together you could use the **Range: through highest** option entering the value 6 in the box. When using these two options you should bear in mind your missing values. If, for example, you used 9 as the missing value, then recoding in this way would result in the missing observation being included in the new category. People who did not specify their religion would be included with those who declared themselves either atheist or agnostic.

The **<u>V</u>alue:** option allows you to specify a single value that you want to recode. The **All <u>o</u>ther values** option is, in effect a "and for everything I haven't yet specified" option which allows you to tell SPSS how to recode all of the values not covered by one of the previous recode instructions

You are less likely to use the **System-missing** or the **System- or <u>u</u>ser-missing** options. System missing values are rather like user-missing values (what in Chapter 2 we simply called missing values). Both are used to indicate that there is no valid value for a variable. However, a system missing value indicates that SPSS rather than you (the "user") has declared a value non-valid – perhaps, for example, because for this participant it is not possible to calculate a valid value for the variable. These two options allow you to recode these two types of missing values but they should be used with caution. Think carefully about the implications of your actions before using these options.

Note that by entering into the **New Value** box, a value which has previously been specified as a missing value (see step 8 above), you can effectively remove a range of values from an analysis by recoding valid responses into missing values. Similarly, by clicking on the **System-missing** option in the **New Value** box you can instruct SPSS to regard any value or range of values as system missing from this point onwards.

> **TIP** Remember, the big advantage of using **Recode into <u>D</u>ifferent Variables** (rather than **Recode into <u>S</u>ame Variable** described below) is that you do not lose anything. If you make an error, the original data are still available in the old variable and you can simply try again.

RECODE INTO SAME VARIABLES

If you are certain that you know what you are doing, and you have a backup of your data file, you might decide that you can over-write the existing data rather than create a new variable. To do this, follow the steps 1 and 2 described on page 125 (**Transform** > **Recode**) but then select **Into Same Variables.** From this point onwards the procedure is very similar to that described above except that you omit step 5 as there is no new variable to name. The results of this recode will over-write the old data in the data table.

CONDITIONAL RECODE

On some occasions you might want to recode a variable only if a particular condition is satisfied for that participant. For example, you might want to perform the recoding of agnostic and atheist religious groups described above, only in the case of participants who were adopted. This can be achieved by using the **If** button which appears on the **Recode into Different Variables** and the **Recode into Same Variables** dialogue boxes. Follow the procedure described above up to and including step 5. Then, follow the new steps described below.

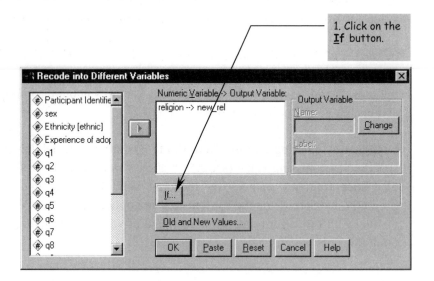

1. Click on the **If** button.

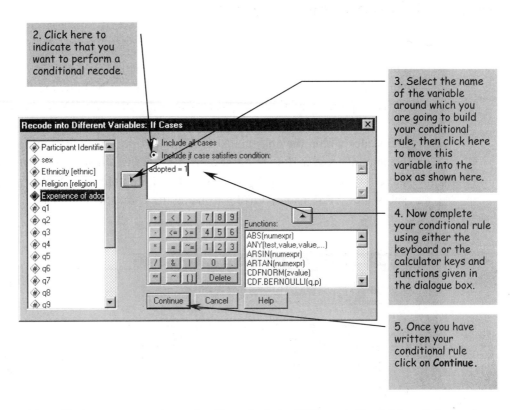

2. Click here to indicate that you want to perform a conditional recode.

3. Select the name of the variable around which you are going to build your conditional rule, then click here to move this variable into the box as shown here.

4. Now complete your conditional rule using either the keyboard or the calculator keys and functions given in the dialogue box.

5. Once you have written your conditional rule click on **Continue**.

This will then return you to the **Recode into Different Variables** dialogue box. Now click on the **Old and New Values** button (see page 126) and follow the instructions given from step 6 onwards on page 126.

TIP   The rules for constructing a conditional rule (or logical expression) are the same as in the **Select If** command described earlier. You can construct quite complex logical expressions by using a combination of the functions provided and the operators (add, subtract etc) available on the calculator style buttons. Some of the less obvious buttons are listed below:

**	Raise to the power (for example, "3**2" is equivalent to $3^2 = 9$)
<=	Less than or equal to
>=	Greater than or equal to
~=	Not equal to
&	And
|	Or
~	Not

Section 6: Computing new variables

On occasions we need to calculate a new variable based on the values for existing variables. A common example would be when you had entered the response given by each participant to each question in a questionnaire. You might now want to calculate the overall score for the questionnaire or several separate scores for the sub-scales within the questionnaire. In our fictitious survey of attitudes to adoption, we administered a 10 item questionnaire which was made up of two sub-scales. We therefore need to add up the responses to all the items that contribute to each of the sub-scales. SPSS can do this for us using the **Compute** command.

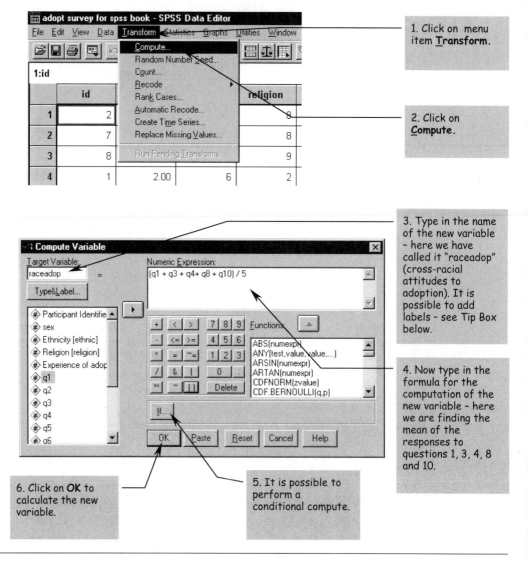

1. Click on menu item **Transform**.

2. Click on **Compute**.

3. Type in the name of the new variable – here we have called it "raceadop" (cross-racial attitudes to adoption). It is possible to add labels – see Tip Box below.

4. Now type in the formula for the computation of the new variable – here we are finding the mean of the responses to questions 1, 3, 4, 8 and 10.

5. It is possible to perform a conditional compute.

6. Click on **OK** to calculate the new variable.

> **TIP** When entering the name of the new variable (see step 3 above) it is possible to enter a variable label to act as a reminder of what the new variable means. Do this by clicking on the **Type&Label** button. You can then either type in a text label, or by selecting the **Use expression as label** option, you can ask SPSS to use your numeric expression as the variable label. In this case the label would be "(q1+q3+q4+q8+q10)/5".

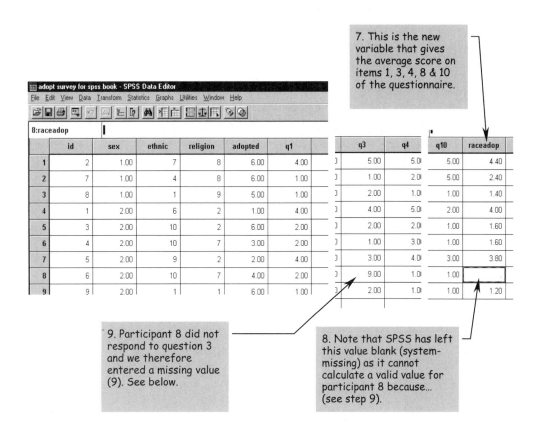

7. This is the new variable that gives the average score on items 1, 3, 4, 8 & 10 of the questionnaire.

9. Participant 8 did not respond to question 3 and we therefore entered a missing value (9). See below.

8. Note that SPSS has left this value blank (system-missing) as it cannot calculate a valid value for participant 8 because... (see step 9).

COMPUTE AND MISSING VALUES

When using **Compute** you must think carefully about missing values. SPSS will not be able to compute the value of the new variable if **any** of the values for the variables involved in the compute statement are missing. In the example above, participant 8 had not answered question 3 and we had entered a missing value (9) in this cell of the data table. As SPSS knows that this is not a valid response it refuses to compute a value for the new variable "raceadop" for this participant. With more complex compute statements involving lots of variables this can be a major problem. One way round this would be to:

1. Recode the missing values to zero (assuming that zero is not a valid response).
2. Count the number of non-zero responses (see Section 7 for a description of the **Count** function).
3. Compute the mean by adding together all the responses and dividing by the number of non-zero responses (as they are now set to zero, missing values will not affect the total).

Section 7: Counting values

Sometimes it is useful to be able to count for each participant how many times a particular value occurs over a range of variables. If, as in our example data set, you have a series of variables which represent the responses to questionnaire items, you might want to find out how many times each participant has answered "Strongly Agree". You could do this by asking SPSS to count the number of times the value 1 (the value used to code the response "Strongly Agree") has occurred in variables Q1 to Q10. Using **Count,** SPSS will create a new variable that will contain a value representing the number of times the value 1 occurs in variable Q1 to Q10.

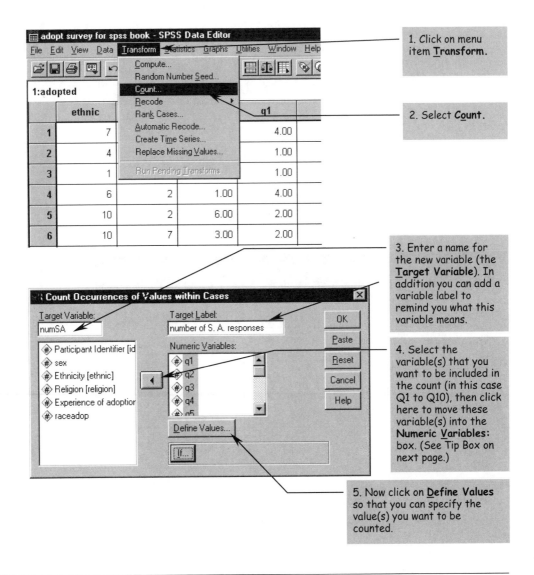

1. Click on menu item **Transform.**

2. Select **Count.**

3. Enter a name for the new variable (the **Target Variable**). In addition you can add a variable label to remind you what this variable means.

4. Select the variable(s) that you want to be included in the count (in this case Q1 to Q10), then click here to move these variable(s) into the **Numeric Variables:** box. (See Tip Box on next page.)

5. Now click on **Define Values** so that you can specify the value(s) you want to be counted.

TIP When selecting more than one variable – as in step 4 above – you can select them all in one go by holding down the shift Key and clicking on the first and then the last of the variables. You can then click on the ▶ button to move them all together.

6. Enter the value (or values) which you want to be counted (the options here are the same as for **Recode** - see Section 5).

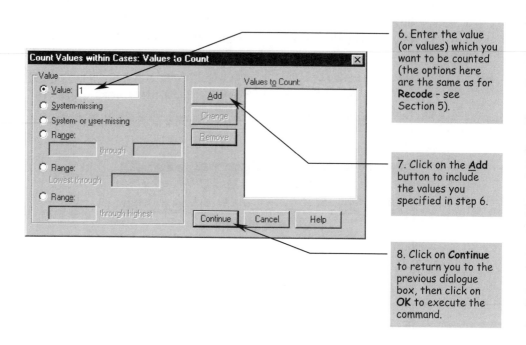

7. Click on the **Add** button to include the values you specified in step 6.

8. Click on **Continue** to return you to the previous dialogue box, then click on **OK** to execute the command.

9. This is the new variable. We can see that participant 1 responded "Strongly Agree" to three of the questionnaire items, whereas participant 2 responded this way to six items.

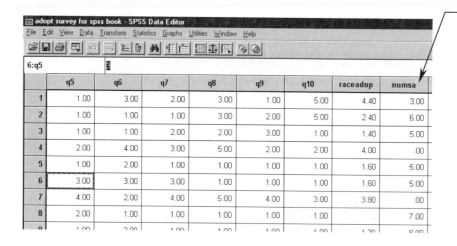

CONDITIONAL COUNT

It is possible to perform a conditional count – which is to only count the occurrences of a value(s) for participants who satisfy some particular criterion. This is done by clicking on the **If** button either before or after you have specified the values to be counted (see step 5 above). This will bring up a dialogue box almost identical to the one we used for the conditional recode described in Section 5. You can now specify your conditional rule and then click on the **Continue** button.

Section 8: Ranking cases

Sometimes it is useful to convert interval or ratio scores into ordinal scores. We might, for example, want to convert the variable "raceadop" (which we calculated using **Compute** in Section 6) into a rank score. That is, we might want to rank all of our participants on the basis of their score on this variable. The participant who had the highest overall raceadop score would be given a rank of 1, the next highest a rank of 2 and so on. The **Rank Cases** command calculates the ranks for us and generates a new variable to contain the ranks. We can rank in either ascending or descending order, and can even rank on the basis of more than one variable.

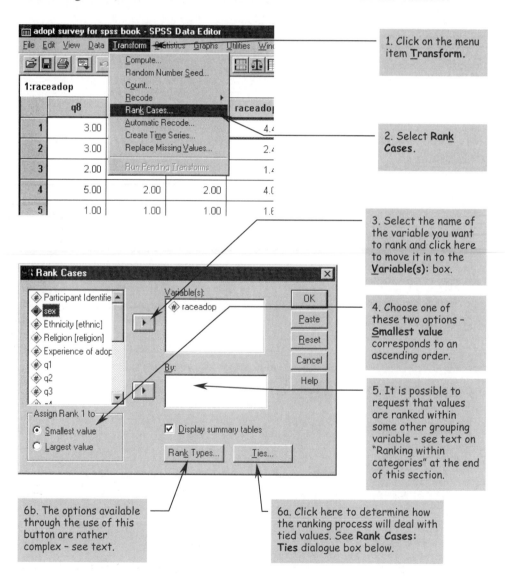

1. Click on the menu item **Transform**.

2. Select **Rank Cases**.

3. Select the name of the variable you want to rank and click here to move it in to the **Variable(s):** box.

4. Choose one of these two options – **Smallest value** corresponds to an ascending order.

5. It is possible to request that values are ranked within some other grouping variable – see text on "Ranking within categories" at the end of this section.

6b. The options available through the use of this button are rather complex – see text.

6a. Click here to determine how the ranking process will deal with tied values. See **Rank Cases: Ties** dialogue box below.

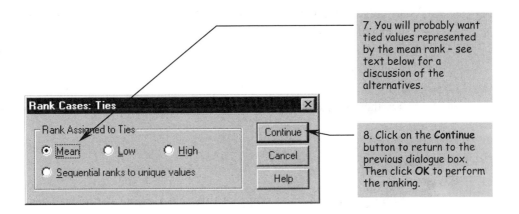

7. You will probably want tied values represented by the mean rank – see text below for a discussion of the alternatives.

8. Click on the **Continue** button to return to the previous dialogue box. Then click **OK** to perform the ranking.

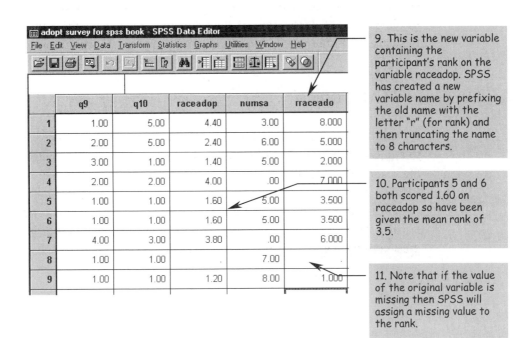

9. This is the new variable containing the participant's rank on the variable raceadop. SPSS has created a new variable name by prefixing the old name with the letter "r" (for rank) and then truncating the name to 8 characters.

10. Participants 5 and 6 both scored 1.60 on raceadop so have been given the mean rank of 3.5.

11. Note that if the value of the original variable is missing then SPSS will assign a missing value to the rank.

RANKING TIED VALUES

SPSS provides four alternative methods of handling tied values. The default, **Mean** method, gives the tied values the mean of the available ranks. You can see this option in operation above where participants 5 and 6 both scored 1.6 and were given a rank of 3.5 – the mean of ranks 3 and 4. This is the ranking method described in most introductory statistics books. The **Low** option assigns the tied participants the lowest of the available ranks – so in this case both would have been ranked 3. The **Highest** option would award both participants the highest of the available ranks – 4 in this case. The **Sequential ranks to unique values** option would assign a rank of 3 to both participant 5 and 6, but would then assign a rank of 4 to participant 2, thus ensuring that all the sequential ranks are awarded – this means that the highest rank will **not** be equal to the number of valid cases (as it would for the other three methods).

Try these options for yourself and compare the results.

TYPES OF RANKING

SPSS provides a wide range of different ranking methods. These are available by clicking on the **Rank Types** button (see step 6b above). These options are rather complex and are beyond the scope of this book. Right-click on each of the options to obtain a brief description of their function, or consult the help index or SPSS manuals for further information. If in doubt leave the **Mean** option selected.

RANKING WITHIN CATEGORIES

By specifying a second variable in the **By** box (see step 5 on page 136) it is possible to request SPSS to rank the scores on the first variable within categories formed by the second variable. For example, if we specified the variable sex in this box, then SPSS would first rank all the male participants and then rank all the female participants. Thus, in this case we would have two participants (one male and one female) with a rank of 1. This can be a very useful function, but it can also cause great confusion and therefore should be used with caution.

Section 9: Other useful functions

Under the **Transform** and **Data** menu items you will find several other useful commands. These are described briefly here. In explaining these commands, we have not made use of the annotated "screen shots" you have become familiar with. Instead, to save space we have described the actions required to execute a command in words only. We describe a series of actions using a simple shorthand notation. So, clicking on the menu item **Transform** then selecting **Compute** would be written as:

Transform ⇒ **Compute**

This notation will also be used in some of the later sections of this book.

AUTOMATIC RECODE

Automatic Recode converts string variables into numeric variables. For example, if you had coded sex as a string variable, using the strings "M" and "F" to code male and female, you may discover that some commands will not work with string variables. **Automatic Recode** will resolve this problem by recoding string variables into numeric variables. The old string variables are recoded in alphabetic order, so in the case above "F" would be recoded as 1 and "M" as 2. Any value or variable labels are transferred. If there were no value labels then the old strings are used as the labels (so, in the case above the value label "F" would be attached to the value 1).

The commands needed are:

Transform ⇒ **Automatic Recode**

Now select the name of the variable to be recoded and move it into the **Variable ->New Name** box. Next specify a new name for the variable, click on **New Name** and finally click on OK .

CATEGORIZE VARIABLES (VERSIONS 9 AND 10 ONLY)

The **Categorize variables** command is a new introduction to SPSS Version 9. It is really an automatic recode function, in that it allows you to recode a continuous variable (for example age) into a categorical variable. For example, we might recode age so that we had five different age categories rather than the actual age of the participants recorded. Note that **Categorize variable** recodes on the basis of the value of the input variable, not the frequency of the values. Thus, the above example will create five categories covering an equal age range, but probably not an equal number of participants in each age category. You can choose the number of categories that your input variable is recoded into.

This command is accessed by:

Transform ⇒ Categorize variables

CREATE TIME SERIES AND REPLACE MISSING VALUES

Time series are special types of data in which measurements are made repeatedly over a period of time. Time series data in SPSS are unusual in that each row of the data file becomes a sampling time rather than a participant. The analysis of time series data is beyond the scope of this book, but the **Create Time Series** and **Replace Missing Values** commands allow you to create new variables based on time series data, and estimate values to replace missing observations respectively.

Chapter Six

Analysis of Variance

An introduction to Analysis of Variance (ANOVA)

One-way between-subjects ANOVA

Two-way between-subjects ANOVA

One-way within-subjects ANOVA

Two-way within-subjects ANOVA

Mixed ANOVA

Some additional points

Planned and unplanned comparisons

Nonparametric equivalents to ANOVA: Kruskal–Wallis and Friedman

Section 1: An introduction to Analysis of Variance (ANOVA)

WHAT IS ANOVA?

ANOVA is an enormously useful statistical procedure that is very widely used in psychological research. The popularity of this statistical procedure is based on two important characteristics:

1. ANOVA will allow us to handle the data from experiments that have designs involving more than 2 conditions. You will remember the *t*-test allowed us to compare the means of two sets of scores (either from two groups of participants – an independent *t*-test or from a repeated measures design involving two conditions – a dependent or paired *t*-test). However, in practice, we may wish to design experiments involving more than two conditions and in these situations, rather than using several *t*-tests to compare all possible differences, we can use a single ANOVA. This single test will tell us whether the change in the independent variable has affected the scores – i.e. whether the different conditions have resulted in significantly different scores. It should be noted that ANOVA cannot tell us precisely which pairs of conditions are significantly different. For example, if the independent variable has three conditions, ANOVA will tell us whether the scores significantly vary across those conditions. However, it will not tell us whether condition 1 is significantly different from condition 2, whether condition 2 is significantly different from condition 3, or whether condition 1 is significantly different from condition 3. Such comparisons of specific means require some additional statistical procedures called planned and unplanned comparisons, which we will cover later in this chapter.

2. ANOVA also allows us to investigate the effect of more than one independent variable. All the experimental designs we have considered so far have involved investigating the effect of just one IV on one DV. ANOVA will allow us to design experiments involving more than one IV. For example, we could examine the effect of participants' sex as well as their age on their memory for a list of words. Here we have two IVs (sex and age) and one DV (memory score). A single ANOVA test will allow us simultaneously to examine the effect of these two IVs. In fact ANOVA can handle any number of IVs in a single experiment – but in practice we rarely include more than three or four for reasons that will become apparent shortly.

This ability to include more than one IV in an experimental design not only saves time but also allows us to investigate how these IVs combine to affect the DV. For example, we might know that two new drugs are each quite safe when administered on their own. However, it could be that when administered together they are lethal. This is an example of a drug interaction. In statistics we are interested in how independent variables interact. That is, we can ask questions about how the sex **and** the age of a participant **combine** to affect memory score – it might be that male participants' performances decline with age but that female participants' performances improve with age. Such an *interaction* between these two variables is clearly of enormous theoretical importance, but it is only by manipulating both variables in one design that we can discover this interaction. A major advantage of ANOVA over the procedures we have looked at so far is that it can reveal such interactions.

WHEN CAN WE USE ANOVA?

In order to legitimately use ANOVA, the following conditions must be met:
1. The dependent variable comprises of interval or ratio data.
2. The populations are normally distributed.
3. The population variances are all equal.
4. In the case of independent groups designs, independent random samples must have been taken from each population.

HOW DOES IT WORK?

We all know that humans vary in performance, both between individuals and within individuals over time. For these reasons, if we conduct a simple experiment comparing, say, the time it takes to learn a list of short words, medium length words and long words, we would not expect all the participants within a condition to take the same amount of time. We naturally accept that some participants will be faster than others (i.e. there will be variation between individuals). We also know that any one participant might take less or more time on one occasion than on other occasions (i.e. there will be variation within individuals). Remember that we can measure the amount of variation within a set of scores with measures of dispersion, such as the standard deviation or the *variance*.

Now let us imagine for a moment that we were RobotoPsychologists – that is, we were interested in the psychology of robots (rather than robots interested in psychology!). If we repeated our learning experiment with a group of R2D2 robots, we would expect all of the robots in one condition to react at exactly the same speed. That is, robots would not vary either between or within individuals. Table 6.1 shows some hypothetical data for robots and for humans.

Table 6.1: Time (in seconds) taken to learn three different lists of words for a group of human and robot participants. The robots show no individual differences and so the variance within each condition is zero.

ROBOTS			
LIST A	*LIST B*	*LIST C*	
10	20	30	
10	20	30	
10	20	30	
10	20	30	
10	20	30	
10	20	30	
10	20	30	
10	20	30	
Mean = 10	*Mean = 20*	*Mean = 30*	*Grand Mean = 20*

HUMANS			
LIST A	*LIST B*	*LIST C*	
30	54	68	
40	58	75	
35	45	80	
45	60	75	
38	52	85	
42	56	90	
36	65	75	
25	52	88	
Mean = 36.375	*Mean = 55.25*	*Mean = 79.50*	*Grand Mean = 57.04*

Let us just consider the data from the humans for the moment. If we asked you to "eye-ball" the raw data and guess whether there was a difference in learning times for the three lists, you would probably have no problem saying that the difference did appear to be significant. In making this judgement you are actually doing something quite sophisticated. What you are doing is deciding whether the natural variation between individuals within the conditions is large or small compared to the variation between individuals across the different conditions. That is you are asking "OK, so not all the participants in the List A condition took the same time, and OK not all the participants in the List B or List C condition took the same time, but is this natural variation (or noise) large or small compared to the difference in times between the three conditions?". In this case participants within each condition might vary from each other by several seconds, but this is small compared to the larger differences between the times produced under the three different list conditions.

Let us look at the robots' data again. Robots perform identically under identical conditions (or at least our robots do), so within each condition every robot has exactly the same learning time. Thus the variance within each condition is zero. But if we compare the performance between the three conditions, it is clear that all the robots were fastest at learning the short words and all took longest to learn the long words. You might conclude that you want to switch from Psychology to RobotoPsychology, but there is also a more important point here. What we want to do is make our human participants' data more like the robots' data – that is we want to reduce the variance down towards zero. In fact all the practices of good experimental design, such as giving all participants the same instructions and testing under identical conditions, are designed to do just this – to reduce the variance within each condition. This good experimental practice will reduce the variance but will not eliminate it – our participants will never behave exactly like the robots. So, if we cannot eliminate the variance perhaps we can account for it. What we need is a statistical procedure that takes account of the variance within the conditions and compares this to the variance between conditions. If the variance between conditions is much larger than the variance within conditions then surely we can say that the IV is having a larger effect on the scores than the individual differences are. Clearly, for the robots the variance within the conditions is zero and the variance between the conditions is quite large. For our humans, the situation is not quite so clear cut, but if we calculate the variances we will find the same basic pattern applies:

Variance between conditions > variance within conditions

This concept of calculating the variance due to nuisance factors such as individual differences and comparing it to the variance due to our manipulation of the IV is central to ANOVA. Exactly how we calculate these variances can get rather complex for some designs, but this does not alter the basic principle that we simply want to ask whether or not the variance in the data brought about by our manipulation of the IV is larger than that brought about by the other nuisance factors such as individual differences. The variance brought about by these nuisance variables is usually referred to as the *error variance*, so we ask whether the error variance is less than the variance due to the manipulation of the IV.

A convenient way of expressing this is to calculate the ratio of the variance due to our manipulation of the IV and the error variance. This ratio is known as the *F*-ratio (named after Fisher). The *F*-ratio is:

$$F = Variance\ due\ to\ manipulation\ of\ IV/Error\ variance$$

If the error variance is small compared to the variance due to the IV (as in the case of our robots where the error variance is zero), then the F-ratio will be a number greater than 1 (a large number divided by a smaller number always gives rise to a number greater than 1). If, on the other hand, the effect of the IV is small, and/or the error variance is large (perhaps because our participants varied considerably or because we did not adequately control the experiment) then the F-ratio will be a number less than 1 (a small number divided by larger number will always result in a number less than 1). Thus, we can now say that the effect of the IV is definitely not significant if the F-ratio is less than 1. This is because the error variance is actually larger than the variance caused by our manipulation of the IV.

So, the F-ratio is simply the ratio of these two estimates of variance. The larger the F-ratio, the greater the effect of the IV compared to the "noise" (error variance) in the data. An F-ratio equal to or less than 1 indicates a non-significant result as it shows that the scores were equally affected or more affected by the nuisance variables (such as individual differences) as they were by the manipulation of the IV.

HOW DO WE FIND OUT IF THE F-RATIO IS SIGNIFICANT?

Once we have calculated the value of the F-ratio and found it is larger than 1, we need to determine whether it is large enough to be regarded as significant. That is, we ask whether the effect of the IV is sufficiently larger than the effect of the nuisance variables to regard the result as significant. When calculating the F-ratio with a calculator, we consult F tables to discover, given the number of observations we made, what value F had to exceed to be considered as significant. When using SPSS to perform ANOVA, the output reports the exact p value for that particular F-ratio. This p value is the probability of getting this F-ratio by chance alone and it needs to be less than 0.05 for the F-ratio to be regarded as significant.

WHAT ABOUT DEGREES OF FREEDOM?

You will remember from performing a t-test, another test of difference, that we need to calculate and report the degrees of freedom associated with our analysis. One complication with ANOVA is that for each F value we must report two sets of degrees of freedom. This is because we need to remember how many observations went into our calculation of the error variance and also how many went into our calculation of the variance due to the manipulation of the IV. As these are the bottom and top halves of the F-ratio equation, these are sometimes referred to as the denominator and numerator degrees of freedom respectively. A good statistics text will explain the calculation of degrees of freedom in detail, but as SPSS calculates and reports these for you, all you need know is to expect two values for each F-ratio. We will look at how to report these degrees of freedom and the F-ratio in more detail later.

WHAT TERMS ARE USED WITH ANOVA?

Different textbooks tend to use slightly different terminologies to describe ANOVA. To avoid the problems this can create we are going to use what we consider to be the simplest terminology.

Factors

These are really independent variables, but as there may well be more than one of them per study, it makes sense to call them factors from now on.

Levels of factors

These are similar to conditions. In the experiments we considered earlier, we had a single IV which was manipulated to create two conditions. We would now describe this as a single factor with two levels. In ANOVA designs a factor can have as many levels as we like. For example we might have a factor of Drug Dosage which might be manipulated to create 4 levels of 0mg; 10mg; 20mg and 30mg.

Between-subjects factors

These are factors whose levels vary between participants, so that each participant will experience only one level of a factor. For example, a participant can be administered either 0mg; 10mg; 20mg or 30mg. This is a factor that is manipulated using an independent groups design, which we will now refer to as a "between-subjects design".

Within-subjects factors

These are factors whose levels vary within a participant, so that each participant will experience two or more levels of a factor. For example, a participant might be administered all four different drug dosages. This is a factor that is manipulated using a repeated measures design, which we will now refer to as a "within-subjects design".

Mixed ANOVA designs

The term "mixed ANOVA design" is used when a design includes one or more within-subjects factors and one or more between-subjects factors.

HOW DO WE DESCRIBE ANOVA DESIGNS?

When describing an ANOVA design we need to specify three things:

1. How many factors are involved in the design.
2. How many levels there are of each factor.
3. Whether each factor is a within or a between-subjects factor.

The number of factors is described by talking about a one-way ANOVA (where there is one factor), a two-way ANOVA (two factors) and so on (for example a six-way ANOVA would have six factors). What this does not tell you is how many levels each factor has. You could describe this in long hand, but there is an easier convention. For example, a three-way ANOVA in which the first factor Sex had two levels, the second factor Age had three levels and the third factor Drug Dosage had 5 levels could be described more simply as a 2*3*5 ANOVA design. Note that in this terminology the number of numerals (three in this case) describes the number of factors, and the values of the numerals indicate the number of levels of each of these factors. Using this terminology we just need to make it clear whether the factors were within or between subject factors. We could do this by writing:

"A 2*3*5 (Sex*Age*Drug dose) mixed ANOVA design was employed where Sex and Age were between-subjects factors and Drug dose was a within-subjects factor."

MAIN EFFECTS AND INTERACTIONS

Using ANOVA we can analyse data from studies that incorporate more than one factor. We can assess both the effect of each of these factors on their own and the interaction between the factors. The term "main effect" is used to describe the independent effect of a factor. For example, in the 2*3*5 ANOVA described above, three main effects will be reported. The main effect of Sex will tell us whether men performed significantly differently from women, irrespective of their age or drug dosage. The main effect of Age will tell us whether age affects performance, irrespective of sex or drug dose. Finally, the main effect of drug dose will tell whether drug dosage affects performance, irrespective of the sex or age of the participants. These main effects simply compare the mean for one level of a factor with the mean of the other level(s) of that factor – for example comparing mean male performance levels to mean female performance levels. Interactions on the other hand assess the combined effect of the factors. An interaction that assesses how two factors combine to affect performance is called a two-way interaction. When three factors are involved, the interaction is known as a three-way interaction.

When attempting to understand the output form the ANOVA command in SPSS, it is very helpful if you know in advance how many results you are looking for.

1. A one-way ANOVA, where the single factor is called A, will give rise to just a single main effect of A.
2. A two-way ANOVA, where the factors are called A and B, will give rise to two main effects (main effect of A and main effect of B, and a single two-way interaction (A*B). This is a total of 3 results (3 F-ratios).
3. A three-way ANOVA, where the factors are called A, B and C, will give rise to three main effects (main effect of A, main effect of B and main effect of C), three two-way interactions (A*B, A*C and B*C) and a single three-way interaction (A*B*C). This is a total of 6 results.
4. A four-way ANOVA, where the factors are called A, B, C, and D, will give rise to four main effects (main effect of A, main effect of B, main effect of C and main effect of D), six two-way interactions (A*B, A*C, A*D, B*C, B*D, and C*D), four three-way interactions (A*B*C, A*B*D, A*C*D and B*C*D), and a single four-way interaction (A*B*C*D). This is a total of 15 results.

You can now see why it is unusual to include more than four factors in a design. The number of possible interactions rises steeply as the number of factors increases. Furthermore, it is unlikely that you hypothesised about the shape of these higher level interactions and if they are significant they can be very hard to describe and/or explain. Using SPSS it is very easy to undertake a four- or even five-way ANOVA, but rather more difficult to explain the results. Our advice is to try to limit yourself to a maximum of three factors.

HOW DO WE CALCULATE THE F-RATIO?

You do not need to know how to calculate the F-ratio, as SPSS will do this for you. However, to fully appreciate the output that SPSS generates, it would be helpful to read this section and to realise why the calculation is dependent on the type of factor manipulated. We show this below with reference to a one-way design.

Let us go back to our learning experiment, and imagine that there are different humans taking part in each condition; that 8 participants were asked to learn list A, another 8 to learn list B and another 8 to learn list C.

Table 6.2: Time (in seconds) taken to learn three different lists of words for the group of human participants in a between-subjects design.

HUMANS			
LIST A	LIST B	LIST C	
30	54	68	
40	58	75	
35	45	80	
45	60	75	
38	52	85	
42	56	90	
36	65	75	
25	52	88	
Mean = 36.375	Mean = 55.25	Mean = 79.50	**Grand Mean = 57.04**

There are two sources of variance of interest here.
1. How do the scores in one group vary from those in the other groups? We can look at how the mean of each column deviates from the grand mean. This provides us with a measure of the variance due to the factor.
2. How do the scores vary within each group? We can look at how each score within a column deviates from the mean for that condition. This provides us with a measure of noise.

Together these two sources of variance must add up to the total variance (the variance between each single score and the grand mean). That is:

$$Var_{(Total)} = Var_{(Between\ Groups)} + Var_{(Within\ Groups)}$$

The box below and overleaf shows the steps involved in calculating both sources of variance. Although you will probably never use a calculator to work out the F-ratio, you may find it helpful to look at the box and familiarise yourself with the procedure.

STEP A

We first calculate the **Sum of Squares (Within groups):** this is the sum of all the squared differences between each individual data point and the mean for that group.
$SS_{(within\ groups)} = (30\text{-}36.375)^2 + (40\text{-}36.375)^2 + (35\text{-}36.375)^2 + (45\text{-}36.375)^2 + (38\text{-}36.375)^2 + (42\text{-}36.375)^2 + (36\text{-}36.375)^2 + (25\text{-}36.375)^2 + (54\text{-}55.25)^2 + (58\text{-}55.25)^2 + (45\text{-}55.25)^2 + (60\text{-}55.25)^2 + (52\text{-}55.25)^2 + (56\text{-}55.25)^2 + (65\text{-}55.25)^2 + (52\text{-}55.25)^2 + (68\text{-}79.5)^2 + (75\text{-}79.5)^2 + (80\text{-}79.5)^2 + (75\text{-}79.5)^2 + (85\text{-}79.5)^2 + (90\text{-}79.5)^2 + (75\text{-}79.5)^2 + (88\text{-}79.5)^2$
$SS_{(within\ groups)} = 953.375$

Then we calculate the **Sum of Squares (Between Groups):** this is the sum of all the squared differences between the means for each condition and the grand mean, multiplied by the number of observations per group.
$SS_{(between\ groups)} = [(36.375\text{-}57.04)^2 + (55.25\text{-}57.04)^2 + (79.5\text{-}57.04)^2]*8 = 7477.583$

Then we calculate the **Sum of Squares (Total):** this is the sum of the squared differences between each individual data point and the grand mean.
Alternatively (more easily) this can be calculated by summing the $SS_{(between\ groups)}$ and the $SS_{(within\ groups)}$.
$SS_{(total)} = 7477.583 + 953.375 = 8430.958$
(If you want to check this you can calculate it the long way: $(30\text{-}57.04)^2 + (40\text{-}57.04)^2 +$ etc. until $+ (88\text{-}57.04)^2 = 8430.958$).

STEP B

We need to figure out the degrees of freedom for each **Sum of Squares**.
For the Sum of Squares (Within Groups):
There are 3 groups and 8 participants per group. We lose one df for each group mean. Thus the df (within) is 24-3 = 21. You could express this, when you have n observations in each of the k groups as: df (within) = k(n-1).
For the Sum of Squares (Between Groups):
There are three groups but we lose one df, so the df (between) is 3-1 = 2. You could express this as: df (between) = k-1.
For Sum of Squares (Total):
The total df is based on 24 scores, we lose one df, so the df (total) is 24-1 = 23. You could express this as: df (total) = nk-1.

continues overleaf

STEP C

Now we can calculate the Mean Square by dividing each Sum of Squares by its df. This provides us with a measure of the average deviation of individual values from their respective mean.

Mean Square (Within groups) (The average variation within the groups)
$MS_{(within\ groups)}$ = 953.375/21 = 45.399

Mean Square (Between groups) (The average variation between groups)
$MS_{(Between\ groups)}$ = 7477.583/2 = 3736.792

STEP D

We now have the two Mean Squares for **the *F*-ratio**:
F = 3736.792/45.399 = 82.354

If you calculate *F* with a calculator, you next look in Tables of *F* to determine whether your calculated *F*-ratio is significant.

Imagine that in our learning experiment, 8 participants took part and each performed in each level of the factor. We would be able to calculate both a mean score for each list and a mean score for each participant; see below.

Table 6.3: Time (in seconds) taken to learn three different lists of words for the group of human participants in a within-subjects design.

HUMANS			
LIST A	LIST B	LIST C	Participant Mean
35	42	64	47
48	60	90	66
36	65	75	58.67
40	55	70	55
38	52	85	58.33
25	42	58	41.67
30	42	60	44
42	60	90	64
Mean = 36.755	Mean = 52.25	Mean = 74.0	Grand Mean = 54.33

The calculation of F for the within-subjects design is more complicated. Again, we want to determine the sources of variance. However, with this design we have repeated observations of each participant as every person performs in every level of the factor. This allows us to separate out participant variance from error variance; we can distinguish between variation caused by individual differences and variation caused by different participants performing differently in the different conditions – the error variance. So, we have three sources of variance and we can ask:

1. How do the scores in one condition vary from those in the other condition? We can compare overall differences between the three lists. As before, we can look at how the mean of each column deviates from the grand mean. This provides us with a measure of the variance due to our manipulation of the factor.
2. How do participants vary in their average scores? We can get an indication of how much individuals differ from each other by looking at how much each participant's average score deviates from the grand mean. This provides us with a measure of participant variance.
3. How much error variance there is? We can work this out by looking at the extent to which each score is not what we would predict from the row and column means. You can also think of this as the variance resulting from different participants responding differently to the change in the factor.

For example, with regard to the score for participant one in list A – we know that his/her mean time is 47 seconds. Participant one is on average 7.33 seconds faster compared with the overall grand mean of 54.33 seconds. The mean for the list A column is 36.75 seconds, so participants are on average 17.58 seconds faster at learning list A than the overall grand mean of 54.22 seconds. So, altogether we would expect participant one to be 17.58+7.33 seconds faster than the grand mean of 54.33 seconds at leaning list A, giving an expected time of 29.42 seconds. The observed score is 35 seconds, which is slower than we would expect. (Looking at participant one's scores, we can see that s/he is relatively faster with lists B and C compared with list A.)

With regard to participant two's score in list A condition – we know that his/her row mean is 66 seconds which is 11.67 seconds slower than the grand mean of 54.33 seconds. So, we would expect participant two to be 17.58 seconds faster at learning list A, but 11.67 seconds slower because this participant is slower on average. Thus, we expect a time of 54.33-17.58+11.67 and this is 48.42 seconds. The observed score is 48 seconds which is close to what we would expect.

The extent to which the observed scores vary from the expected scores reflects the extent to which participants are inconsistent and, as illustrated above, provides us with a measure of error variance.

Using SPSS to calculate the *F*-ratio

The calculation of the *F*-ratio for a within-subjects factor is tricky and as you will see the SPSS output is quite complex. SPSS Versions 8, 9 and 10 will give you much more information than just the *F*-ratio statistic, because they use the General Linear Model (GLM) procedure. Analysis of variance has many similarities to a different statistical test called multiple regression (see Chapter 7). Analysis of variance can be considered to be a special case of multiple linear regression, which itself is a special case of the general linear model. This is why you will see both analysis of variance and multiple regression statistics in the SPSS output.

Now let us see how to perform the various different types of ANOVA using SPSS.

Section 2: One-way between-subjects ANOVA

EXAMPLE STUDY: THE EFFECTS OF WITNESS MASKING

To practise the use of the one-way between-subjects ANOVA we shall consider an applied experiment, which looked at the effects of masking the face of a witness. There is growing awareness that the identity of witnesses in sensitive cases should be protected, especially in light of the move towards televising live court cases. The technology to mask a witness's face is available and has been used in America. Towell, Kemp and Pike (1996) reported the results of a study investigating the effect that masking might have on jurors' memory for witness's testimony and on jurors' perceptions of the witness's credibility. The testimony of an alleged victim of rape presented in a televised trial in America was shown to participants.

The design employed was a one-way between-subjects ANOVA design. The between-subjects factor, presentation condition had four levels: unmasked, grey blob, pixelation and negation. These were operationalised by showing some participants the witness unmasked, so that her face was fully visible; some with her face masked by a grey blob, some with her face masked by pixelation and some with her face negated (white and black was reversed). One of the dependent variables was the percentage of facts from the testimony correctly remembered by the participants. The hypothesis was that there would be a negative effect of masking on memory. Results revealed that participants' memory for the victim's testimony was affected by presentation condition; whilst negating the face did not lower memory compared to the unmasked condition, both masking with a grey blob and pixelation impaired memory. For the purposes of this book, we have created a data file that will reproduce some of these findings. (These data are available in the Appendix.)

SPSS provides two ways of carrying out a one way, between-subjects ANOVA, one using the **General Factorial** command and one using the **One-Way ANOVA** command. The first command can also be used to perform a multi-between-subjects ANOVA. The second command will only permit analysis of a one-way ANOVA design, but does have the advantage of a much simpler output. Both methods allow you to do planned and unplanned comparisons to evaluate the differences between pairs of group means (these are covered in Section 8 of this chapter).

We will now describe both methods.

To perform the one-way ANOVA:

For SPSS Versions 9 and 10, click on **Analyze** ⇒ **General Linear Model** ⇒ **Univariate.**

For SPSS Version 8, click on **Statistics** ⇒ **General Linear Model** ⇒ **GLM General Factorial.**

You will then see a dialogue box like this:

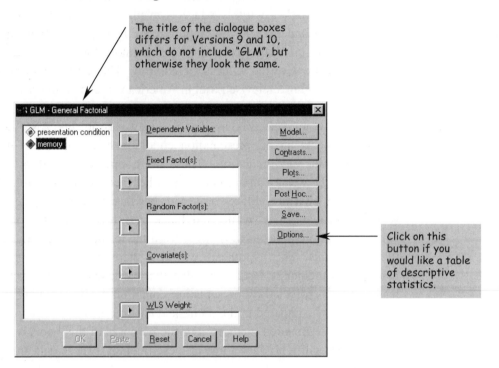

The title of the dialogue boxes differs for Versions 9 and 10, which do not include "GLM", but otherwise they look the same.

Click on this button if you would like a table of descriptive statistics.

Select the dependent variable "memory" and click on ▶ next to the **Dependent Variable** box ("memory" will move into the **Dependent Variable** box). Next click on the variable "presentation condition". This is the grouping variable (i.e. the between-subjects factor) so click on ▶ next to the **Fixed Factor(s)** box and "presentation condition" will appear in the box. As explained in the SPSS help files, the levels of a fixed factor include all the levels about which conclusions are desired. It is rare in psychological research to choose the levels of a factor by a random procedure; however were we to do so, then this could be regarded to increase the generalisability of our findings as we would have chosen the levels in an unbiased way.

If you wish, you can click on the **Options** button and ask for descriptive statistics to be included in the output. Below is the dialogue box you will see.

> **TIP** In the **Options** dialogue box, you can ask for **Estimates of effect size.** The output will then include the eta-squared statistic, which tells you the proportion of total variance accounted for by the factor.

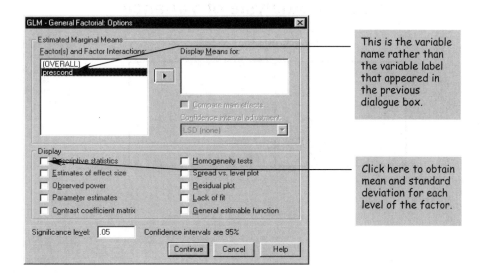

This is the variable name rather than the variable label that appeared in the previous dialogue box.

Click here to obtain mean and standard deviation for each level of the factor.

Click on **Continue** to return to the **General Factorial** dialogue box. Click on [OK] and SPSS will calculate the test for you.

See the next two pages for an example of the output using the **General Factorial** command, which includes the means, standard deviations and N (number of scores) obtained by clicking on **Descriptive statistics**.

> **TIP** Means, standard errors and 95% confidence intervals for each level of a factor can also be obtained by clicking on the factor/variable name in the **Estimated Marginal Means** box and then clicking on [▶]. You should only use this option if the number of participants in each level is the same. The estimated means are inaccurate with an unequal sample size.

Obtained Using Menu Items: <u>G</u>eneral Linear Model > Univariate (Versions 9 and 10) or GLM – <u>G</u>eneral Factorial (Version 8)

Univariate Analysis of Variance

Between-Subjects Factors

		Value Label	N
presentation condition	1	unmasked	10
	2	greyblob	10
	3	pixelated	10
	4	negated	10

SPSS reminds you of the factor that you are analysing, what the levels of that factor are, and the number of participants in each level.

This table will appear if you requested **Descriptive statistics** in the **General Factorial: Options** dialogue box.

Descriptive Statistics

Dependent Variable: MEMORY

presentation condition	Mean	Std. Deviation	N
unmasked	66.7000	5.3344	10
greyblob	55.7000	3.8020	10
pixelated	57.7000	5.4171	10
negated	67.2000	4.5898	10
Total	61.8250	7.0014	40

The mean and the standard deviation (SD) for each level of the factor.

The Total mean and SD: that is, for all participants regardless of which condition they were in.

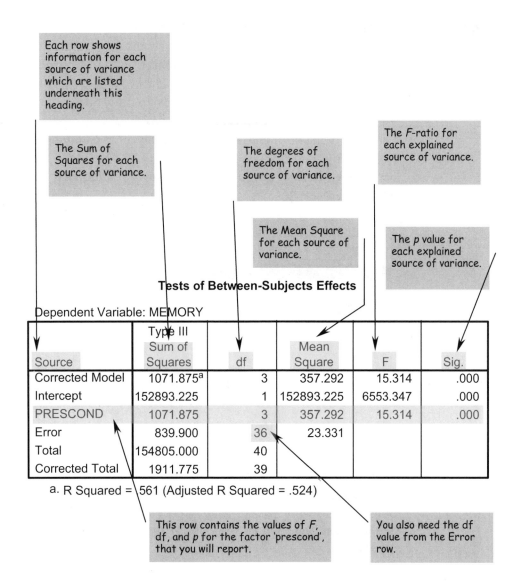

Each row shows information for each source of variance which are listed underneath this heading.

The Sum of Squares for each source of variance.

The degrees of freedom for each source of variance.

The *F*-ratio for each explained source of variance.

The Mean Square for each source of variance.

The *p* value for each explained source of variance.

Tests of Between-Subjects Effects

Dependent Variable: MEMORY

Source	Type III Sum of Squares	df	Mean Square	F	Sig.
Corrected Model	1071.875[a]	3	357.292	15.314	.000
Intercept	152893.225	1	152893.225	6553.347	.000
PRESCOND	1071.875	3	357.292	15.314	.000
Error	839.900	36	23.331		
Total	154805.000	40			
Corrected Total	1911.775	39			

a. R Squared = .561 (Adjusted R Squared = .524)

This row contains the values of *F*, df, and *p* for the factor 'prescond', that you will report.

You also need the df value from the Error row.

In a report you would write: There was a significant effect of the presentation condition ($F_{(3,36)} = 15.314$, $p < 0.0005$).

To identify which pair(s) of conditions significantly differed, you would carry out planned or unplanned comparisons as appropriate (see Section 8).

As stated earlier, one-way between-subjects ANOVA can be carried out in two different ways in SPSS. This is the second way.

To get the **One-Way ANOVA** dialogue box:
For SPSS Versions 9 and 10 click on **Analyze** ⇒ **Compare Means** ⇒ **One-Way ANOVA**.
For SPSS Version 8 click on **Statistics** ⇒ **Compare Means** ⇒ **One-Way ANOVA**.

You will then see this dialogue box:

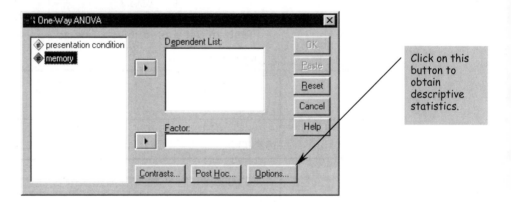

Click on this button to obtain descriptive statistics.

Follow the same procedure as before, selecting "memory" as your dependent variable and "presentation condition" as your factor.

See the next page for an example of the output using the **One-Way ANOVA** command.

SPSS OUTPUT FOR ONE-WAY BETWEEN-SUBJECTS ANALYSIS OF VARIANCE

Obtained Using Menu Items: Compare <u>M</u>eans > <u>O</u>ne-Way ANOVA

Oneway

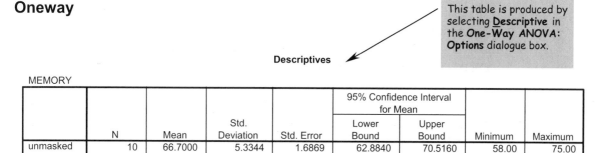

This table is produced by selecting <u>**Descriptive**</u> in the **One-Way ANOVA: Options** dialogue box.

Descriptives

MEMORY

	N	Mean	Std. Deviation	Std. Error	95% Confidence Interval for Mean		Minimum	Maximum
					Lower Bound	Upper Bound		
unmasked	10	66.7000	5.3344	1.6869	62.8840	70.5160	58.00	75.00
greyblob	10	55.7000	3.8020	1.2023	52.9802	58.4198	48.00	61.00
pixelated	10	57.7000	5.4171	1.7130	53.8249	61.5751	51.00	68.00
negated	10	67.2000	4.5898	1.4514	63.9166	70.4834	58.00	74.00
Total	40	61.8250	7.0014	1.1070	59.5858	64.0642	48.00	75.00

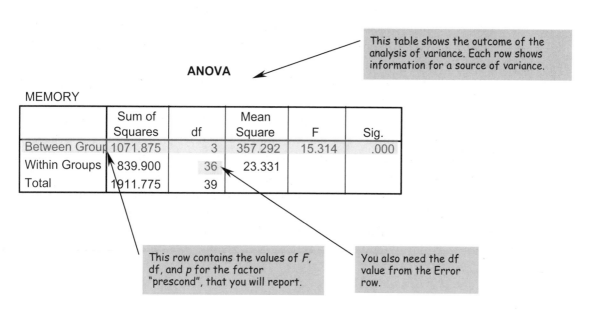

This table shows the outcome of the analysis of variance. Each row shows information for a source of variance.

ANOVA

MEMORY

	Sum of Squares	df	Mean Square	F	Sig.
Between Groups	1071.875	3	357.292	15.314	.000
Within Groups	839.900	36	23.331		
Total	1911.775	39			

This row contains the values of *F*, df, and *p* for the factor "prescond", that you will report.

You also need the df value from the Error row.

In a report you would write: There was a significant effect of presentation condition ($F_{(3,36)} = 15.314, p < 0.0005$).

Section 3: Two-way between-subjects ANOVA

EXAMPLE STUDY: THE EFFECT OF DEFENDANT'S ATTRACTIVENESS AND SEX ON SENTENCING

To practise how to analyse data from the two-way between-subjects ANOVA design, we will return to the issue outlined earlier, concerning the relationship between a defendant's attractiveness and the sentence awarded. By using an ANOVA design, we were able to consider not only attractiveness but also the gender of the defendant. In the study described here, the testimony of a hypothetical defendant describing a murder and admitting guilt was presented as written text to 60 participants. 20 participants simply received the written text with no photograph attached, 20 participants received the text and a photograph of an attractive defendant and 20 participants received the text and a photograph of an unattractive defendant. The photograph was of either a man or a woman. Participants were asked to indicate how many years in jail the defendant should receive as punishment.

The design employed was a 3*2 between-subjects ANOVA design. The first between-subjects factor was the knowledge about attractiveness which had three levels; the factor is operationalised as showing either no photograph of defendant (so no knowledge about attractiveness), a photograph of an attractive defendant and a photograph of an unattractive defendant. The second between-subjects factor was same or different sex; operationalised by showing a photograph of the defendant of the same or opposite sex as the participant. Sex of the defendant was also given in the written text, for the participants who received no photograph. The dependent variable was the sentence given, operationalised as how many years the defendant should spend in years, ranging from a minimum of 3 to a maximum of 25. The hypothesis tested was that the unattractive defendant would be sentenced more harshly and that the length of sentence given might also depend on the sex of the participant. (These data are available in the Appendix.)

The sequence to perform a two way between-subjects (and any multi-way between-subjects) ANOVA is:

For SPSS Versions 9 and 10, click on **Analyze** ⇒ **General Linear Model** ⇒ **Univariate.**

For SPSS Version 8, click on **Statistics** ⇒ **General Linear Model** ⇒ **GLM General Factorial.**

You should now be looking at a dialogue box like this:

These are the two between-subjects factors.

This is your dependent variable.

The dependent variable is the sentence the participants awarded, so click on "Sentence awarded in years" and then on the ► button to add it to the box labelled **Dependent Variable**. This is a two-way ANOVA and the two factors are "Attractiveness of defendant" and "Same or different sex" (whether the defendant was same or different sex to the participant). Both these factors need to be added to the **Fixed Factor(s)** box. A quick way to do this is to highlight both factors by clicking on "Attractiveness of defendant" and dragging the cursor down to "Same or different sex"; then click on the ► button to bring them into the box.

Click on ok and SPSS will carry out the test. The output, which is explained after we describe how to obtain a graph, includes means, standard deviations and N (the number of scores). These were obtained by clicking on **Descriptive statistics** in the **Options** dialogue box.

You will find that there is a significant effect of attractiveness of defendant and you may wish to display the means for this variable as a graph (shown in the annotated output on page 166).

CREATING A BAR CHART

To obtain such a chart, click on **Graphs** on the menu bar. This will give you a choice of graphs. Bar charts are frequently used to display the results of ANOVA, so click on **Bar** to get the following dialogue box.

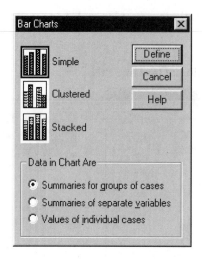

Click on **Simple** and then on Define. You will then see the following dialog box. We have selected "Attractiveness of defendant" as the **Category Axis** and "Sentence awarded" as the **Variable**.

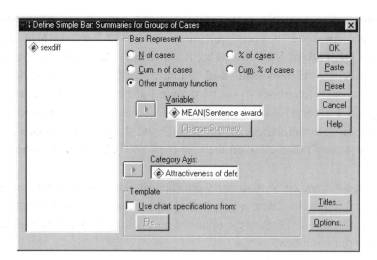

All of the two-way between-subjects ANOVA output and the chart are shown on the next two pages.

Obtained Using Menu Items: General Linear Model > Univariate (Versions 9 and 10) or GLM – General Factorial (Version 8)

Univariate Analysis of Variance

Between-Subjects Factors

		Value Label	N
SEXDIFF	1	Same sex as defendant	30
	2	Opposite sex to defendant	30
Attractiveness of defendant	1	Attractive	20
	2	Unattractive	20
	3	No picture	20

SPSS reminds you of the factors that you are analysing, what the levels of each factor are, and the number of participants in each level.

Descriptive Statistics

This table was produced by requesting **Descriptive statistics** in the **General Factorial: Options** dialogue box.

Dependent Variable: Sentence awarded (in years)

SEXDIFF	Attractiveness of defendant	Mean	Std. Deviation	N
Same sex as defendant	Attractive	7.50	1.78	10
	Unattractive	11.20	2.30	10
	No picture	14.50	1.27	10
	Total	11.07	3.40	30
Opposite sex to defendant	Attractive	7.50	2.42	10
	Unattractive	10.30	2.06	10
	No picture	13.50	1.65	10
	Total	10.43	3.19	30
Total	Attractive	7.50	2.06	20
	Unattractive	10.75	2.17	20
	No picture	14.00	1.52	20
	Total	10.75	3.29	60

These rows show descriptives for each level of the factor "attract", collapsing across the levels of the other factor, "sexdiff".

Each of these six rows shows the descriptives for one of the conditions of the study. Thus, the first row is for participants who were given a photo of an attractive defendant and who were the same sex as that defendant.

These two rows show descriptives for each level of the factor "sexdiff", collapsing across the levels of the other factor, "attract".

This table shows the outcome of the analysis of variance. Each row shows information for a source of variance.

Tests of Between-Subjects Effects

Dependent Variable: Sentence awarded (in years)

Source	Type III Sum of Squares	df	Mean Square	F	Sig.
Corrected Model	431.550[a]	5	86.310	22.658	.000
Intercept	6933.750	1	6933.750	1820.236	.000
SEXDIFF	6.017	1	6.017	1.579	.214
ATTRACT	422.500	2	211.250	55.457	.000
SEXDIFF * ATTRACT	3.033	2	1.517	.398	.674
Error	205.700	54	3.809		
Total	7571.000	60			
Corrected Total	637.250	59			

a. R Squared = .677 (Adjusted R Squared = .647)

This row shows information about the main effect of the factor "sexdiff".

This row shows information about the main effect of the factor "attract".

This row shows information about the interaction between the factors "sexdiff" and "attract".

In a report you would write, at appropriate points:

The main effect of whether the sex of the defendant was the same as or different from the sex of the participant was not significant ($F_{(1,54)} = 1.579$, $p = 0.214$).

There was a significant main effect of knowledge about attractiveness ($F_{(2,54)} = 55.457$, $p < 0.0005$), see graph below.

There was no significant interaction between the factor of knowledge about attractiveness and the factor of same or different sex ($F_{(2,54)} = 0.398$, $p = 0.674$).

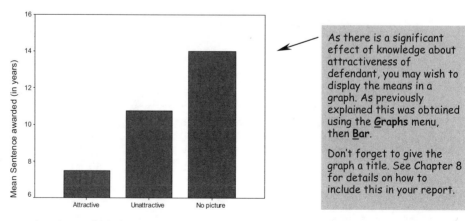

As there is a significant effect of knowledge about attractiveness of defendant, you may wish to display the means in a graph. As previously explained this was obtained using the **Graphs** menu, then **Bar**.

Don't forget to give the graph a title. See Chapter 8 for details on how to include this in your report.

Section 4: One-way within-subjects ANOVA

EXAMPLE STUDY: THE STROOP EFFECT

Many experiments have been conducted to investigate the Stroop effect. The most common way of demonstrating this effect is to show participants the names of colours printed in an incongruous colour (e.g. the word "red" written in green ink) and ask them to name the colour of the ink. Results show that this is not an easy task because of our tendency to read the word, which then interferes with the task of naming the colour of the ink. In one experiment with undergraduate students, we devised three lists. One list was incongruent and contained four words with strong colour associations (grass, coal, blood, sky) repeated three times in a random order, each time in a different incongruent colour ink (e.g. "grass" printed in black, red and blue ink). One list was congruent and contained the same four words repeated three times in a random order, each time in their congruent colour ink (e.g. "grass" printed in green ink). The third list was neutral and contained 4 new words, matched in word length to the original words, and repeated three times. These words were not associated with any particular colour and were printed in one of the four different colour inks (e.g. "table" written in green).

The design employed was a one-way within-subjects ANOVA design. The within-subjects factor, the list, had three levels: incongruent, congruent and neutral. The dependent variable was the time taken in seconds to name the colour of the ink of the 12 words in the list. The hypothesis was that there would be an effect of list on performance. (These data are available in the Appendix.)

To perform the one-way within-subjects ANOVA:
For SPSS Versions 9 and 10, click on **Analyze** ⇒ **General Linear Model** ⇒ **Repeated Measures.**
For SPSS Version 8, click on **Statistics** ⇒ **General Linear Model** ⇒ **GLM Repeated Measures.**

You are then presented with a dialogue box like this:

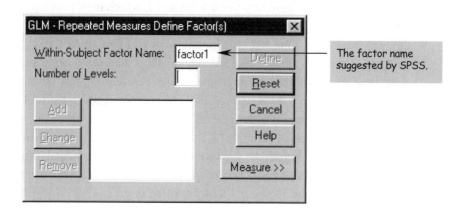

Factor1 is not a very helpful name for a factor, so we shall change it to something that describes the factor we are looking at. Change the factor name by highlighting factor1 and typing the word "list". We then need to tell SPSS how many levels there are –in this case 3 – incongruent, congruent and neutral. Type the number "3" in the Number of Levels box and click on ▭Add▭ button to finish this part of the operation. The dialogue box will now look like this:

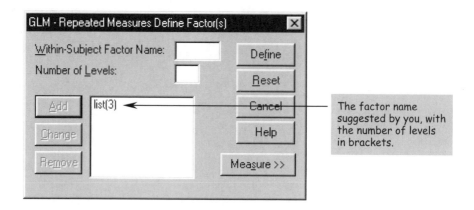

Next, click on the [Define] button.

You will see another dialogue box that will look like this:

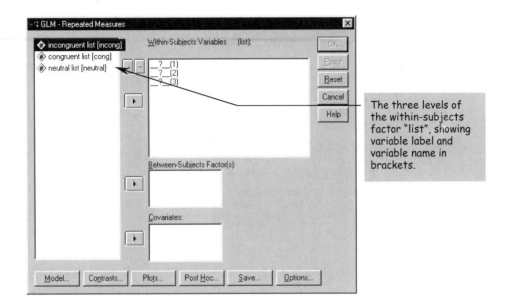

The three levels of the within-subjects factor "list", showing variable label and variable name in brackets.

You need to move the variable names into the **Within-Subjects Variables** box. It is worth thinking about whether they should be entered in any particular order, as SPSS does a trend test. For this study, we would expect the time taken to name the ink colour for all the words in the list to be shortest for the congruent list, longer for the neutral list, and longest for the incongruent list, so enter them in that order.

Click on "congruent list [cong]" and then click on [▶]. This level of the factor will be inserted in the **Within-Subjects Variables** box in the first factor position (i.e. next to the 1 in brackets). Continue by clicking on "neutral list [neutral]" and on [▶] and "incongruent list [incong]" and [▶]. Again, you can click on the **Options** button and ask for descriptives for the three levels of this factor. Click on [OK] and SPSS will calculate the ANOVA.

You will find that there is a significant effect of list, and you may wish to include in your results section an error bar graph, which displays the mean for each condition and a vertical bar representing the 95% confidence intervals of the mean.

CREATING AN ERROR BAR GRAPH

To obtain such a chart, click on **Graphs** on the menu bar and select **Error Bar**. You will see the following dialog box:

Click on **Simple** and click on the circle next to **Summaries of separate variables.** Next click on ⌊**Define**⌋. You will then see the following dialog box. This box shows you that we have selected the three levels of "list" in a specific order to reflect the trend in the means.

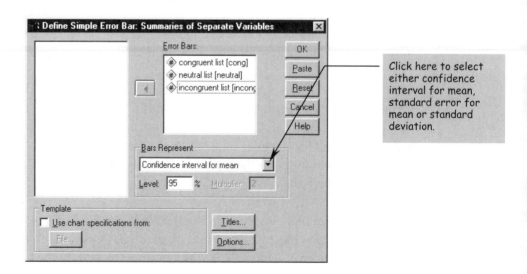

All of the one-way within-subjects ANOVA output and the error-bar chart are shown on the next two pages.

SPSS OUTPUT FOR ONE-WAY WITHIN-SUBJECTS ANALYSIS OF VARIANCE

Obtained Using Menu Items: <u>G</u>eneral Linear Model > <u>R</u>epeated Measures (Versions 9 and 10) or GLM – <u>R</u>epeated Measures (Version 8)

Within-Subjects Factors

Measure: MEASURE_1

LIST	Dependent Variable
1	CONG
2	NEUTRAL
3	INCONG

On this page we show all of the output, reduced to fit the page. The shaded tables are the parts of the output that are normally required in an undergraduate course: these tables appear full size and annotated on the following two pages.
See Section 7 for information about the other tables.

Descriptive Statistics

	Mean	Std. Deviation	N
congruent list	8.9000	.7379	10
neutral list	11.1000	1.1972	10
incongruent list	14.4000	1.5055	10

Multivariate Tests [b]

Effect		Value	F	Hypothesis df	Error df	Sig.
LIST	Pillai's Trace	.920	45.993[a]	2.000	8.000	.000
	Wilks' Lambda	.080	45.993[a]	2.000	8.000	.000
	Hotelling's Trace	11.498	45.993[a]	2.000	8.000	.000
	Roy's Largest Root	11.498	45.993[a]	2.000	8.000	.000

a. Exact statistic

b.
Design: Intercept
Within Subjects Design: LIST

Mauchly's Test of Sphericity [b]

Measure: MEASURE_1

Within Subjects Effect	Mauchly's W	Approx. Chi-Square	df	Sig.	Greenhouse-Geisser	Huynh-Feldt	Lower-bound
					Epsilon[a]		
LIST	.892	.914	2	.633	.903	1.000	.500

Tests the null hypothesis that the error covariance matrix of the orthonormalized transformed dependent variables is proportional to an identity matrix.

a. May be used to adjust the degrees of freedom for the averaged tests of significance. Corrected tests are displayed in the layers (by default) of the Tests of Within Subjects Effects table.

b.
Design: Intercept
Within Subjects Design: LIST

This section appears in the Output Viewer as it is shown here. When you print it, however, it may split into two separate tables. See Chapter 8 for information on how to format tables for printing.

Tests of Within-Subjects Effects

Measure: MEASURE_1

Source		Type III Sum of Squares	df	Mean Square	F	Sig.
LIST	Sphericity Assumed	153.267	2	76.633	68.741	.000
	Greenhouse-Geisser	153.267	1.805	84.906	68.741	.000
	Huynh-Feldt	153.267	2.000	76.633	68.741	.000
	Lower-bound	153.267	1.000	153.267	68.741	.000
Error(LIST)	Sphericity Assumed	20.067	18	1.115		
	Greenhouse-Geisser	20.067	16.246	1.235		
	Huynh-Feldt	20.067	18.000	1.115		
	Lower-bound	20.067	9.000	2.230		

Tests of Within-Subjects Contrasts

Measure: MEASURE_1

Source	LIST	Type III Sum of Squares	df	Mean Square	F	Sig.
LIST	Linear	151.250	1	151.250	102.736	.000
	Quadratic	2.017	1	2.017	2.663	.137
Error(LIST)	Linear	13.250	9	1.472		
	Quadratic	6.817	9	.757		

Tests of Between-Subjects Effects

Measure: MEASURE_1
Transformed Variable: Average

Source	Type III Sum of Squares	df	Mean Square	F	Sig.
Intercept	3944.533	1	3944.533	1957.765	.000
Error	18.133	9	2.015		

General Linear Model

Within-Subjects Factors

Measure: MEASURE_1

LIST	Dependent Variable
1	CONG
2	NEUTRAL
3	INCONG

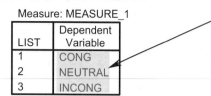

These are the names for each level of the factor "LIST". If there is a meaningful order by which you entered them into the **Repeated Measures** dialogue box (see page 169), then the table Tests of Within-Subjects Contrasts, shown on the next page, will also be relevant.

Descriptive Statistics

	Mean	Std. Deviation	N
congruent list	8.9000	.7379	10
neutral list	11.1000	1.1972	10
incongruent list	14.4000	1.5055	10

Useful descriptives that you can incorporate into your report, obtained by ticking **Descriptive statistics** in the **Repeated Measures: Options** dialogue box.

This table shows the outcome of the analysis of variance.

For information about the non-highlighted rows see Section 7.

Tests of Within-Subjects Effects

Measure: MEASURE_1

Source		Type III Sum of Squares	df	Mean Square	F	Sig.
LIST	Sphericity Assumed	153.267	2	76.633	68.741	.000
	Greenhouse-Geisser	153.267	1.805	84.906	68.741	.000
	Huynh-Feldt	153.267	2.000	76.633	68.741	.000
	Lower-bound	153.267	1.000	153.267	68.741	.000
Error(LIST)	Sphericity Assumed	20.067	18	1.115		
	Greenhouse-Geisser	20.067	16.246	1.235		
	Huynh-Feldt	20.067	18.000	1.115		
	Lower-bound	20.067	9.000	2.230		

This row is the one you will normally use. It gives the values for the factor "LIST" which was a within-subjects factor with three levels (the three types of list).

You also need the df for the Error term.

In a report you would write: There was a significant effect of the type of list ($F_{(2,18)}$ = 68.741, $p < 0.0005$).

Tests of Within-Subjects Contrasts

This table shows the outcome of two trend tests.

Measure: MEASURE_1

Source	LIST	Type III Sum of Squares	df	Mean Square	F	Sig.
LIST	Linear	151.250	1	151.250	102.736	.000
	Quadratic	2.017	1	2.017	2.663	.137
Error(LIST)	Linear	13.250	9	1.472		
	Quadratic	6.817	9	.757		

This row is for the linear trend test.

This row is for the quadratic trend test.

For these data there is a significant linear trend ($F_{(1,9)}$ =102.736, p < 0.0005) over the mean values for each level of the factor, illustrated in the figure below. For the congruent list, the participants take the shortest time to name the ink colour of the 12 words; for the neutral list they take a longer time; and for the incongruent list they take the longest time. Note that the Tests of Within-Subjects Contrasts table shows only whether a trend is significant or not. It is not a test of whether the individual conditions significantly differ from one another; for that you need planned or unplanned comparisons (see Section 8).

For these data there is no significant quadratic trend ($F_{(1,9)}$ = 2.663, p = 0.137). A linear trend test is used to see if the points tend to fall onto a straight line (as here). A quadratic trend test looks for a "U" shaped or inverted "U" shaped trend. If you entered the three levels in the order "cong", "incong" and "neutral", then the quadratic trend would be significant. You might like to try this. (See Howell, 1997, Section 12.13.)

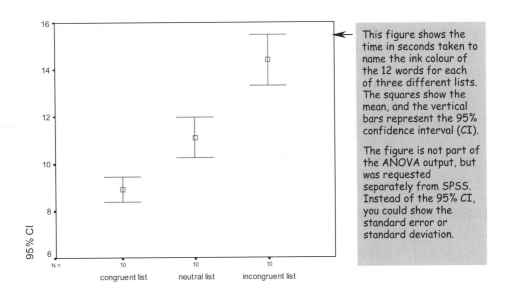

This figure shows the time in seconds taken to name the ink colour of the 12 words for each of three different lists. The squares show the mean, and the vertical bars represent the 95% confidence interval (CI).

The figure is not part of the ANOVA output, but was requested separately from SPSS. Instead of the 95% CI, you could show the standard error or standard deviation.

Section 5: Two-way within-subjects ANOVA

EXAMPLE STUDY: THE EFFECTS OF TWO MEMORY TASKS ON FINGER TAPPING PERFORMANCE

To practise a two-way within-subjects ANOVA, we shall look at an experiment carried out to examine the effects of two memory tasks on tapping performance. Research has identified that right index finger tapping is largely controlled by the left hemisphere, and left index finger tapping by the right hemisphere. If a cognitive task is performed at the same time as this finger-tapping task, then the way in which the cognitive task interferes with such tapping could reflect the extent to which either hemisphere is involved in controlling the cognitive task. Many studies that required participants to tap as fast as possible with their index finger whilst also performing a verbal task, found that right-hand tapping was disrupted more than left-hand tapping. This result is compatible with the notion that the left side of the brain controls both right-hand tapping and many verbal tasks. In a study published by Towell, Burton and Burton (1994), participants were asked to tap with each hand whilst memorising either the words presented to them on a screen (a verbal memory task) or the position of the words on the screen (a visuo-spatial memory task). Memorising the words should disrupt right-hand tapping more than left-hand tapping. Whereas, because the right side of the brain controls many visuo-spatial tasks, memorising the positions of words should disrupt left-hand tapping more than right-hand tapping.

The design employed was a 2*2 within-subjects ANOVA. Each factor had two levels; the first was tapping hand (left or right hand) and the second was the memory task (memorising the words or memorising the positions). All participants were tested under each possible combination of the two factors. The dependent variable was a percentage change score, showing the extent to which tapping is slowed down by the concurrent performance of the memory task. The hypothesis tested was that there would be an interaction between tapping hand and memory task. This hypothesis was supported and for the purposes of this book, we have created a data file that will reproduce some of the findings of the above paper. (These data are available in the Appendix.)

LABELLING WITHIN-SUBJECTS FACTORS

Consider the factors and levels in this example; they could be set out as in Table 6.4 below. As each factor has two levels, there are four conditions, each with one level of one factor and one level for the other factor. The name that will be given, in the SPSS data file, to each column containing the data for each condition can then incorporate a number for each level of each factor, as shown in the bottom row of Table 6.4. In these column names:

"h1s1" means tapping hand 1 (left) and stimulus for task 1 (memorising words)
"h2s2" means tapping hand 2 (right) and stimulus for task 2 (memorising positions)

Table 6.4: An illustration of the numbering system for within-subjects factors.

Factor 1	Tapping Hand			
Levels	Left		Right	
Factor 2	Memory Task		Memory Task	
Levels	Words	Position	Words	Position
Column name, SPSS data file, for conditions	h1s1	h1s2	h2s1	h2s2

You should jot down a rough table such as this before entering the data for any design with two or more within-subjects factors. This will help you when you define the within-subjects factors, because you will find that the numbers that you have used for the column names will match with the numbers that SPSS uses when requesting variable selection.

HOW TO DO IT

The two-way within-subjects ANOVA is performed in the following way:
For SPSS Versions 9 and 10, click on **Analyze** ⇒ **General Linear Model** ⇒ **Repeated Measures.**
For SPSS Version 8, click on **Statistics** ⇒ **General Linear Model** ⇒ **GLM Repeated Measures.**

You are then presented with dialogue box like this:

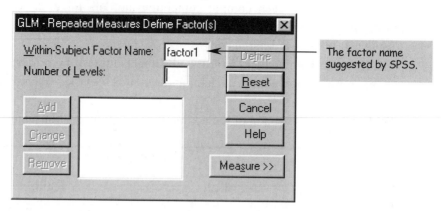

The factor name suggested by SPSS.

Factor1 is obviously not a very helpful factor name, and so we shall change it to something that describes the factor we are looking at. Our first factor describes the hand used, so we will call this "hand". Change the label by highlighting factor1 and typing the word "hand". We then need to tell SPSS how many levels there are, which in this case is 2 – left and right. Type the number "2" in the **Number of Levels** box and click on ⬚ to finish this part of the operation. As this is a two way ANOVA, there is another factor. In this experiment it is the type of memory task, which has two levels. Again, click in the **Within-Subject Factor Name** box and type in the name of this factor "task". Click in the **Number of Levels** box and type in "2" and again click on ⬚. The dialogue box will now look like this:

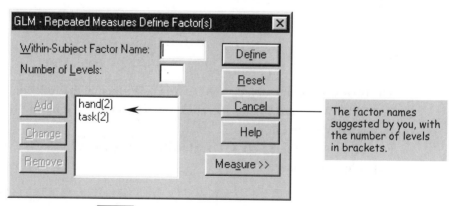

The factor names suggested by you, with the number of levels in brackets.

Now click on ⬚ Define ⬚ button and you will be confronted with the dialogue box below – this looks a bit complicated so take a little time to think about what is required.

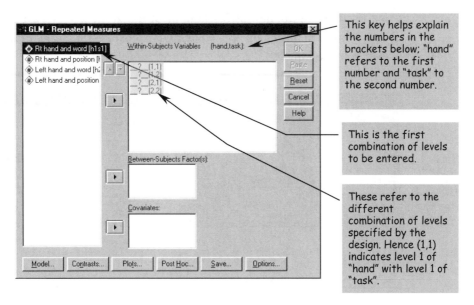

This key helps explain the numbers in the brackets below; "hand" refers to the first number and "task" to the second number.

This is the first combination of levels to be entered.

These refer to the different combination of levels specified by the design. Hence (1,1) indicates level 1 of "hand" with level 1 of "task".

SPSS requires you to select the variables in the correct order and enter these into the **Within-Subjects Variables** box. This will be easy for you because they were labelled in such a way to make the correct order obvious. The variable names are given in brackets after the variable labels. The variable name "h1s1" refers to the condition where the level "hand 1" (the right hand) is combined with the level "stimulus 1" (memorising words).

Click on "Rt hand and word [h1s1]", then click on ▶ to add it to the list in the **Within-Subjects Variables** box, where it should appear in place of the _?_ next to the slot (1,1). Repeat this for the "Rt hand and position [h1s2]" variable, which should go into the slot next to (1,2) and for "Left hand and word [h2s1]"(next to 2,1) and "Left hand and position [h2s2]"(next to 2,2).

Once you have completed this, OK will become active (i.e. will no longer be greyed out) indicating that you have entered sufficient information for SPSS to carry out the analysis.

We recommend that in addition you obtain the means by clicking on **Options** to obtain the **General Factorial Options** dialogue box. Move "hand", "task" and "hand*task" into the box labelled **Display Means for:**. Click on **Continue** to return to the **General Factorial,** and click on OK. SPSS will perform the calculations. If, however, you wish to obtain an interaction graph, then follow the steps outlined below.

Click on the **Plots** button at the bottom of the **Repeated Measures** dialogue box above. This will bring up the **Repeated Measures: Profile Plots** dialogue box shown below on the left.

 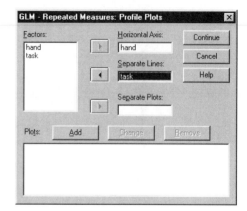

Select which factor should be placed on the horizontal axis of your line graph and which you wish to display as lines on the graph, by highlighting the factors and clicking on the relevant arrow keys. Once you have done this, the dialogue box will change as shown above. Click on the **Add** button, which is now active, and the interaction graph you have requested will appear in the Viewer window.

Click on **Continue** and you will return to the **Repeated Measures** dialogue box. Click on OK to obtain the ANOVA output, shown over the next four pages. The interaction graph will appear at the end of the output.

Obtained Using Menu Items: <u>G</u>eneral Linear Model > <u>R</u>epeated Measures (Versions 9 and 10) or GLM – <u>R</u>epeated Measures (Version 8).

General Linear Model

Within-Subjects Factors

Measure: MEASURE_1

HAND	TASK	Dependent Variable
1	1	H1S1
	2	H1S2
2	1	H2S1
	2	H2S2

On this page and the next page we show all of the output, reduced to fit the page. The shaded tables are the parts of the output that you would normally require: these tables appear full size and are annotated on pages 181 and 182.

For information about other tables see Section 7.

Multivariate Tests[b]

Effect		Value	F	Hypothesis df	Error df	Sig.
HAND	Pillai's Trace	.006	.133[a]	1.000	23.000	.719
	Wilks' Lambda	.994	.133[a]	1.000	23.000	.719
	Hotelling's Trace	.006	.133[a]	1.000	23.000	.719
	Roy's Largest Root	.006	.133[a]	1.000	23.000	.719
TASK	Pillai's Trace	.078	1.955[a]	1.000	23.000	.175
	Wilks' Lambda	.922	1.955[a]	1.000	23.000	.175
	Hotelling's Trace	.085	1.955[a]	1.000	23.000	.175
	Roy's Largest Root	.085	1.955[a]	1.000	23.000	.175
HAND * TASK	Pillai's Trace	.173	4.807[a]	1.000	23.000	.039
	Wilks' Lambda	.827	4.807[a]	1.000	23.000	.039
	Hotelling's Trace	.209	4.807[a]	1.000	23.000	.039
	Roy's Largest Root	.209	4.807[a]	1.000	23.000	.039

a. Exact statistic

b.
Design: Intercept
Within Subjects Design: HAND+TASK+HAND*TASK

Mauchly's Test of Sphericity [b]

Measure: MEASURE_1

Within Subjects Effect	Mauchly's W	Approx. Chi-Square	df	Sig.	Epsilon[a]		
					Greenhouse-Geisser	Huynh-Feldt	Lower-bound
HAND	1.000	.000	0	.	1.000	1.000	1.000
TASK	1.000	.000	0	.	1.000	1.000	1.000
HAND * TASK	1.000	.000	0	.	1.000	1.000	1.000

Tests the null hypothesis that the error covariance matrix of the orthonormalized transformed dependent variables is proportional to an identity matrix.

a. May be used to adjust the degrees of freedom for the averaged tests of significance. Corrected tests are displayed in the layers (by default) of the Tests of Within Subjects Effects table.

b.
Design: Intercept
Within Subjects Design: HAND+TASK+HAND*TASK

Tests of Within-Subjects Effects

Measure: MEASURE_1

Source		Type III Sum of Squares	df	Mean Square	F	Sig.
HAND	Sphericity Assumed	2.295	1	2.295	.133	.719
	Greenhouse-Geisser	2.295	1.000	2.295	.133	.719
	Huynh-Feldt	2.295	1.000	2.295	.133	.719
	Lower-bound	2.295	1.000	2.295	.133	.719
Error(HAND)	Sphericity Assumed	398.267	23	17.316		
	Greenhouse-Geisser	398.267	23.000	17.316		
	Huynh-Feldt	398.267	23.000	17.316		
	Lower-bound	398.267	23.000	17.316		
TASK	Sphericity Assumed	70.906	1	70.906	1.955	.175
	Greenhouse-Geisser	70.906	1.000	70.906	1.955	.175
	Huynh-Feldt	70.906	1.000	70.906	1.955	.175
	Lower-bound	70.906	1.000	70.906	1.955	.175
Error(TASK)	Sphericity Assumed	834.213	23	36.270		
	Greenhouse-Geisser	834.213	23.000	36.270		
	Huynh-Feldt	834.213	23.000	36.270		
	Lower-bound	834.213	23.000	36.270		
HAND * TASK	Sphericity Assumed	21.441	1	21.441	4.807	.039
	Greenhouse-Geisser	21.441	1.000	21.441	4.807	.039
	Huynh-Feldt	21.441	1.000	21.441	4.807	.039
	Lower-bound	21.441	1.000	21.441	4.807	.039
Error(HAND*TASK)	Sphericity Assumed	102.585	23	4.460		
	Greenhouse-Geisser	102.585	23.000	4.460		
	Huynh-Feldt	102.585	23.000	4.460		
	Lower-bound	102.585	23.000	4.460		

Tests of Within-Subjects Contrasts

Measure: MEASURE_1

Source	HAND	TASK	Type III Sum of Squares	df	Mean Square	F	Sig.
HAND	Linear		2.295	1	2.295	.133	.719
Error(HAND)	Linear		398.267	23	17.316		
TASK		Linear	70.906	1	70.906	1.955	.175
Error(TASK)		Linear	834.213	23	36.270		
HAND * TASK	Linear	Linear	21.441	1	21.441	4.807	.039
Error(HAND*TASK)	Linear	Linear	102.585	23	4.460		

Tests of Between-Subjects Effects

Measure: MEASURE_1
Transformed Variable: Average

Source	Type III Sum of Squares	df	Mean Square	F	Sig.
Intercept	2544.862	1	2544.862	33.553	.000
Error	1744.438	23	75.845		

Estimated Marginal Means

1. HAND

Measure: MEASURE_1

HAND	Mean	Std. Error	95% Confidence Interval Lower Bound	Upper Bound
1	4.994	1.017	2.890	7.098
2	5.303	.952	3.334	7.273

2. TASK

Measure: MEASURE_1

TASK	Mean	Std. Error	95% Confidence Interval Lower Bound	Upper Bound
1	6.008	1.137	3.655	8.361
2	4.289	1.021	2.178	6.401

3. HAND * TASK

Measure: MEASURE_1

HAND	TASK	Mean	Std. Error	95% Confidence Interval Lower Bound	Upper Bound
1	1	6.326	1.352	3.530	9.123
	2	3.662	.967	1.662	5.662
2	1	5.690	1.122	3.369	8.011
	2	4.916	1.248	2.334	7.499

This table shows the outcome of the analysis of variance.

For information about the non-highlighted rows see Section 7.

Tests of Within-Subjects Effects

Measure: MEASURE_1

Source		Type III Sum of Squares	df	Mean Square	F	Sig.
HAND	Sphericity Assumed	2.295	1	2.295	.133	.719
	Greenhouse-Geisser	2.295	1.000	2.295	.133	.719
	Huynh-Feldt	2.295	1.000	2.295	.133	.719
	Lower-bound	2.295	1.000	2.295	.133	.719
Error(HAND)	Sphericity Assumed	398.267	23	17.316		
	Greenhouse-Geisser	398.267	23.000	17.316		
	Huynh-Feldt	398.267	23.000	17.316		
	Lower-bound	398.267	23.000	17.316		
TASK	Sphericity Assumed	70.906	1	70.906	1.955	.175
	Greenhouse-Geisser	70.906	1.000	70.906	1.955	.175
	Huynh-Feldt	70.906	1.000	70.906	1.955	.175
	Lower-bound	70.906	1.000	70.906	1.955	.175
Error(TASK)	Sphericity Assumed	834.213	23	36.270		
	Greenhouse-Geisser	834.213	23.000	36.270		
	Huynh-Feldt	834.213	23.000	36.270		
	Lower-bound	834.213	23.000	36.270		
HAND * TASK	Sphericity Assumed	21.441	1	21.441	4.807	.039
	Greenhouse-Geisser	21.441	1.000	21.441	4.807	.039
	Huynh-Feldt	21.441	1.000	21.441	4.807	.039
	Lower-bound	21.441	1.000	21.441	4.807	.039
Error(HAND*TASK)	Sphericity Assumed	102.585	23	4.460		
	Greenhouse-Geisser	102.585	23.000	4.460		
	Huynh-Feldt	102.585	23.000	4.460		
	Lower-bound	102.585	23.000	4.460		

This table shows the outcome of trend tests. Each factor only has two levels, and so:
1. only linear tests can be carried out, and not quadratic;
2. the values are simply those for the analysis of variance.
If, however, you have at least one factor with three or more levels, then this table would be useful as shown in the one-way within ANOVA example.

Tests of Within-Subjects Contrasts

Measure: MEASURE_1

Source	HAND	TASK	Type III Sum of Squares	df	Mean Square	F	Sig.
HAND	Linear		2.295	1	2.295	.133	.719
Error(HAND)	Linear		398.267	23	17.316		
TASK		Linear	70.906	1	70.906	1.955	.175
Error(TASK)		Linear	834.213	23	36.270		
HAND * TASK	Linear	Linear	21.441	1	21.441	4.807	.039
Error(HAND*TASK)	Linear	Linear	102.585	23	4.460		

These three tables give the descriptives requested in the **Repeated Measures: Options** dialogue box: "HAND", "TASK", and "HAND*TASK" were moved into the box labelled **Display Means for** (see page 177).

Estimated Marginal Mean

1. HAND

Measure: MEASURE_1

HAND	Mean	Std. Error	95% Confidence Interval Lower Bound	95% Confidence Interval Upper Bound
1	4.994	1.017	2.890	7.098
2	5.303	.952	3.334	7.273

This table shows descriptives for each level of the factor "HAND", collapsed across the other factor "TASK". We used the code 1 = left and 2 = right, so the first row is for the right hand, and the second row is for the left hand.

2. TASK

Measure: MEASURE_1

TASK	Mean	Std. Error	95% Confidence Interval Lower Bound	95% Confidence Interval Upper Bound
1	6.008	1.137	3.655	8.361
2	4.289	1.021	2.178	6.401

This table shows descriptives for each level of the factor "TASK" collapsed across the two levels of the factor "HAND".

3. HAND * TASK

Measure: MEASURE_1

HAND	TASK	Mean	Std. Error	95% Confidence Interval Lower Bound	95% Confidence Interval Upper Bound
1	1	6.326	1.352	3.530	9.123
	2	3.662	.967	1.662	5.662
2	1	5.690	1.122	3.369	8.011
	2	4.916	1.248	2.334	7.499

This table shows descriptives for each of the conditions of the study. Thus, the first row gives details of performance when participants were tapping with their right hand while memorising words. The bottom row gives details of performance when participants were tapping with their left hand while memorising the positions of the words.

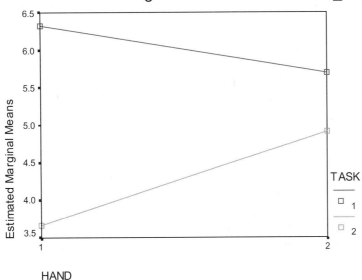

Estimated Marginal Means of MEASURE_1

In a report you would write, at appropriate points:

The main effect of tapping hand was not significant ($F_{(1,23)} = 0.133$, $p = 0.719$).
The main effect of type of task was not significant ($F_{(1,23)} = 1.955$, $p < 0.175$).
There was a significant interaction between tapping hand and type of task ($F_{(1,23)} = 4.807$, $p = 0.039$). This interaction is displayed in the graph above, showing that right-hand tapping was disrupted more by memorising words than memorising positions, and that this effect of type of task was reduced for left-hand tapping.

Section 6: Mixed ANOVA

In this section, we show you how to perform an ANOVA that involves both between- and within-subjects factors in the same experiment. We shall do so by referring to a study employing a three-way mixed design.

EXAMPLE STUDY: THE EFFECTS OF INVERSION, NEGATION AND PRIMING ON THE PERCEPTION OF FACE-LIKE PATTERNS

It has previously been demonstrated that faces are peculiarly difficult to recognise when inverted (upside-down) or when in photographic negative (negated). In an earlier published study, Kemp, McManus and Pigott (1990) demonstrated that negation and inversion also make it more difficult to detect minor changes to the appearance of a face, brought about by moving the features (the eyes being moved up, down, in or out). The current study is a further investigation of these effects, designed to see whether non-face patterns (three dots arranged in the positions of the eyes and the mouth to make a face-like pattern) are also affected by these transformations. Participants were shown three such patterns at a time. One of these patterns showed the dots in their original location. The participants were required to decide which of the other two patterns had been modified.

The design employed was a 2*2*2 mixed ANOVA design. The first factor was the within-subjects factor of negation, with two levels, operationalised by showing face-like dot patterns as normal images or in photographic negative. The second factor was the within-subjects factor of orientation, with two levels, operationalised by showing the face-like dot patterns upright or inverted. The third factor was the between-subjects factor of priming where some participants were primed by being asked to perform this task on faces before taking part in the experiment whereas others were not.

The dependent variable was the percentage of correct judgements made by the participants. The hypothesis tested was that the effects of negation and inversion would only be apparent in the group that was primed.

For the purposes of this book, we have created a data file that will reproduce some of the findings of this later study. In the data file, the columns holding the data for the combination of levels of the two within-subjects factors have been named using the numbering systems that we described in Section 5. (These data are available in the Appendix.)

To perform the three-way mixed ANOVA, follow the sequence used for any ANOVA with within-subjects factors:

For SPSS Versions 9 and 10, click on **Analyze** ⇒ **General Linear Model** ⇒ **Repeated Measures.**

For SPSS Version 8, click on **Statistics** ⇒ **General Linear Model** ⇒ **GLM Repeated Measures.**

You are then presented with the dialogue box shown below.

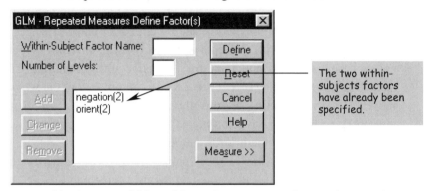

The two within-subjects factors have already been specified.

To specify the two within-subjects factors, enter the word "negation" to replace the default **factor1** in the **Within-Subject Factor Name** box and enter "2" in the **Number of Levels** box and click on ⎡Add⎤. Now type "orient" in the **Within-Subject Factor Name** box and "2" in the **Number of Levels** box and again click on ⎡Add⎤. The dialogue box will now look like the one shown above. Click on ⎡Define⎤ and you will be presented with the dialogue box shown below:

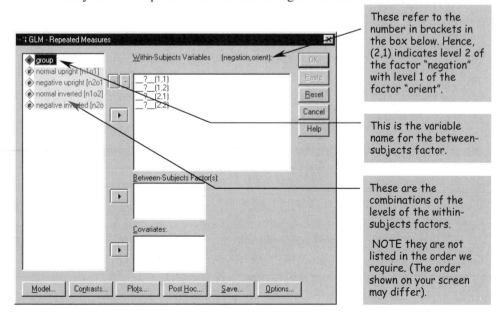

These refer to the number in brackets in the box below. Hence, (2,1) indicates level 2 of the factor "negation" with level 1 of the factor "orient".

This is the variable name for the between-subjects factor.

These are the combinations of the levels of the within-subjects factors.

NOTE they are not listed in the order we require. (The order shown on your screen may differ).

Because this is a mixed design, a between-subjects factor has to be specified. Click on "group" and then click on ▶ next the **Between-Subjects Factor(s)** box. Now select the remaining variables in the correct order and enter these into the **Within-Subjects Variables** box. Again, they were labelled in such a way to make the correct order obvious. The variable names are given in brackets after the variable labels. The variable name "n1o1" refers to the condition where the first level of the factor "negation" (normal) is combined with the first level of the factor "orientation" (upright).

Click on "normal upright [n1o1]" and click on ▶ to add it to the list in the **Within-Subjects Variables** box, where it should appear in place of the _?_ next to the slot (1,1). Repeat this for the "normal inverted [n1o2]" variable, which should go into the slot next to (1,2) and then for "negative upright [n2o1]" (next to 2,1) and "negative inverted [n2o2]" (next to 2,2). If you put one in the wrong place, you can move it by highlighting it and then clicking on the up or down arrow, as appropriate. Once you have completed this, OK will become active, indicating that you have entered sufficient information for SPSS to carry out the analysis and you can click on OK. After a short pause, SPSS will calculate the ANOVA and produce the output that is explained on the next three pages.

SPSS OUTPUT FOR THREE-WAY MIXED ANALYSIS OF VARIANCE

Obtained Using Menu Items: <u>G</u>eneral Linear Model > <u>R</u>epeated Measures (Versions 9 and 10) or GLM – <u>R</u>epeated Measures (Version 8)

General Linear Model

Within-Subjects Factors

Measure: MEASURE_1

NEGATION	ORIENT	Dependent Variable
1	1	N1O1
	2	N1O2
2	1	N2O1
	2	N2O2

On this page we show the first four tables, reduced to fit the page. On the following two pages we show the remaining three tables: they hold the information that you are most likely to need.

Between-Subjects Factors

		Value Label	N
GROUP	1.00	unprimed	38
	2.00	primed	23

If you requested **De<u>s</u>criptive statistics** in the **Repeated Measures: Options** dialogue box, the Descriptive Statistics table would appear here.

Multivariate Tests[b]

Effect		Value	F	Hypothesis df	Error df	Sig.
NEGATION	Pillai's Trace	.002	.137[a]	1.000	59.000	.713
	Wilks' Lambda	.998	.137[a]	1.000	59.000	.713
	Hotelling's Trace	.002	.137[a]	1.000	59.000	.713
	Roy's Largest Root	.002	.137[a]	1.000	59.000	.713
NEGATION * GROUP	Pillai's Trace	.006	.384[a]	1.000	59.000	.538
	Wilks' Lambda	.994	.384[a]	1.000	59.000	.538
	Hotelling's Trace	.007	.384[a]	1.000	59.000	.538
	Roy's Largest Root	.007	.384[a]	1.000	59.000	.538
ORIENT	Pillai's Trace	.009	.539[a]	1.000	59.000	.466
	Wilks' Lambda	.991	.539[a]	1.000	59.000	.466
	Hotelling's Trace	.009	.539[a]	1.000	59.000	.466
	Roy's Largest Root	.009	.539[a]	1.000	59.000	.466
ORIENT * GROUP	Pillai's Trace	.038	2.319[a]	1.000	59.000	.133
	Wilks' Lambda	.962	2.319[a]	1.000	59.000	.133
	Hotelling's Trace	.039	2.319[a]	1.000	59.000	.133
	Roy's Largest Root	.039	2.319[a]	1.000	59.000	.133
NEGATION * ORIENT	Pillai's Trace	.048	3.006[a]	1.000	59.000	.088
	Wilks' Lambda	.952	3.006[a]	1.000	59.000	.088
	Hotelling's Trace	.051	3.006[a]	1.000	59.000	.088
	Roy's Largest Root	.051	3.006[a]	1.000	59.000	.088
NEGATION * ORIENT * GROUP	Pillai's Trace	.051	3.185[a]	1.000	59.000	.079
	Wilks' Lambda	.949	3.185[a]	1.000	59.000	.079
	Hotelling's Trace	.054	3.185[a]	1.000	59.000	.079
	Roy's Largest Root	.054	3.185[a]	1.000	59.000	.079

a. Exact statistic

b. Design: Intercept+GROUP
Within Subjects Design: NEGATION+ORIENT+NEGATION*ORIENT

For information about these two tables see Section 7.

Mauchly's Test of Sphericity[b]

Measure: MEASURE_1

Within Subjects Effect	Mauchly's W	Approx. Chi-Square	df	Sig.	Epsilon[a]		
					Greenhouse-Geisser	Huynh-Feldt	Lower-bound
NEGATION	1.000	.000	0	.	1.000	1.000	1.000
ORIENT	1.000	.000	0	.	1.000	1.000	1.000
NEGATION * ORIENT	1.000	.000	0	.	1.000	1.000	1.000

Tests the null hypothesis that the error covariance matrix of the orthonormalized transformed dependent variables is proportional to an identity matrix.

a. May be used to adjust the degrees of freedom for the averaged tests of significance. Corrected tests are displayed in the layers (by default) of the Tests of Within Subjects Effects table.

b. Design: Intercept+GROUP
Within Subjects Design: NEGATION+ORIENT+NEGATION*ORIENT

This table shows the outcome of any part of the mixed ANOVA that incorporates a within-subjects factor. See Section 7 for an explanation of the 2nd-4th rows of each cell.

Tests of Within-Subjects Effects

Measure: MEASURE_1

Source		Type III Sum of Squares	df	Mean Square	F	Sig.
NEGATION	Sphericity Assumed	9.470	1	9.470	.137	.713
	Greenhouse-Geisser	9.470	1.000	9.470	.137	.713
	Huynh-Feldt	9.470	1.000	9.470	.137	.713
	Lower-bound	9.470	1.000	9.470	.137	.713
NEGATION * GROUP	Sphericity Assumed	26.587	1	26.587	.384	.538
	Greenhouse-Geisser	26.587	1.000	26.587	.384	.538
	Huynh-Feldt	26.587	1.000	26.587	.384	.538
	Lower-bound	26.587	1.000	26.587	.384	.538
Error(NEGATION)	Sphericity Assumed	4079.831	59	69.150		
	Greenhouse-Geisser	4079.831	59.000	69.150		
	Huynh-Feldt	4079.831	59.000	69.150		
	Lower-bound	4079.831	59.000	69.150		
ORIENT	Sphericity Assumed	33.631	1	33.631	.539	.466
	Greenhouse-Geisser	33.631	1.000	33.631	.539	.466
	Huynh-Feldt	33.631	1.000	33.631	.539	.466
	Lower-bound	33.631	1.000	33.631	.539	.466
ORIENT * GROUP	Sphericity Assumed	144.622	1	144.622	2.319	.133
	Greenhouse-Geisser	144.622	1.000	144.622	2.319	.133
	Huynh-Feldt	144.622	1.000	144.622	2.319	.133
	Lower-bound	144.622	1.000	144.622	2.319	.133
Error(ORIENT)	Sphericity Assumed	3678.712	59	62.351		
	Greenhouse-Geisser	3678.712	59.000	62.351		
	Huynh-Feldt	3678.712	59.000	62.351		
	Lower-bound	3678.712	59.000	62.351		
NEGATION * ORIENT	Sphericity Assumed	201.313	1	201.313	3.006	.088
	Greenhouse-Geisser	201.313	1.000	201.313	3.006	.088
	Huynh-Feldt	201.313	1.000	201.313	3.006	.088
	Lower-bound	201.313	1.000	201.313	3.006	.088
NEGATION * ORIENT * GROUP	Sphericity Assumed	213.273	1	213.273	3.185	.079
	Greenhouse-Geisser	213.273	1.000	213.273	3.185	.079
	Huynh-Feldt	213.273	1.000	213.273	3.185	.079
	Lower-bound	213.273	1.000	213.273	3.185	.079
Error(NEGATION*ORIENT)	Sphericity Assumed	3950.946	59	66.965		
	Greenhouse-Geisser	3950.946	59.000	66.965		
	Huynh-Feldt	3950.946	59.000	66.965		
	Lower-bound	3950.946	59.000	66.965		

From the highlighted rows, and associated error dfs, you can report the following: The main effect of negation was not significant ($F_{(1,59)} = 0.137, p = 0.713$). The group by negation interaction was not significant ($F_{(1,59)} = 0.384, p = 0.538$). The main effect of orientation was not significant ($F_{(1,59)} = 0.539, p < 0.466$). The orientation by group interaction was not significant ($F_{(1,59)} = 2.319, p = 0.133$). The negation by orientation interaction was not significant ($F_{(1,59)} = 3.006, p = 0.088$). The three-way interaction between negation, orientation and group was not significant ($F_{(1,59)} = 3.185, p = 0.079$).

Tests of Within-Subjects Contrasts

Measure: MEASURE_1

Source	NEGATION	ORIENT	Type III Sum of Squares	df	Mean Square	F	Sig.
NEGATION	Linear		9.470	1	9.470	.137	.713
NEGATION * GROUP	Linear		26.587	1	26.587	.384	.538
Error(NEGATION)	Linear		4079.831	59	69.150		
ORIENT		Linear	33.631	1	33.631	.539	.466
ORIENT * GROUP		Linear	144.622	1	144.622	2.319	.133
Error(ORIENT)		Linear	3678.712	59	62.351		
NEGATION * ORIENT	Linear	Linear	201.313	1	201.313	3.006	.088
NEGATION * ORIENT *	Linear	Linear	213.273	1	213.273	3.185	.079
Error(NEGATION*ORIENT)	Linear	Linear	3950.946	59	66.965		

Tests of Between-Subjects Effects

Measure: MEASURE_1
Transformed Variable: Average

Source	Type III Sum of Squares	df	Mean Square	F	Sig.
Intercept	990995.86	1	990995.86	5833.883	.000
GROUP	193.383	1	193.383	1.138	.290
Error	10022.271	59	169.869		

In this example there is only one between-subjects factor. If there had been two, then each main effect and the two-way interaction between the factors would appear in this table. From the highlighted row, and the error df, you can report:

The main effect of priming was not significant ($F_{(1,59)} = 1.138$, $p = 0.290$).

> **TIP** If you requested **Display <u>M</u>eans for** using the **Repeated Measures: Options** dialogue box, then the tables of Estimated Marginal Means will appear here, at the end of the output. For this example, there would be seven tables of descriptives:
> three tables: one for each of the three factors, showing decriptives for each level of a factor ignoring the other factors;
> three tables: one for each of the three two-way interactions, showing descriptives for each combination of levels of two of the factors ignoring the third factor;
> and one table for the three-way interaction, showing descriptives for each of the eight conditions.
> These means are very useful to help you interpret the results of the ANOVA.

Section 7: Some additional points

The within-subjects Analysis of Variance output contains several sections that describe statistical concepts that are beyond those normally covered in an undergraduate psychology degree. However, for those readers who want to understand the entire output these sections are described below.

TEST OF BETWEEN-SUBJECTS EFFECTS

The fact that the output for a within-subjects (repeated measures) ANOVA contains details of between-subjects effects often confuses students. In fact this part of the output can usually be ignored. In effect what SPSS is doing is assuming that **participant** is an additional, between-subjects factor in the analysis. Hence for a 2*2 within-subjects analysis SPSS actually reports an N*2*2 analysis where N is the number of participants. One way to think of this is to say that the part of the output reporting between-subjects effects is asking "did all participants perform the same?". It is in the nature of Psychology that participants are very variable in almost all tasks and hence you will find that the F-ratio is invariably very high and highly significant. As we are not normally interested in this question of whether the participants are all performing in the same way (we usually want to know about general trends across groups of participants) we can ignore this section of the output. Indeed, you will very rarely see this result reported in psychological papers.

MAUCHLY'S TEST OF SPHERICITY

If you have two or more levels of a within-subjects factor, SPSS will print a test called the Mauchly's test of Sphericity. For ANOVAs with only two levels, the contents of the table showing this test (see page 187) are not useful, but with more than two levels they can be valuable. The Mauchly's test of Sphericity is a statistical test to determine whether the data entered into the ANOVA meets certain assumptions. This is rather like the Levene's equality of variance test that we described when looking at the independent t-test. With the within-subjects ANOVA, the assumption being tested is effectively that the correlations between all the variables are roughly the same. A chi value is estimated to test the significance of the Mauchly's test of Sphericity procedure (hence the output reports "Approx. Chi-square"). The significance of this value of chi is reported. If it is significant (i.e. less than 0.05) then the assumptions behind the normal within-subjects ANOVA have been violated. When this does occur there are two things you can do: Corrections using Epsilon, or Multivariate Tests.

Corrections using Epsilon

SPSS provides three estimates of a statistic called **Epsilon** that can be used to correct for a violation of these assumptions (see page 188). The greater the violation the smaller will be the value of Epsilon. To adjust the F ratio, both numerator and denominator degrees of freedom must be multiplied by Epsilon before the p value is calculated. However, SPSS Versions 8, 9 and 10 compute the correction for you and report the corrected values of p in the "Tests of Within-Subjects Effects" table.

All you need to do is decide which of the three estimates of Epsilon you need to use. Greenhouse–Geisser Epsilon is probably the most appropriate value to use, but if you have relatively few participants this can tend to be rather too conservative (i.e. its use will decrease the chances of finding a significant result) – in these cases the Huynh–Feldt Epsilon may be preferable. The third estimate (called the "Lower-bound Epsilon") is a minimum value for Epsilon that will give the most conservative correction. SPSS gives corrected values in the table. When reporting any result, make it clear which you have used.

> **TIP** When, as in the example on page 187, the Mauchly's test of Sphericity is not significant, the Epsilon will be zero and all the entries in the Tests of Within-Subjects Effects table will be identical.

Multivariate Tests

A second solution is to use what is called the **multivariate approach** (as opposed to the normal procedure that we have been describing up to now which is known as the univariate approach – just to confuse us, SPSS refers to this as the averaged test of significance). The multivariate approach makes fewer assumptions about the data and hence is more appropriate when the Mauchly's test of Sphericity is significant. In the Multivariate Tests table, SPSS reports four different multivariate statistics: Pilliai's Trace, Wilks' Lambda, Hotelling's Trace and Roy's Largest Root (see page 187). Each of these tests reports a value of F with associated degrees of freedom and a significance value. You will probably find that there is little difference between the significance of F reported by these four procedures – pick one of them and report it! The multivariate values of F are always lower than the univariate values, and hence if a result is not significant by the univariate method it cannot be significant for the multivariate method. For this reason SPSS does not report the multivariate estimates when the univariate test is non-significant.

> **TIP**   Remember, if your within-subjects factor has only two levels, then the multivariate estimates and the Epsilon corrected values in the Tests of Within-Subjects Effects table are all identical to the Sphericity Assumed values. This is because with only 2 levels of a factor there is only one correlation that can be calculated and hence you cannot be violating the assumptions described above.

IN SUMMARY

1. If the Mauchly's test of Sphericity is reported, look to see if it is significant.
2. If not significant (i.e. $p > 0.05$) then report the univariate results as described in the main text.
3. If the Mauchly's test of Sphericity is significant then either:
   a. Use the values for your chosen Epsilon from the Tests of Within-subjects Effects table

   or:

   b. Adopt a multivariate approach and report one of the four statistics given in the Multivariate Tests table.
4. Either way, when reporting the result, make it clear which solution you have adopted.

Section 8: Planned and unplanned comparisons

You have by now gathered that a significant F-ratio in ANOVA tells us that the dependent variable varies with the levels of the factor. However, unless the factor has only two levels, ANOVA does not tell us which means are different from which other means. If there are only two levels and there is a significant main effect of that factor, then the mean for one level must be significantly different from the mean for the other level. For a factor with more than two levels, a significant F-ratio tells us the dependent variable varies with the levels of the factor, but we need to turn to other devices to analyse the data in more detail. These can allow us to compare means or groups of means in a variety of ways and help us understand and interpret the results. When deciding on which tests to use to make these comparisons, we need to be clear whether they are:

1. Planned (*a priori*) comparisons. These are decided upon before the data was collected. The researcher has predicted which means will differ significantly from each other.
2. Unplanned (*a posteriori or post-hoc*) comparisons. Here differences among means are explored after the data has been collected.

Why should this matter? We need to use different tests for these two kinds of comparisons because the probability of a Type I error is smaller when the comparisons are planned in advance. Type I error involves **incorrectly** rejecting a null hypothesis, thus concluding that there is a significant effect when in fact the means differ due to chance. When making multiple comparisons, we run the risk of Type I errors. Howell (1987) gives the following example: assume that we give a group of males and a group of females 50 words and ask them to give us as many associations to these words as possible in 1 minute. For each word, we then test whether there is a significant difference in the number of associations given by male and female participants. We could run 50 more or less independent t tests, but we would run the risk that 2.5 of these (50*0.05) will be declared "significant" by chance.

Why is there a greater risk of making a Type I error when carrying out unplanned comparisons? Consider the following. Imagine an experiment to look at the effect of five different levels of noise on memory that employed a one-way ANOVA design. You will have five means (one for each condition) and could do a total of ten comparisons (you could compare mean 1 to mean 2; mean 1 to mean 3; mean 1 to mean 4 etc.). Assume that the null hypothesis is true, and that noise does not affect memory, but that by chance two of the means are far enough apart to lead us erroneously to reject the null hypothesis, thus the data contain one Type I error. If you had planned your single comparison in advance, you would have a probability of 0.1 of hitting on the one comparison out of 10 that involves the Type I error. But if you first look at the data, you are certain to make a Type I error since you are likely to test the largest difference you can observe.

UNPLANNED COMPARISONS IN SPSS

Unplanned or *post-hoc* comparisons are easy to perform in SPSS and you can do as many as you like, with two restrictions: firstly, if any factor has two levels, SPSS will not perform the post-hoc tests because the main effect is sufficient; secondly, they can only be used to compare levels from between-subjects factors (remember that SPSS automatically performs trend tests on within-subjects factors). There is a range of post-hoc tests to choose from. They can be used in conjunction with the **One-Way ANOVA** or the **General Factorial** command. To obtain the dialogue box to perform such comparisons, simply click on the **Post Hoc** button in either dialogue box.

One-way ANOVA   **General Factorial**

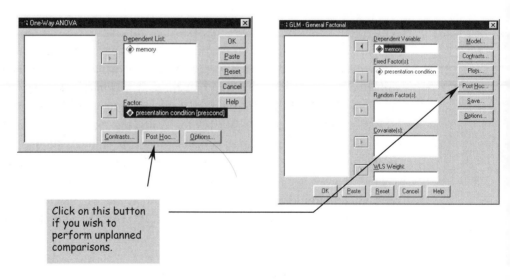

Click on this button if you wish to perform unplanned comparisons.

You will then see the **Post Hoc Multiple Comparisons** dialogue box.

One-way ANOVA   **General Factorial**

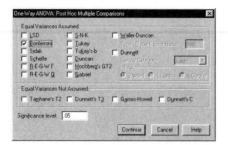   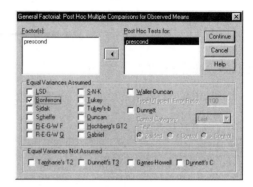

Which test you select depends on how cautious you wish to be. We have selected **Bonferroni** and overleaf you can see the output. We have used the data from the study described in Section 2 of this chapter, which employed a one-way between-subjects ANOVA design. (These data are available in the Appendix.)

TIP   You can also do unplanned comparisons on any between-subjects factor (with 3 or more levels) in a mixed design. There is a post-hoc button in the **Repeated Measures** dialogue box. In a mixed design, the post-hoc output can only be applied to the between-subjects factor(s).

Post-Hoc Tests

Multiple Comparisons

Dependent Variable: MEMORY
Bonferroni

This heading and the **Multiple Comparisons** table will appear after all the other tables in the ANOVA output.

(I) presentation condition	(J) presentation condition	Mean Difference (I-J)	Std. Error	Sig.	95% Confidence Interval	
					Lower Bound	Upper Bound
unmasked	greyblob	11.0000*	2.160	.000	4.9690	17.0310
	pixelated	9.0000*	2.160	.001	2.9690	15.0310
	negated	-.5000	2.160	1.000	-6.5310	5.5310
greyblob	unmasked	-11.0000*	2.160	.000	-17.0310	-4.9690
	pixelated	-2.0000	2.160	1.000	-8.0310	4.0310
	negated	-11.5000*	2.160	.000	-17.5310	-5.4690
pixelated	unmasked	-9.0000*	2.160	.001	-15.0310	-2.9690
	greyblob	2.0000	2.160	1.000	-4.0310	8.0310
	negated	-9.5000*	2.160	.001	-15.5310	-3.4690
negated	unmasked	.5000	2.160	1.000	-5.5310	6.5310
	greyblob	11.5000*	2.160	.000	5.4690	17.5310
	pixelated	9.5000*	2.160	.001	3.4690	15.5310

*. The mean difference is significant at the .05 level.

SPSS prints a complete matrix (as it does for correlations). You have to pick out the comparisons required, and ignore the repetitions.

As our factor had four levels there are six possible comparisons. Their p values are highlighted here.

If you had requested post hoc tests for two factors from the **General Factorial** dialogue box, then two tables would be printed, one for each factor.

In a report you would write:

Employing the Bonferroni post-hoc test, significant differences were found between the unmasked and greyblob conditions ($p < 0.0005$), between the unmasked and pixelated conditions ($p = 0.001$), between the greyblob and negated conditions ($p < 0.0005$), and between the pixelated and negated conditions ($p = 0.001$). There was no significant difference between the unmasked and negated conditions ($p = 1$), or between the greyblob and pixelated conditions ($p = 1$).

Or, to abbreviate:

There was no significant difference between the unmasked and negated conditions, or between the greyblob and pixelated conditions (for both, $p = 1$). The greyblob and pixelated conditions were each significantly different from each of the unmasked and negated conditions (all $p \leq 0.001$).

Generally, for planned comparisons the technique of linear contrasts is used, which allows us to compare one level, or set of levels, with another level or set of levels. The simplest way of doing this is to assign weights to each. These weights are known as coefficients. This technique is available on SPSS which uses the t-statistic to test specific contrasts. Indeed, the print-out will give you two t-values, one for "assume equal variances" and one for "does not assume equal". Since the variances of the groups being compared should be broadly similar (otherwise you should not be using ANOVA), you can "assume equal variances", but check both values and their significance. A point to note here is that the overall main effect does not have to be significant for you to test for specific differences using planned comparisons.

By assigning weights (or coefficients) we can make three sorts of comparisons:
1. We can compare one condition with one other condition
2. We can compare one condition with the mean of two or more other conditions
3. We can compare the mean of one set of conditions with the mean of another set of conditions.

In all three of these cases we assign a weight of zero to a condition (or conditions) that we do not want to be included in the comparison. Conditions (or groups of conditions) that are to be compared with each other are assigned opposite signs (positive or negative). In all cases the sum of the weights must be zero.

So, suppose you had four conditions, C1 C2 C3 and C4. If you wanted to compare only conditions 1 and 3 you could assign the weights: **1, 0, -1, 0.**

If you wanted to compare the average of the first 2 conditions with the third condition you could assign the weights: **1, 1, -2, 0.**

If you wanted to compare the mean of the first two groups with the mean of the last two groups you could use the weights: **1, 1, -1, -1.**

TIP   If you wish to perform more than one planned comparison on the same set of data, then you need to check that the comparisons are independent of one another, that they are non-overlapping – these are called **orthogonal** comparisons. You can do this by taking each pair of comparisons and checking that the products of the coefficients assigned to each level sum to zero (see any good statistics text).

To carry out a planned comparison, you need to click on the "Contrasts" button at the bottom of the **One-Way ANOVA** dialogue box. You will then see the following dialogue box:

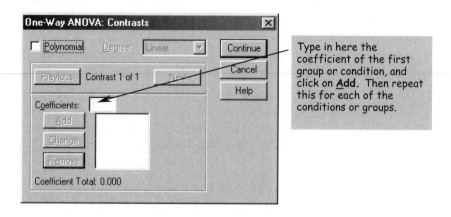

Type in here the coefficient of the first group or condition, and click on **Add**. Then repeat this for each of the conditions or groups.

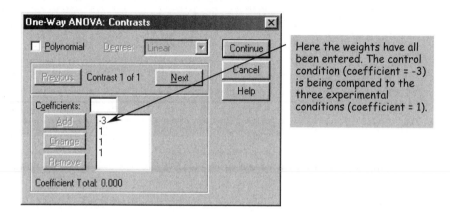

Here the weights have all been entered. The control condition (coefficient = -3) is being compared to the three experimental conditions (coefficient = 1).

The dialogue box above shows a planned comparison for the data from the one-way between-subjects ANOVA experiment, where the control group (who were shown the witness giving evidence with her face visible) is compared with the three experimental groups (who were all shown the witness giving evidence with her face masked). A linear contrast is requested and the coefficients have been entered, first for group 1, then groups 2, 3 and 4. (These data are available in the Appendix.)The output overleaf shows that this comparison is significant.

> **TIP**   Contrasts are available for the other ANOVA commands, but they are much more complicated and beyond the scope of this book. They comprise a range of specific contrasts, and you can use the SPSS Help function to find out more about them.

SPSS OUTPUT FOR CONTRASTS

These tables will appear after all the other tables in the ANOVA output.

Contrast Coefficients

Contrast	presentation condition			
	unmasked	greyblob	pixelated	negated
1	-3	1	1	1

SPSS reminds you of the weights that you assigned to the levels of the factors in your contrast. If you had requested an additional contrast, then there would be two rows in this table.

Contrast Tests

		Contrast	Value of Contrast	Std. Error	t	df	Sig. (2-tailed)
MEMORY	Assume equal variances	1	-19.5000	5.2912	-3.685	36	.001
	Does not assume equal	1	-19.5000	5.6654	-3.442	13.818	.004

This row contains the values of *t*, *df*, and *p* for the contrast that you requested, and assuming equal variance.

In a report you would write:

A planned comparison revealed that participants who saw the witness's face unmasked remembered significantly more of her testimony than the participants in the three masking conditions ($t = 3.685$, df = 36, $p = 0.001$)

Note that the contrast test can only tell you whether the conditions that you compared are significantly different or not; for the **direction** of the difference. In order to fully interpret the result, you will need to obtain descriptive statistics for the conditions or groups compared.

Section 9: Nonparametric equivalents to ANOVA: Kruskal–Wallis and Friedman

EXAMPLE STUDY: THE COGNITIVE INTERVIEW

To explore the use of the non-parametric equivalents of the one-way ANOVA, we shall look at a study investigating the use of the Cognitive Interview. One application of memory research has been the adoption of the use of the Cognitive Interview (CI) by many police forces in Britain. This provides the police officer with a toolkit of mnemonic techniques to assist recall by a witness or victim, so that as full and accurate account as possible of a crime incident can be recorded. Research has demonstrated that the CI elicits more information than the standard police interview. Newlands (1997) investigated the effect the CI has on perpetrator identification, and examined whether the CI affected the confidence with which a participant made an identification. There is evidence to suggest that the more one talks about a facial image, the harder it is to maintain that image in one's mind's eye. A mock crime scenario was seen by 60 participants, 20 of whom were then interviewed using the CI, 20 using the standard police interview (SI) and 20 participants were simply asked to visualise the face of the perpetrator. Participants were then asked to identify the perpetrator from a photo array. Three confidence ratings were provided by participants: confidence in decision after viewing the video, after being interviewed or visualising the face and finally after making an identification.

Two hypotheses were tested: that CI and SI interviews affect a participant's confidence at making an identification compared with a visualisation condition, and that confidence levels decline after attempting to make an identification. The design employed had two factors; the between-subjects factor of condition (CI, SI or visualisation) and the within-subjects factor of time of confidence rating (before and after interview/visualisation and after identification). The dependent variable was measured on an ordinal scale and is the confidence rating, operationalised as the response on a 7-point scale where point 1 was "complete confidence" and point 7 "complete guess".

For the purposes of this book, we have created a data file that will reproduce some of the findings from this study. We have used this same data file to demonstrate both of the nonparametric equivalents of ANOVA. (These data are available in the Appendix.)

THE KRUSKAL–WALLIS TEST

The Kruskal–Wallis test is a nonparametric equivalent of the one-way between-subjects analysis of variance. It was employed here to test the hypothesis that the CI and SI interviews affect a participant's confidence at making an identification compared with the visualisation condition. The second confidence rating was therefore the dependent variable and condition the between-subjects factor.

How to perform the Kruskal–Wallis

The sequence to perform the Kruskal–Wallis is:
For SPSS Versions 9 and 10, click on **Analyze** ⇒ **Nonparametric Tests**
For SPSS Version 8, click on **Statistics** ⇒ **Nonparametric Tests**
Click on **K Independent Samples**.

The following dialogue box then appears:

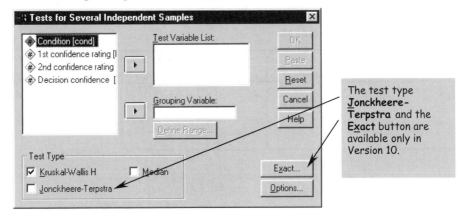

Click on the name of the dependent variable. Three confidence ratings were obtained "1st confidence rating" (before interview), "2nd confidence rating" (after interview) and "decision confidence" (identification confidence). Of interest here was whether the type of interview influenced the 2nd confidence rating. This rating was therefore entered into the **Test Variable List** box. "Condition [cond]" (interview condition) was entered into the grouping variable box, and the **Define Range** button was used to specify its minimum and maximum values (1 and 3). The output on the next page shows the results of comparing the three interview conditions.

Obtained by Using Menu Items: <u>N</u>onparametric Tests > <u>K</u> Independent Samples

NPar Tests

Descriptives, from the **Options** button in the dialogue box. The first row is for the confidence rating; however it is for all 60 participants regardless of the between-subjects condition they were in.
For a report, descriptives for each group separately, obtained using **Custom Tables**, would be much more useful (see Chapter 2).

Descriptive Statistics

	N	Mean	Std. Deviation	Minimum	Maximum
2nd confidence rating	60	2.98	1.28	1	6
Condition	60	2.00	.82	1	3

Kruskal–Wallis Test

Ranks

	Condition	N	Mean Rank
2nd confidence rating	CI	20	41.72
	Visualisation	20	12.45
	SI	20	37.33
	Total	60	

Information about the calculations for the Kruskal-Wallis: it can be considered as an extension of the Mann-Whitney U test. See the annotated output of that test for an explanation of this part.

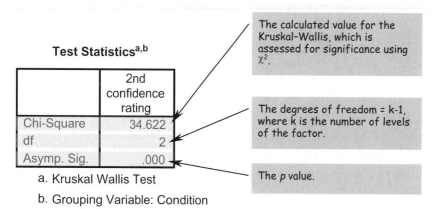

Test Statistics[a,b]

	2nd confidence rating
Chi-Square	34.622
df	2
Asymp. Sig.	.000

a. Kruskal Wallis Test

b. Grouping Variable: Condition

The calculated value for the Kruskal-Wallis, which is assessed for significance using χ^2.

The degrees of freedom = k-1, where k is the number of levels of the factor.

The *p* value.

In a report you would write:

For the second confidence rating there was a significant effect of interview condition ($\chi^2 = 34.622$, df = 2, $p < 0.0005$).

THE FRIEDMAN TEST

The Friedman test is the nonparametric equivalent of the one-way within-subjects analysis of variance. Confusingly, the Friedman test is sometimes referred to as the Friedman two-way ANOVA (this is because for a within-subjects analysis of variance, the participants are also considered to be a factor). The Friedman test was employed here to test the hypothesis that participants' confidence levels declined after attempting to make an identification, regardless of the condition in which they participated.

How to perform the Friedman test

The sequence to perform the Friedman test is:
For SPSS Versions 9 and 10, click on **Analyze** ⇒ **Nonparametric Tests**
For SPSS Version 8, click on **Statistics** ⇒ **Nonparametric Tests**
Click on **K Related Samples.**

You will see the following dialogue box:

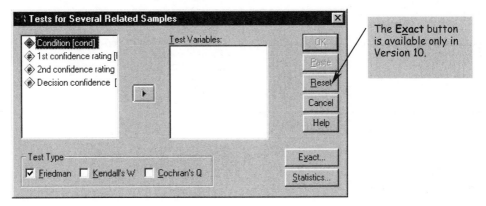

Click on the variables you would like to compare. Of interest here was the comparison of the three confidence ratings given by participants, as it was predicted that confidence levels would decline after attempting to make an identification. To perform this comparison, "1st confidence rating" (before interview), "2nd confidence rating" (after interview) and "decision confidence" (identification confidence) were entered into the **Test Variables** box. These are the levels of the within-subjects factor. The output is shown on the next page.

Obtained by Using Menu Items: <u>N</u>onparametric Tests > K Related <u>S</u>amples

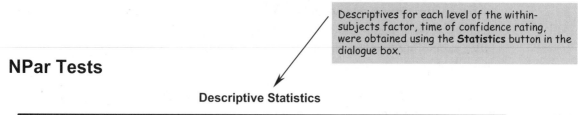

Descriptives for each level of the within-subjects factor, time of confidence rating, were obtained using the **Statistics** button in the dialogue box.

NPar Tests

Descriptive Statistics

	N	Mean	Std. Deviation	Minimum	Maximum
1st confidence rating	60	1.78	.72	1	3
2nd confidence rating	60	2.98	1.28	1	6
Decision confidence	60	3.9500	1.3952	1.00	7.00

Friedman Test

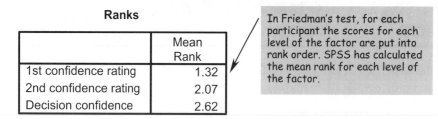

Ranks

	Mean Rank
1st confidence rating	1.32
2nd confidence rating	2.07
Decision confidence	2.62

In Friedman's test, for each participant the scores for each level of the factor are put into rank order. SPSS has calculated the mean rank for each level of the factor.

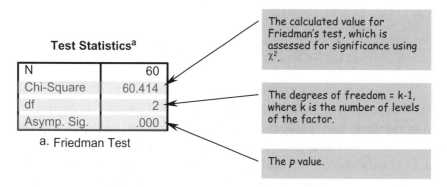

The calculated value for Friedman's test, which is assessed for significance using χ^2.

Test Statistics[a]

N	60
Chi-Square	60.414
df	2
Asymp. Sig.	.000

a. Friedman Test

The degrees of freedom = k-1, where k is the number of levels of the factor.

The *p* value.

In a report you would write:

Confidence varied significantly across the three assessment points ($\chi^2 = 60.414$, df $= 2$, $p < 0.0005$).

Chapter Seven

Multiple regression

An introduction to multiple regression

Performing a multiple regression on SPSS

Section 1: An introduction to multiple regression

WHAT IS MULTIPLE REGRESSION?

Multiple regression is a statistical technique that allows us to predict someone's score on one variable on the basis of their scores on several other variables. An example might help. Suppose we were interested in predicting how much an individual enjoys their job. Variables such as salary, extent of academic qualifications, age, sex, number of years in full-time employment and socio-economic status might all contribute towards job satisfaction. If we collected data on all of these variables, perhaps by surveying a few hundred members of the public, we would be able to see how many and which of these variables gave rise to the most accurate prediction of job satisfaction. We might find that job satisfaction is most accurately predicted by type of occupation, salary and years in full-time employment, with the other variables not helping us to predict job satisfaction.

When using multiple regression in psychology, many researchers use the term "independent variables" to identify those variables that they think will influence some other "dependent variable". We prefer to use the term "predictor variables" for those variables that may be useful in predicting the scores on another variable that we call the "criterion variable". Thus, in our example above, type of occupation, salary and years in full-time employment would emerge as significant predictor variables, which allow us to estimate the criterion variable – how satisfied someone is likely to be with their job. As we have pointed out before, human behaviour is inherently noisy and therefore it is not possible to produce totally accurate predictions, but multiple regression allows us to identify a set of predictor variables which together provide a useful estimate of a participant's likely score on a criterion variable.

HOW DOES MULTIPLE REGRESSION RELATE TO CORRELATION AND ANALYSIS OF VARIANCE?

In a previous section (Chapter 4, Section 2), we introduced you to correlation and the regression line. If two variables are correlated, then knowing the score on one variable will allow you to predict the score on the other variable. The stronger the correlation, the closer the scores will fall to the regression line and therefore the more accurate the prediction. Multiple regression is simply an extension of this principle, where we predict one variable on the basis of several other variables. Having more than one predictor variable is useful when predicting human behaviour, as our actions, thoughts and emotions are all likely to be influenced by some combination of several factors. Using multiple regression we can test theories (or models) about precisely which set of variables is influencing our behaviour.

As we discussed in Chapter 6, Section 1, on Analysis of Variance, human behaviour is rather variable and therefore difficult to predict. What we are doing in both ANOVA and multiple regression is seeking to account for the variance in the scores we observe. Thus, in the example above, people might vary greatly in their levels of job satisfaction. Some of this variance will be accounted for by the variables we have identified. For example, we might be able to say that salary accounts for a fairly large percentage of the variance in job satisfaction, and hence it is very useful to know someone's salary when trying to predict their job satisfaction. You might now be able to see that the ideas here are rather similar to those underlying ANOVA. In ANOVA we are trying to determine how much of the variance is accounted for by our manipulation of the independent variables (relative to the percentage of the variance we cannot account for). In multiple regression we do not directly manipulate the IVs but instead just measure the naturally occurring levels of the variables and see if this helps us predict the score on the dependent variable (or criterion variable). Thus, ANOVA is actually a rather specific and restricted example of the general approach adopted in multiple regression.

To put this another way, in ANOVA we can directly manipulate the factors and measure the resulting change in the dependent variable. In multiple regression we simply measure the naturally occurring scores on a number of predictor variables and try to establish which set of the observed variables gives rise to the best prediction of the criterion variable.

A current trend in statistics is to emphasise the similarity between multiple regression and ANOVA, and between correlation and the t-test. All of these statistical techniques are basically seeking to do the same thing – explain the variance in the level of one variable on the basis of the level of one or more other variables. These other variables might be manipulated directly in the case of controlled experiments, or be observed in the case of surveys or observational studies, but the underlying principle is the same. Thus, although we have given separate chapters to each of these procedures they are fundamentally all the same procedure. This underlying single approach is called the General Linear Model – a term you first encountered when we were undertaking ANOVA in Chapter 6, Section 1.

WHEN SHOULD I USE MULTIPLE REGRESSION?

1. You can use this statistical technique when exploring linear relationships between the predictor and criterion variables – that is, when the relationship follows a straight line. (To examine non-linear relationships, special techniques can be used.)

2. The criterion variable that you are seeking to predict should be measured on a continuous scale (such as interval or ratio scale). There is a separate regression method called logistic regression that can be used for dichotomous dependent variables (not covered here).

3. The predictor variables that you select should be measured on a ratio, interval, or ordinal scale. A nominal predictor variable is legitimate but only if it is dichotomous, i.e. there are no more that two categories. For example, sex is acceptable (where male is coded as 1 and female as 0) but gender identity (masculine, feminine and androgynous) could not be coded as a single variable. Instead, you would create three different variables each with two categories (masculine/not masculine; feminine/not feminine and androgynous/not androgynous). The term dummy variable is used to describe this type of dichotomous variable.

4. Multiple regression requires a large number of observations. The number of cases (participants) must substantially exceed the number of predictor variables you are using in your regression. The absolute minimum is that you have five times as many participants as predictor variables. A more acceptable ratio is 10:1, but some people argue that this should be as high as 40:1 for some statistical selection methods (see page 210).

TERMINOLOGY

There are certain terms we need to clarify to allow you to understand the results of this statistical technique.

Beta (standardised regression coefficients)

The beta value is a measure of how strongly each predictor variable influences the criterion variable. The beta is measured in units of standard deviation. For example, a beta value of 2.5 indicates that a change of one standard deviation in the predictor variable will result in a change of 2.5 standard deviations in the criterion variable. Thus, the higher the beta value the greater the impact of the predictor variable on the criterion variable.

When you have only one predictor variable in your model, then beta is equivalent to the correlation coefficient between the predictor and the criterion variable. This equivalence makes sense, as this situation is a correlation between two variables. When you have more than one predictor variable, you cannot compare the contribution of each predictor variable by simply comparing the correlation coefficients. The beta regression coefficient is computed to allow you to make such comparisons and to assess the strength of the relationship between each predictor variable to the criterion variable.

R, R Square, Adjusted R Square

R is a measure of the correlation between the observed value and the predicted value of the criterion variable. In our example this would be the correlation between the levels of job satisfaction reported by our participants and the levels predicted for them by our predictor variables. R Square (R^2) is the square of this measure of correlation and indicates the proportion of the variance in the criterion variable which is accounted for by our model – in our example the proportion of the variance in the job satisfaction scores accounted for by our set of predictor variables (salary, etc.). In essence, this is a measure of how good a prediction of the criterion variable we can make by knowing the predictor variables. However, R square tends to somewhat over-estimate the success of the model when applied to the real world, so an Adjusted R Square value is calculated which takes into account the number of variables in the model and the number of observations (participants) our model is based on. This Adjusted R Square value gives the most useful measure of the success of our model. If, for example we have an Adjusted R Square value of 0.75 we can say that our model has accounted for 75% of the variance in the criterion variable.

DESIGN CONSIDERATIONS

Multicollinearity

When choosing a predictor variable you should select one that might be correlated with the criterion variable, but that is not strongly correlated with the other predictor variables. However, correlations amongst the predictor variables are not unusual. The term multicollinearity (or collinearity) is used to describe the situation when a high correlation is detected between two or more predictor variables. Such high correlations cause problems when trying to draw inferences about the relative contribution of each predictor variable to the success of the model. SPSS provides you with a means of checking for this and we describe this below.

Selection methods

There are different ways that the relative contribution of each predictor variable can be assessed. In the "simultaneous" method (which SPSS calls the **Enter** method), the researcher specifies the set of predictor variables that make up the model. The success of this model in predicting the criterion variable is then assessed.

In contrast, "hierarchical" methods enter the variables into the model in a specified order. The order specified should reflect some theoretical consideration or previous findings. If you have no reason to believe that one variable is likely to be more important than another you should not use this method. As each variable is entered into the model its contribution is assessed. If adding the variable does not significantly increase the predictive power of the model then the variable is dropped.

In "statistical" methods, the order in which the predictor variables are entered into (or taken out of) the model is determined according to the strength of their correlation with the criterion variable. Actually there are several versions of this method, called forward selection, backward selection and stepwise selection. In **Forward** selection, SPSS enters the variables into the model one at a time in an order determined by the strength of their correlation with the criterion variable. The effect of adding each is assessed as it is entered, and variables that do not significantly add to the success of the model are excluded.

In **Backward** selection, SPSS enters all the predictor variables into the model. The weakest predictor variable is then removed and the regression re-calculated. If this significantly weakens the model then the predictor variable is re-entered – otherwise it is deleted. This procedure is then repeated until only useful predictor variables remain in the model.

Stepwise is the most sophisticated of these statistical methods. Each variable is entered in sequence and its value assessed. If adding the variable contributes to the model then it is retained, but all other variables in the model are then re-tested to see if they are still contributing to the success of the model. If they no longer contribute significantly they are removed. Thus, this method should ensure that you end up with the smallest possible set of predictor variables included in your model.

In addition to the **Enter**, **Stepwise**, **Forward** and **Backward** methods, SPSS also offers the **Remove** method in which variables are removed from the model in a block – the use of this method will not be described here.

How to choose the appropriate method?

If you have no theoretical model in mind, and/or you have relatively low numbers of cases, then it is probably safest to use **Enter**, the simultaneous method. Statistical procedures should be used with caution and only when you have a large number of cases. This is because minor variations in the data due to sampling errors can have a large effect on the order in which variables are entered and therefore the likelihood of them being retained. However, one advantage of the **Stepwise** method is that it should always result in the most parsimonious model. This could be important if you wanted to know the minimum number of variables you would need to measure to predict the criterion variable. If for this, or some other reason, you decide to select a statistical method, then you should really attempt to validate your results with a second independent set of data. The can be done either by conducting a second study, or by randomly splitting your data set into two halves (see Chapter 5, Section 3). Only results that are common to both analyses should be reported.

Section 2: Performing a multiple regression on SPSS

EXAMPLE STUDY

In an investigation of children's spelling, a colleague of ours, Corriene Reed, decided to look at the importance of several psycholinguistic variables on spelling performance. Previous research has shown that age of acquisition has an effect on children's reading and also on object naming. A total of 64 children, aged between 7 and 9 years, completed standardised reading and spelling tests and were then asked to spell 48 words that varied systematically according to certain features such as age of acquisition, word frequency, word length, and imageability. Word length and age of acquisition emerged as significant predictors of whether the word was likely to be spelt correctly.

Further analysis was conducted on the data to determine whether the spelling performance on this list of 48 words accurately reflected the children's spelling ability as estimated by a standardised spelling test. Children's chronological age, their reading age, their standardised reading score and their standardised spelling score were chosen as the predictor variables. The criterion variable was the percentage correct spelling score attained by each child using the list of 48 words.

For the purposes of this book, we have created a data file that will reproduce some of the findings from this second analysis. As you will see, the standardised spelling score derived from a validated test emerged as a strong predictor of the spelling score achieved on the word list. The data file contains only a subset of the data collected and is used here to demonstrate multiple regression. (These data are available in the Appendix.)

HOW TO PERFORM THE TEST

For SPSS Versions 9 and 10, click on **Analyze** ⇒ **Regression** ⇒ **Linear**
For SPSS Version 8, click on **Statistics** ⇒ **Regression** ⇒ **Linear**

You will then be presented with the **Linear Regression** dialogue box shown below. You now need to select the criterion (dependent) and the predictor (independent) variables.

We have chosen to use the percentage correct spelling score ("spelperc") as our criterion variable. As our predictor variables we have used chronological age

("age"), reading age ("readage"), standardised reading score ("standsc"), and standardised spelling score ("spellsc").

As we have a relatively small number of cases and do not have any strong theoretical predictions, we recommend you select **Enter** (the simultaneous method). This is usually the safest to adopt.

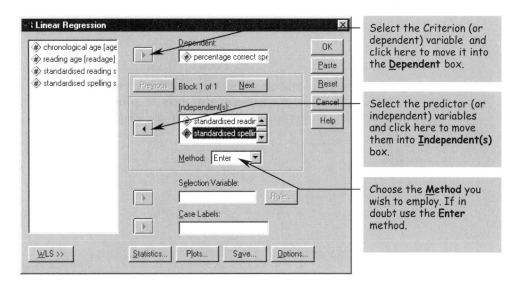

Now click on the Statistics button. This will bring up the **Linear Regression: Statistics** dialogue box shown below

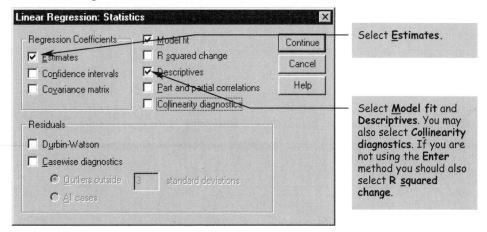

The **Collinearity diagnostics** option gives some useful additional output that allows you to assess whether you have a problem with collinearity in your data. The **R squared change** option is useful if you have selected a statistical method such as

stepwise as it makes clear how the power of the model changes with the addition or removal of a predictor variable from the model.

When you have selected the statistics options you require, click on the **Continue** button. This will return you to the **Linear Regression** dialogue box. Now click on the [OK] button. The output that will be produced is illustrated on the following pages.

Tip   The SPSS multiple regression option was set to **Exclude cases listwise**. Hence, although the researcher collected data from 52 participants, SPSS analysed the data from only the 47 participants who had no missing values.

Obtained Using Menu Items: **Regression** > **Linear** (Method = Enter)

Descriptive Statistics

	Mean	Std. Deviation	N
percentage correct spelling	59.7660	23.9331	47
chronological age	93.4043	7.4910	47
reading age	89.0213	21.3648	47
standardised reading score	95.5745	17.7834	47
standardised spelling score	107.0851	14.9882	47

This first table is produced by the **Descriptives** option.

This second table gives details of the correlation between each pair of variables. We do not want strong correlations between the criterion and the predictor variables. The values here are acceptable.

Correlations

		percentage correct spelling	chronological age	reading age	standardised reading score	standardised spelling score
Pearson Correlation	percentage correct spelling	1.000	-.074	.623	.778	.847
	chronological age	-.074	1.000	.124	-.344	-.416
	reading age	.623	.124	1.000	.683	.570
	standardised reading score	.778	-.344	.683	1.000	.793
	standardised spelling score	.847	-.416	.570	.793	1.000
Sig. (1-tailed)	percentage correct spelling	.	.311	.000	.000	.000
	chronological age	.311	.	.203	.009	.002
	reading age	.000	.203	.	.000	.000
	standardised reading score	.000	.009	.000	.	.000
	standardised spelling score	.000	.002	.000	.000	.
N	percentage correct spelling	47	47	47	47	47
	chronological age	47	47	47	47	47
	reading age	47	47	47	47	47
	standardised reading score	47	47	47	47	47
	standardised spelling score	47	47	47	47	47

Variables Entered/Removed[b]

Model	Variables Entered	Variables Removed	Method
1	standardised spelling score, chronological age, reading age, standardised reading score[a]	.	Enter

a. All requested variables entered.

b. Dependent Variable: percentage correct spelling

This third table tells us about the predictor variables and the method used. Here we can see that all of our predictor variables were entered simultaneously (because we selected the Enter method.

Model Summary

Model	R	R Square	Adjusted R Square	Std. Error of the Estimate
1	.923[a]	.852	.838	9.6377

a. Predictors: (Constant), standardised spelling score, chronological age, reading age, standardised reading score

This table is important. The Adjusted R Square value tells us that our model accounts for 83.8% of variance in the spelling scores – a very good model!

ANOVA[b]

Model		Sum of Squares	df	Mean Square	F	Sig.
1	Regression	22447.277	4	5611.819	60.417	.000[a]
	Residual	3901.149	42	92.884		
	Total	26348.426	46			

a. Predictors: (Constant), standardised spelling score, chronological age, reading age, standardised reading score

b. Dependent Variable: percentage correct spelling

This table reports an ANOVA, which assesses the overall significance of our model. As $p < 0.05$ our model is significant.

Coefficients[a]

Model		Unstandardized Coefficients		Standardized Coefficients	t	Sig.
		B	Std. Error	Beta		
1	(Constant)	-232.079	30.500		-7.609	.000
	chronological age	1.298	.252	.406	5.159	.000
	reading age	-.162	.110	-.144	-1.469	.149
	standardised reading score	.530	.156	.394	3.393	.002
	standardised spelling score	1.254	.165	.786	7.584	.000

a. Dependent Variable: percentage correct spelling

The Standardized Beta Coefficients give a measure of the contribution of each variable to the model. A large value indicates that a unit change in this predictor variable has a large effect on the criterion variable. The *t* and Sig (*p*) values give a rough indication of the impact of each predictor variable – a big absolute *t* value and small *p* value suggests that a predictor variable is having a large impact on the criterion variable. If you requested **Collinearity diagnostics** these will also be included in this table – see next page.

Collinearity diagnostics

If you requested the optional **Collinearity diagnostics**, these will be shown in an additional two columns of the Coefficients table (the last table shown above) and a further table (titled Collinearity diagnostics) that is not shown here. Ignore this extra table and simply look at the two new columns.

Coefficients^a

Model		Unstandardized Coefficients		Standardized Coefficients	t	Sig.	Collinearity Statistics	
		B	Std. Error	Beta			Tolerance	VIF
1	(Constant)	-232.079	30.500		-7.609	.000		
	chronological age	1.298	.252	.406	5.159	.000	.568	1.759
	reading age	-.162	.110	-.144	-1.469	.149	.365	2.737
	standardised reading score	.530	.156	.394	3.393	.002	.262	3.820
	standardised spelling score	1.254	.165	.786	7.584	.000	.329	3.044

a. Dependent Variable: percentage correct spelling

The tolerance values are a measure of the correlation between the predictor variables and can vary between 0 and 1. The closer to zero the tolerance value is for a variable, the stronger the relationship between this and the other predictor variables. You should worry about variables that have a very low tolerance. SPSS will not include a predictor variable in a model if it has a tolerance of less that 0.0001. However, you may want to set your own criteria rather higher – perhaps excluding any variable that has a tolerance level of less than 0.01. VIF is an alternative measure of collinearity (in fact it is the reciprocal of tolerance) in which a large value indicates a strong relationship between predictor variables.

Reporting the results

When reporting the results of a multiple regression analysis, you want to inform the reader about the proportion of the variance accounted for by your model, the significance of your model and the significance of the predictor variables. In the results section, we would write:

Using the enter method, a significant model emerged ($F_{4,42}$=60.417, $p < 0.0005$. Adjusted R square = .838. Significant variables are shown below:

Predictor Variable	Beta	p
Chronological age	.406	$p < 0.0005$
Standardised reading score	.394	$p = 0.002$
Standardised spelling score	.786	$p < 0.0005$

(Reading age was not a significant predictor in this model.)

OUTPUT FROM MULTIPLE REGRESSION USING STEPWISE METHOD

Obtained Using Menu Items: **Regression** > **Linear** (Method = Stepwise)

Reproduced below are the key parts of the output produced when you the **Stepwise** method is selected. When using this method you should also select the **R Squared Change** option in the **Linear Regression: Statistics** dialogue box (see page 213).

Variables Entered/Removed[a]

Model	Variables Entered	Variables Removed	Method
1	standardised spelling score		Stepwise (Criteria: Probability-of-F-to-enter <= .050, Probability-of-F-to-remove >= .100).
2	chronological age		Stepwise (Criteria: Probability-of-F-to-enter <= .050, Probability-of-F-to-remove >= .100).
3	standardised reading score		Stepwise (Criteria: Probability-of-F-to-enter <= .050, Probability-of-F-to-remove >= .100).

a. Dependent Variable: percentage correct spelling

> This table shows us the order in which the variables were entered and removed form our model. We can see that in this case three variables were added and none were removed.

> Here we can see that model 1, which included only standardised spelling score accounted for 71% of the variance (Adjusted R^2=0.711). The inclusion of chronological age into model 2 resulted in an additional 9% of the variance being explained (R^2 change = 0.094). The final model 3 also included standardised reading score, and this model accounted for 83% of the variance (Adjusted R^2=0.833).

Model Summary

Model	R	R Square	Adjusted R Square	Std. Error of the Estimate	Change Statistics R Square Change	F Change	df1	df2	Sig. F Change
1	.847[a]	.717	.711	12.8708	.717	114.055	1	45	.000
2	.900[b]	.811	.802	10.6481	.094	21.747	1	44	.000
3	.919[c]	.844	.833	9.7665	.034	9.302	1	43	.004

a. Predictors: (Constant), standardised spelling score

b. Predictors: (Constant), standardised spelling score, chronological age

c. Predictors: (Constant), standardised spelling score, chronological age, standardised reading score

ANOVA[d]

Model		Sum of Squares	df	Mean Square	F	Sig.
1	Regression	18893.882	1	18893.882	114.055	.000[a]
	Residual	7454.543	45	165.657		
	Total	26348.426	46			
2	Regression	21359.610	2	10679.805	94.193	.000[b]
	Residual	4988.815	44	113.382		
	Total	26348.426	46			
3	Regression	22246.870	3	7415.623	77.744	.000[c]
	Residual	4101.556	43	95.385		
	Total	26348.426	46			

a. Predictors: (Constant), standardised spelling score

b. Predictors: (Constant), standardised spelling score, chronological age

c. Predictors: (Constant), standardised spelling score, chronological age, standardised reading score

d. Dependent Variable: percentage correct spelling

> This table reports the ANOVA result for the three models.

Coefficients[a]

Model		Unstandardized Coefficients B	Unstandardized Coefficients Std. Error	Standardized Coefficients Beta	t	Sig.	Collinearity Statistics Tolerance	Collinearity Statistics VIF
1	(Constant)	-85.032	13.688		-6.212	.000		
	standardised spelling score	1.352	.127	.847	10.680	.000	1.000	1.000
2	(Constant)	-209.328	28.959		-7.228	.000		
	standardised spelling score	1.576	.115	.987	13.679	.000	.827	1.209
	chronological age	1.075	.230	.336	4.663	.000	.827	1.209
3	(Constant)	-209.171	26.562		-7.875	.000		
	standardised spelling score	1.197	.163	.750	7.349	.000	.348	2.875
	chronological age	1.092	.211	.342	5.162	.000	.827	1.210
	standardised reading score	.406	.133	.301	3.050	.004	.371	2.698

a. Dependent Variable: percentage correct spelling

> Here SPSS reports the Beta, t and sig (p) values for each of the models. These were explained in the output from the **Enter** method.

Excluded Variables[d]

Model		Beta In	t	Sig.	Partial Correlation	Collinearity Statistics Tolerance	Collinearity Statistics VIF	Collinearity Statistics Minimum Tolerance
1	chronological age	.336[a]	4.663	.000	.575	.827	1.209	.827
	reading age	.208[a]	2.249	.030	.321	.675	1.481	.675
	standardised reading score	.288[a]	2.317	.025	.330	.371	2.696	.371
2	reading age	.036[b]	.395	.695	.060	.517	1.933	.435
	standardised reading score	.301[b]	3.050	.004	.422	.371	2.698	.348
3	reading age	-.144[c]	-1.469	.149	-.221	.365	2.737	.262

a. Predictors in the Model: (Constant), standardised spelling score

b. Predictors in the Model: (Constant), standardised spelling score, chronological age

c. Predictors in the Model: (Constant), standardised spelling score, chronological age, standardised reading score

d. Dependent Variable: percentage correct spelling

> This table gives statistics for the variables that were excluded from each model.

Thus, the final model to emerge from the **Stepwise** analysis contains only three predictor variables. The predictor variable reading age, which was not significant in the **Enter** analysis, was also not included in the **Stepwise** analysis as it did not significantly strengthen the model.

REPORTING THE RESULTS

In your results section, you would report the significance of the model by citing the F and the associated p value, along with the adjusted R square, which indicates the strength of the model. So, for the final model reported above, we would write:

Adjusted R square = .833; $F_{3,43} = 77.7$, $p < 0.0005$ (using the stepwise method). Significant variables are shown below.

Predictor Variable	Beta	p
Standardised spelling score:	.750	$p < 0.0005$
Chronological age	.342	$p < 0.0005$
Standardised reading score	.301	$p = 0.004$

(Reading age was not a significant predictor in this model.)

Chapter Eight

Beyond the basics

The syntax window
Option settings in SPSS
Getting help in SPSS
Printing from SPSS
Incorporating SPSS output into other
  documents
Graphing tips
Interactive charts

Section 1: The syntax window

The dialogue boxes you have been using to control SPSS are a "front end" to the programme. They provide you, the user, with an easy way to interface with the programme. When you click on the [OK] button, this front end translates all your selections into a series of text commands telling SPSS what to do. You may have noticed these text commands, because, depending on your option settings, they may appear in the output window, just before the analysis is reported (we have not included this text in the output reproduced in earlier chapters). For example, when you performed the one-way analysis of variance described in Chapter 6, Section 2, you may have noticed the following lines of text appeared on the printout

```
ONEWAY
     Score BY group
     /STATISTICS DESCRIPTIVES
     /MISSING ANALYSIS.
```

It is these commands that SPSS has executed to perform the oneway ANOVA. These lines of text will be very familiar to anyone who used an old (pre-Windows) version of SPSS. Before the Windows versions of SPSS, the user had to write these commands directly. Users had to learn obscure rules of syntax that governed the exact structure of the command lines, and even the smallest error, such as missing a full stop, would result in a string of equally obscure error messages. The greatest strength of the Windows versions is that you can usually ignore all these commands. However, occasionally it is useful to go back to the old methods and control SPSS directly. It is a bit like programming your videocassette recorder (VCR) at home. Usually you will use the code number published in the newspapers to control which programme the VCR records. Sometimes, however, you want to do something a bit different – perhaps recording only the second half of a programme. In this situation, you will want to talk directly to the VCR and independently set the channel and start and stop times. In this section, we describe how to programme SPSS directly using these commands. When used appropriately the techniques described here can save a great deal of time and effort.

THE PASTE BUTTON AND THE SYNTAX WINDOW

You may have noticed that the dialogue boxes used to execute an analysis (those that include the [OK] button) also contain a button marked [Paste]. If you click on this button, the analysis is not executed, but rather you are switched to a new window called the SPSS Syntax Editor window. The command lines needed to execute your analysis are pasted into this window. You could now select a second analysis, (perhaps a *t*-test comparing two of the groups included in the ANOVA) and click on the `Paste` button again. In this way you can build up a sequence of commands in the syntax editor window, without executing any of them. Finally, when you have selected all the analyses you want, you can execute or "Run" the commands. This might seem like an odd thing to want to do, but there are at least two reasons for wanting to work this way.

Repeating actions

You may choose to work in the syntax editor window because you need to repeat a complex command several times. For example, when analysing the data from the adoption survey described in Chapter 5, we might need to compute 20 new variables, each of which is the mean of ten existing variables. This would be a tedious procedure using the dialogue boxes, but would be easy to perform using syntax commands (this example is demonstrated later in this section).

Tweaking the parameters of a command

Another reason for choosing to work in the syntax editor window is that some of the options or parameters associated with certain commands can only be accessed using the syntax commands. In order to keep the number of buttons manageable the SPSS programmers have pre-set certain features of the commands. Occasionally you might want to alter one of these settings. This can only be done using the command syntax.

Details of the additional features of a command that can be accessed only via the syntax window are described in special help screens that can be accessed via the **Help** button on the dialogue box (see next page).

To access details of the features of a command available only via the command syntax

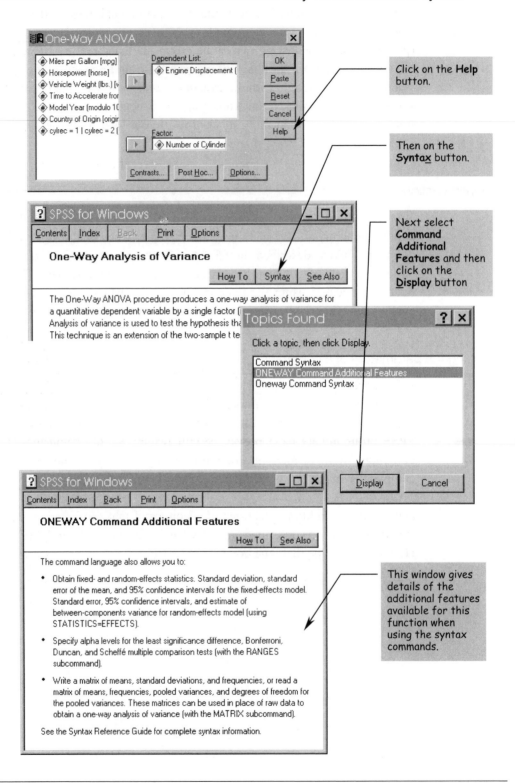

Click on the **Help** button.

Then on the **Syntax** button.

Next select **Command Additional Features** and then click on the **Display** button

This window gives details of the additional features available for this function when using the syntax commands.

THE SYNTAX WINDOW

The Syntax Editor window (or simply the syntax window) allows you to build up the syntax commands you require and then execute them. This window acts like a very simple word processor that allows you to edit the syntax for the commands you want to execute. The **Edit** menu provides access to all the normal text editing functions such as cut, paste, find and replace, delete etc. Careful use of these functions can allow you quickly to build up a long and complex set of syntax commands. The "tool bar" displayed across the top of the syntax window includes a number of useful buttons. The use of some of the special buttons is described below.

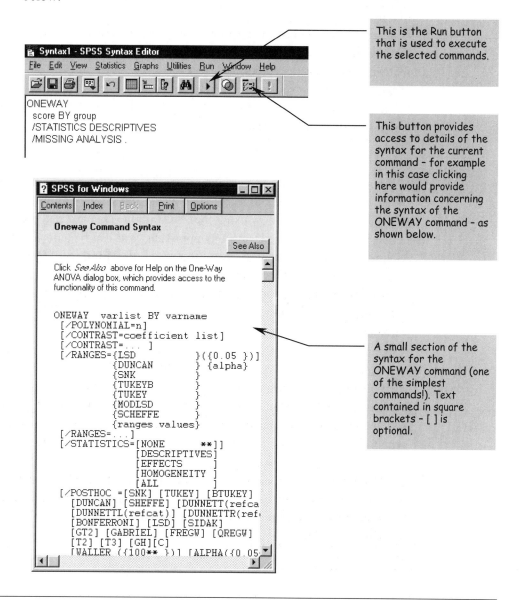

This is the Run button that is used to execute the selected commands.

This button provides access to details of the syntax for the current command – for example in this case clicking here would provide information concerning the syntax of the ONEWAY command – as shown below.

A small section of the syntax for the ONEWAY command (one of the simplest commands!). Text contained in square brackets – [ ] is optional.

Once you get used to the way it is presented, the syntax help can be very useful. There are a few rules you need to remember when starting to write syntax commands.

1. Each new command must start on a new line of text. In practice, leaving several blank lines between commands makes the text easier to understand.
2. Each command must end with a full stop or period mark (.).
3. Sub-commands or options are usually separated by the forward slash mark (/). It is a good idea (but not essential) to start each sub-command on a new line and to slightly indent it.
4. You can split a command over several lines – it is safest to break the line at the start of a new sub-command.
5. Each line of text must be no more than 80 characters long (this seems to be an historic hangover from the days when SPSS was programmed using punch cards that were 80 characters wide).
6. Make sure that you spell your variable names correctly (i.e. exactly as they appear in the data editor window). Misspelling a variable name is one of the most common sources of errors when running syntax commands.

In practice, it is quite rare to write a piece of syntax "from scratch". It is more usual to use the dialogue boxes to select an analysis and set the options, and to then paste this into the syntax window using the **Paste** button. This text can then be copied and edited before being run. Using this approach, you can be sure that the syntax and spelling will be correct. By careful use of the **Find** and **Replace** commands (available from the **Edit** menu) you can copy the syntax of a command, and change the variable(s) very quickly and accurately to build up a series of analyses. An example is given below. In this example we are seeking to compute 20 new variables. Each of these variables is the mean of a block of 10 questionnaire responses. The original variables were given names that reflect the block and question number. For example, B1Q3 is the third question in the first block, while B9Q8 is the eighth question in the ninth block. We could use the dialogue boxes to perform all these computes, but this would be a very laborious task. Because of the way the variables have been named, it would be much easier to produce a series of syntax commands to perform these computes. This could be done as follows:

1. Using the Compute dialogue box, enter the details needed to compute the new variable "b1mean" (see Chapter 5 for details of the compute command).
2. Click on the **Paste** button to paste the syntax commands into the syntax editor window (see below).
3. Select (highlight) this block of text and copy it once.

4. Move the cursor to the start of the second block and use the **Replace** function to change all instances of the string "b1" to "b2" (click on the **Find Next** button, and then click the **Replace** button repeatedly until all the changes are made – do not use the **Replace All** button).

5. Paste a new copy of the command into the window (you can do this using the keyboard by typing "<Ctrl> V"). Now repeat step 4 to replace "b1" with "b3".

6. Continue in this way until you have ten blocks of syntax each instructing SPSS to compute the mean of the 10 variables in that block.

7. Move the cursor to the top of the syntax editor window and select all the text in the window.

8. Click on the Run button. The 10 new variables will be computed and appended to your data file.

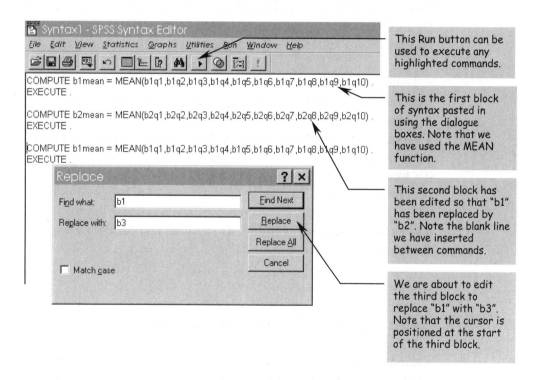

SAVING AND OPENING SYNTAX FILES

Once completed, a syntax file can be saved to disk. If the syntax window is the active window (i.e. if you are currently working in this window), you can simply save the contents of the window as a syntax file by selecting **Save As** from the **File** menu. SPSS will automatically add the suffix ".sps" to the end of the file name. We strongly recommend that you accept this default suffix.

RUNNING COMMANDS IN THE SYNTAX WINDOW

Once you have written and saved your syntax commands you can execute, or run them. You can do this using either the Run button or by selecting one of the options from the **Run** menu. It is important to note that the Run button only executes the highlighted (selected) commands – select all the commands you want to run before clicking on this button. The **Run** menu includes several options:

All – this option executes all of the commands in the syntax window
Selection – this option executes any commands that are selected or highlighted (i.e. the same as the Run button)
Current – this option executes only the current command (defined by the position of the cursor.
To End – this option runs all commands from the current command to the end of the syntax window

The chosen commands will then be executed and the output window will display the results of your analysis.

SYNTAX FILES AND THE PRODUCTION FACILITY

The production facility allows you to pre-programme jobs in SPSS. The production facility runs specified syntax files and directs output towards specified files. This facility is designed for very large analyses that are performed regularly on a changing data file (for example an analysis of that day's sales data for a large supermarket chain) and is not likely to be of use to psychologists.

THE JOURNAL FILE

SPSS records all the analyses you undertake during a session in a special file called a journal file. The journal file for a session will include the full syntax of all the commands you have executed, together with any error messages or warnings that SPSS might have issued. By default, SPSS saves the journal file at the end of each session using the file name "spss.jnl" (usually located in the C:\temp directory). This file is a very useful source of syntax commands for insertion into a syntax file.

Before opening the file, check that someone has not altered the default location or name of the file (or even switched the journal off). To do this select **Options** from the **Edit** menu and click on the **General** tab. You can now see (and if you wish change) the name and location of the journal file. You should also check that the **Record syntax in journal** option is selected (the box should contain a tick). You can also choose whether the file should be overwritten (the default option) or appended. If you select **Append** the file will contain the syntax of all of the commands you ever issue and will grow in length with each SPSS session – probably not a very good idea. Make a note of the name and location of the journal file and click on the **OK** button.

Open the journal file by selecting **Open** from the **File** menu. Enter the full file name and path into the **File Name** box (for example C:\temp\spss.jnl). You can now edit this file. For example, you might wish to copy some of the command syntax from this file into the syntax window.

> **TIP** You may need to perform the same set of analyses several times over. Here is an easy way to produce the syntax file you need. First perform the analyses using the dialogue boxes, and then edit the journal file to remove warnings and other messages. Now save the journal file with a new name and the suffix ".sps" (that of a syntax file). You can load and run this syntax file as many times as required.

Multiple Viewer and Syntax windows

It is possible to open simultaneously multiple viewer and syntax windows. When more than one window is open, SPSS will direct the output or syntax towards what is called the designated window. You designate a window by clicking on the button marked by an exclamation point (on the tool bar of the syntax and viewer windows).

> **TIP** It might sound useful to have several output windows open at the same time, but in our experience you always end up with the output in the wrong window. It is probably easier to work with just one window and then edit the output into two separate files once the analysis is complete.

Section 2: Option settings in SPSS

There are a number of options that can be set in SPSS. These control such things as the appearance of the various windows, the way variables are listed in dialogue boxes, the appearance of output and the location of files. In this section we describe how to access these options and highlight a few that you might like to alter.

> **TIP**   If your screen looks different from the screen shots included in this book, this may be because some of these options settings are different. In particular, if your variables are always listed differently from ours, it may be that the Variable Lists options in your copy of SPSS are set differently to ours (see below).

CHANGING OPTION SETTINGS

The option settings can be accessed from any of the various SPSS windows. Select **Edit** > **Options**. This will bring up the **Options** dialogue box shown below. This style of dialogue box has a series of tabs across the top (rather like the tabs on index cards). The various options available are grouped together, and clicking on a tab presents you with one of these groups of options.

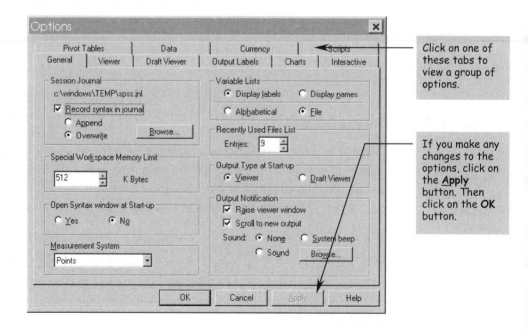

Click on one of these tabs to view a group of options.

If you make any changes to the options, click on the **Apply** button. Then click on the **OK** button.

SOME USEFUL OPTION SETTINGS

Below are just a few of the more useful options. We will leave you to explore all the others for yourself (use the Help button if you require an explanation of an option).

The General Tab

Most of the useful options are on this tab. In particular you might want to change the Variable Lists settings. These alter the way in which variables are listed in the dialogue boxes.

Selecting the **Display labels** option will cause SPSS to list the variable labels (with the variable name given in brackets). If a variable does not have a label then the name is listed. When the **Display names** option is selected, only the variable names are listed in the dialogue boxes. The **Alphabetical** and **File** options control the order in which the variables are listed. Most users prefer to have the variables listed in File order, as they will then be in the same (hopefully) logical order that they were entered into the data file. However, when working with very large data files (e.g. from a survey), having the variables listed in alphabetical order can help you locate a particular variable quickly.

The **Session Journal** options available on this tab are described at the end of Section 1.

The Data Tab

The **Display Format For New Numeric Variables** on the Data Tab allows you to alter the default settings of the width and number of decimal places used to display a new variable. It might be useful to change this setting if you needed to create a large number of variables using the same settings. Remember, this setting alters only the way the number is displayed on screen, not the number of decimal places used when performing calculations.

The Output Labels Tab

Here you can select whether you want variable labels, variable names, or both variable labels and variable names to appear in output. Similarly, you can choose to display either value labels, values, or both value labels and values. You might like to experiment with these settings.

Section 3: Getting help in SPSS

It might seem odd to wait until the last part of the book before describing how to use the SPSS Help system, but we hope that up to now our instructions will have provided all the assistance you needed! However, from now on you are on your own, and will probably need to make use of the extensive Help files provided with SPSS when trying to use functions or commands not covered in this book.

SPSS comes with several different sources of help.

WHAT'S THIS?

One of the easiest and most useful ways of accessing help is using the right mouse button. This is particularly useful if you need some help to understand output. In the output window, select a table by double clicking on it (a hatched outline will appear to show it is selected). You can now move the mouse over any of the column or row titles in the table and click the right-hand mouse button. Select **What's This?** from the menu of options that will appear. A brief explanation of that feature of the output is provided (see below).

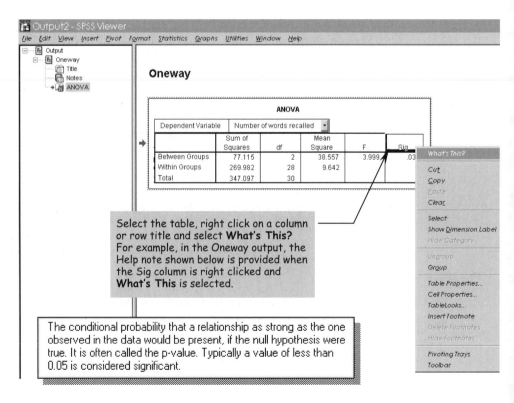

The same technique can often be applied to get help when using Dialogue boxes. For example, when using the one-way dialogue box you can right-click on the **Dependent List** and select **What's This?** (see below).

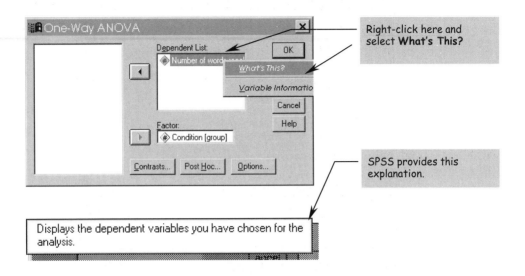

THE HELP BUTTON IN DIALOGUE BOXES

Each dialogue box includes a Help button. Click on this button to view a help window containing a more detailed description of the statistical procedure and the options available within SPSS. This help window will include a number of other buttons linking to further help pages (including the Syntax button described earlier in this chapter).

THE HELP MENU

Ask Me help

The **Help** menu gives access to several sources of help, including **Ask Me** help. If you type a question into this dialogue box, SPSS will list topics that contain information relevant to your request. For example, if you type in the question "How do I do a chi-square" SPSS will list related help files for you to read (see below).

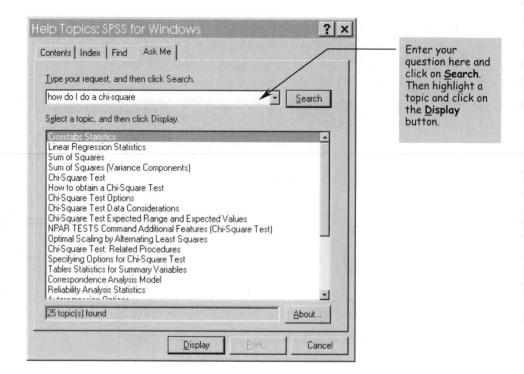

Enter your question here and click on **Search**. Then highlight a topic and click on the **Display** button.

Other Help topic tabs

The other tabs available in this help dialogue box (**Contents, Index** and **Find**) provide various different routes to access the Help information. **Find** allows you to search for single words, while **Contents** provides help organised under topic headings. The **Index** tab gives access to a full alphabetical index to all the help information.

The Results Coach

When viewing output in the output window, double click on a table to select it. Now select **Results Coach** from the **Help** menu. SPSS will open a slide-show style tutorial explaining the output. Work through this help using the **Next** button.

The Statistics Coach

This is another slide-show style presentation availbe from the **Help** menu. The **Statistics Coach** asks a number of questions about your data and the type of analysis you want to perform. It then suggests a suitable statistical procedure. This can act as a useful reminder of suitable procedures, but is no substitute for a basic knowledge of these procedures.

Section 4: Printing from SPSS

It is possible to print the contents of the various windows used by SPSS. In this section we describe how to print output in the form of tables and charts, data and syntax files.

PRINTING OUTPUT FROM THE OUTPUT VIEWER WINDOW

The output viewer window displays the results of your analysis in the form of text, tables or charts, so this is likely to be the first thing you want to print out. To do this, first make the output viewer the active window (if it is not already) by selecting it from the **Window** menu. Now either click on the printer icon on the tool bar across the top of the page, or select **Print** from the **File** menu. The Print dialogue box contains several options.

1. The **All visible output** option prints any output that you could see by scrolling up or down in the output window (i.e. not hidden output).
2. The **All output** option prints all the output in the viewer window, regardless of whether or not it is hidden. (Your computer may not show this option.)
3. The **Selection** option prints only the output that is selected or highlighted. To select a section of output click and drag the mouse over it or hold down the shift key while moving the cursor up or down.

The first of these options is the default setting. However, the **Selection** option can be very useful and can save you printing out large amounts of unwanted analysis – especially from some of the more complex procedures such as a within-subjects analysis of variance.

Adjusting the appearance of the output

Selecting **Page Setup** from the **File** menu will bring up the **Page Setup** dialogue box. You can use this dialogue box to set the paper size and margins, and to select whether you want to print in landscape or portrait orientation. This last option can be useful if you have wide tables that you would like to be printed without being split.

The **Options** button on the Page Setup dialogue box allows you to include text in the headers or footers of the printout. If you share a printer, it might be useful to have your name and/or the name of the project on every page of output. The default setting is to have the page number appearing in the footer. We recommend that you retain this feature – it can be very useful when you drop a pile of printout!

The changes you make in the Page Setup dialogue box affect only the output produced from the output viewer window. If after changing these settings you save the output your settings will be retained with the file.

> **TIP** It may be worth checking the appearance of your output before you commit it to paper. You can do this by selecting **Print Preview** from the **File** menu.

PRINTING OUT A DATA FILE

It is sometimes useful to keep a printed record of your data file. You may be required to include a printed copy of the raw data in an appendix to a report, and researchers should keep the data from any published study for several years after publication.

To obtain a printed copy of your data first make the Data Editor window the active window then select **Print** from the **File** menu. The data file is printed as it appears in the data editor window. If you have selected to display value labels then these will be printed in place of the actual values.

> **TIP** The **Fonts** option under the **View** menu allows you to change the size and appearance of the font used to both display and print the data. It might be possible to squeeze a file containing a large number of variables onto a single sheet of paper by reducing the font size.

PRINTING A SYNTAX FILE

When the syntax window is active, a syntax file can be printed out either by clicking on the printer icon on the toolbar or by selecting **Print** from the **File** menu.

SPECIAL OUTPUT OPTIONS FOR PIVOT TABLES

If you double-click on a pivot table (the name SPSS gives to a table of results displayed in the output viewer window), the table will become highlighted with a special shaded boarder. Once a pivot table is selected in this way, a special set of pivot table menu items will be displayed at the top of the window. These menus can be used to adjust the appearance of the table prior to printing it. A huge number of options are available, including rotating the table (swapping rows and columns) adding or removing grid lines and scaling the table to fit the size of paper being used. Below we have described a few of the most useful actions.

1. From the **Pivot** menu select **Transpose Rows and Columns** to swap the rows and columns of a table.
2. From the **Format** menu select **Table Properties.** The tab-style dialogue boxes displayed will allow you to alter the appearance of the table. The **Printing** tab contains two very useful options (**Rescale wide to fit page** and **Rescale long to fit page**), which force SPSS to automatically adjust the size of print so that table will fit the page without being split.
3. From the **Format** menu select **Table Looks.** You can now select a style for your table from a list of pre-programmed styles. You can also edit the existing styles to suit your exact requirements. This new style can be saved and applied to any table.

> **TIP**   The academic styles are particularly appropriate for a research report.

4. From the **Format** menu select **Autofit.** This will resize the columns and rows of the table to a size that is appropriate for their contents. This usually makes the table slightly smaller and much neater.

> **TIP**   Before using the either of the rescale options (described in point 2 above), you could apply the Autofit option. This will remove any redundant spaces from the table before it is rescaled.

5. From the **Insert** menu select **Caption.** This will allow you to insert a text caption inside the table.
6. From the View menu select Gridlines to either add or remove gridlines from the table.
7. Select a set of table cells by clicking and dragging over them. From the **Format** menu select **Cell Properties** to adjust the way values are displayed in a cell. Alternatively, select **Set Data Cell Widths** to set the width of the cells.

> **TIP**   Once a pivot table is selected, it is possible to adjust the width of a column by clicking on and dragging the grid line dividing the columns. Double-clicking on a cell allows you to change the cell contents. This is useful if you want to edit the value labels used in a table, but otherwise should be used with caution!

Section 5: Incorporating SPSS output into other documents

The output produced by recent versions SPSS is of such a high quality that you might want to incorporate it directly into your word-processed research report, particularly if you have formatted it as described in Section 4.

CUTTING AND PASTING OBJECTS INTO WORD PROCESSOR DOCUMENTS

It is very easy to paste a pivot table or a chart (graph) from SPSS into another application such as a word processing package. Select the section of output you want by clicking on it once and select **Copy** from the **Edit** menu. Now switch to your word processor, move the cursor to the correct point in the document, and select **Paste Special** from the **Edit** menu. From the Paste Special dialogue box select **Picture**. The SPSS output will now be pasted into your document as a picture.

> **TIP**   You can adjust the size of the picture you have pasted by dragging the "handles". It is best to use the corner handles so that you do not change the aspect ratio of the table. If the aspect ratio changes (that is if you stretch the table out of shape) the text will probably not fit into the cells correctly.

If you are using SPSS Version 9 or 10 you can copy and paste several tables at the same time. While holding down the control key click on the required tables. Now select **Copy objects** form the **Edit** menu. You can now switch to your word processor and select **Paste** from the **Edit** menu to paste the tables into your document.

> **TIP**   Users of SPSS Version 8 also should be able to copy and paste multiple objects using this technique. However, when we attempt to do this the output is incomplete. This problem seems to have been resolved in later versions.

EMBEDDING SPSS OBJECTS INTO OTHER APPLICATIONS

Pivot Tables and Interactive Charts (but not standard charts, see Section 7) can also be "embedded" into another application. An embedded object remains part of SPSS and can be activated and edited. This means that, for example, by double clicking on an embedded pivot tale you can edit the table (as described in Section 4). However, using embedded objects can be rather tricky. Before you can export an object for embedding, you must run a special programme file (see SPSS manual or help files for details). Once you have run this file you can copy the object in the normal way. When you go to paste the object into your new application, select **Paste <u>S</u>pecial** from the **<u>E</u>dit** menu. You will see that the list of format options now includes a special SPSS format. In our experience embedding objects in this way is more trouble than it is worth

> **TIP**   Don't bother trying to use embedded objects. Instead, edit the table from within SPSS before copying and pasting it into your word processor document.

Section 6: Graphing tips

SPSS is capable of producing very high quality charts. Chart production facilities were further enhanced in Version 8 of SPSS when a new type of chart – the interactive chart – was introduced.

Rather than include a separate chapter covering the production of charts, we have described how to produce the three most common types of charts in the chapters covering the analysis of the data linked to these chart types.

1. The production of scattergrams was introduced in Chapter 4, which also covered the analysis of data from correlational designs
2. The production of bar graphs was introduced in Chapter 6 where we described one-way analysis of variance.
3. The production of more complex line graphs was also covered in Chapter 6 alongside a description of how to undertake within-subjects analysis of variance.

These charts were all produced using the standard chart facility in SPSS. In the final section of this chapter, we will introduce you to interactive charts.

SELECTING THE CHART TYPE

SPSS provides a variety of useful mechanisms to help you select the appropriate chart type for your graph.

To access this help, from the **Graphs** menu select **Gallery**. If you know the type of chart (bar, line pie etc) you want to produce, click on the appropriate chart icon. Alternatively, if you are not sure which type of chart is best to display your data, click on the **See Also** button at the top of the window and select **Chart Galleries By Data Structure**. You can now select the option that best describes your data set and follow the instructions to produce the chart. These two options are illustrated on the following page.

If you know what type of chart to produce, but need help to produce it

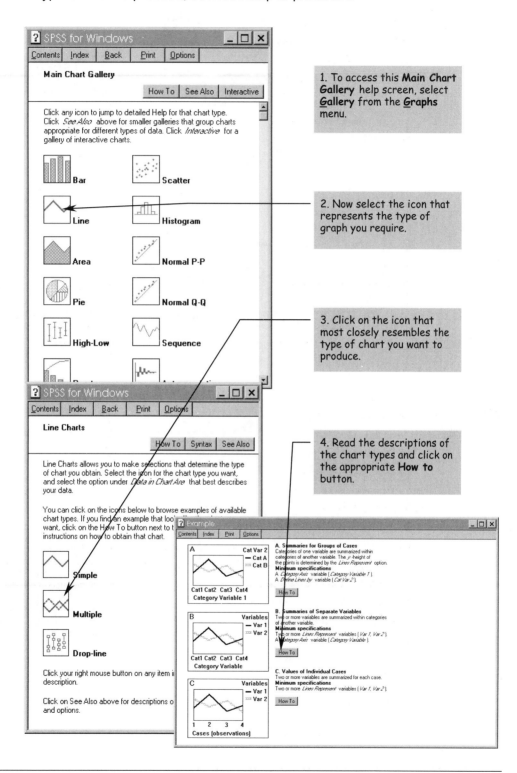

1. To access this **Main Chart Gallery** help screen, select **Gallery** from the **Graphs** menu.

2. Now select the icon that represents the type of graph you require.

3. Click on the icon that most closely resembles the type of chart you want to produce.

4. Read the descriptions of the chart types and click on the appropriate **How to** button.

If you need help to choose an appropriate type of graph for your data

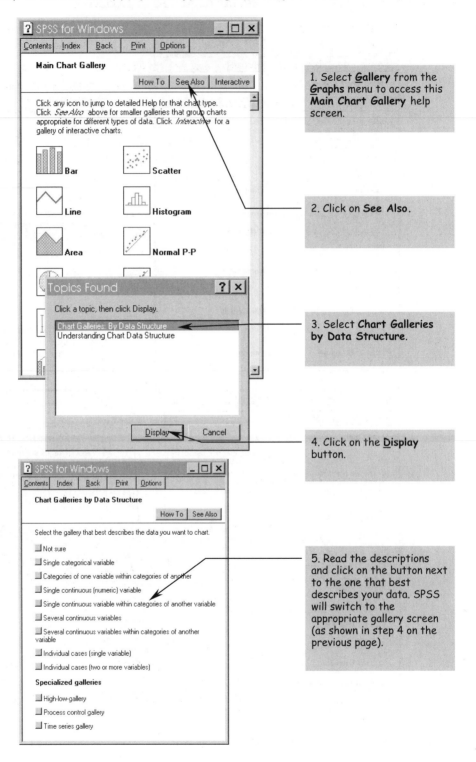

1. Select **Gallery** from the **Graphs** menu to access this **Main Chart Gallery** help screen.

2. Click on **See Also**.

3. Select **Chart Galleries by Data Structure**.

4. Click on the **Display** button.

5. Read the descriptions and click on the button next to the one that best describes your data. SPSS will switch to the appropriate gallery screen (as shown in step 4 on the previous page).

Most chart types require you to define what is to be displayed in the chart. For example, the relevant dialogue box for line charts is illustrated below. If your research employed a repeated measures or within-subjects design, you will have a different SPSS data variable for each level of the independent variable. In these circumstances the **Summaries of separate variables** option is likely to be the most appropriate as it plots the values for two or more data variables on one chart. If, on the other hand, your study employed an independent groups or between-subjects design, you will want to compare the average level of the dependent variable for one group of participants with the average level for another group. In such cases the **Summaries for groups of cases** option is the most appropriate. The third option, **Values of individual cases**, is not very likely to be of use in psychological research. This option allows you to plot the value of one or more variables for each of your participants. This chart type is often sketched by psychology students despite the fact that it tells us almost nothing and generally should be avoided!

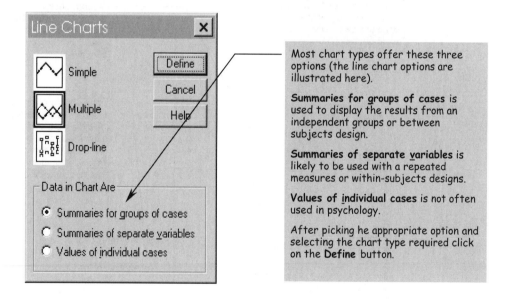

Most chart types offer these three options (the line chart options are illustrated here).

Summaries for groups of cases is used to display the results from an independent groups or between subjects design.

Summaries of separate variables is likely to be used with a repeated measures or within-subjects designs.

Values of individual cases is not often used in psychology.

After picking he appropriate option and selecting the chart type required click on the **Define** button.

Next you are asked to decide which data variables are to be assigned to which axis of the chart. In the above example, if we selected the **Multiple** chart type and the **Summaries for groups of case** options, then the dialogue box shown below would be presented.

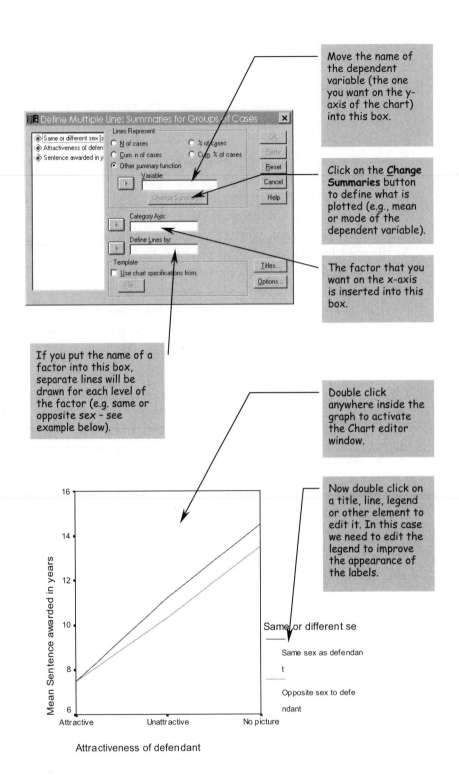

Move the name of the dependent variable (the one you want on the y-axis of the chart) into this box.

Click on the **Change Summaries** button to define what is plotted (e.g., mean or mode of the dependent variable).

The factor that you want on the x-axis is inserted into this box.

If you put the name of a factor into this box, separate lines will be drawn for each level of the factor (e.g. same or opposite sex – see example below).

Double click anywhere inside the graph to activate the Chart editor window.

Now double click on a title, line, legend or other element to edit it. In this case we need to edit the legend to improve the appearance of the labels.

Once a chart has been drawn, it can be edited. Double-click anywhere inside the chart to activate the Chart Editor Window. The menus and tool bar in this window can be used to improve the initial appearance of the chart. Items such as chart titles, subtitles, legends, axis titles, labels, line characteristics and markers can all be altered either through the menus or by double-clicking directly on the item.

Once the editing is complete, close the chart editor window. The changes made to the chart will now be reflected in the appearance of the chart in the output viewer window. This chart can now either be printed or cut and pasted into another document (see Section 5 of this chapter).

Alternatively, charts can be exported in a variety of file formats. To export a chart double-click on the chart to activate the chart editor window, and select **Export Chart** from the **File** menu. Now select the appropriate file format and enter a filename for the exported chart.

By employing all these options, it is possible to produce a very high quality chart to incorporate into a research report.

Section 7: Interactive charts

THE DIFFERENCE BETWEEN INTERACTIVE CHARTS AND STANDARD CHARTS

Interactive charts are a new development in SPSS. At present not all of the standard types of chart (those listed under the **Graphs** menu) can be produced as interactive charts. However, the most common chart types can be produced as interactive charts, and there are some advantages producing charts in this way.

The main differences between standard and interactive charts are as follows:

1. Interactive charts are more flexible. With standard charts, once you have defined the chart all that you can change is the appearance of the elements. With an interactive chart you can change everything. You can even change your mind about the type of graph you want or which variables you want to use.
2. If you edit a standard chart, a new chart editor window is opened, whereas an interactive chart is edited in the output viewer window.
3. In an interactive chart right-clicking on a chart or element of a chart gives access to special functions (in standard charts right-clicking accesses the **What's This** help function).
4. In interactive charts you can choose whether SPSS lists variables by name or by label.
5. In interactive charts, variables can be "dragged and dropped" (in all other parts of SPSS, variables must be highlighted and then moved by clicking on the appropriate arrow button).
6. Interactive charts can be embedded into other applications or exported, or cut and pasted into another document. Standard charts cannot be embedded.
7. All types of interactive charts can be produced as 3-D charts and can be rotated in all three dimensions.
8. Interactive charts utilise the distinction between Scale, Ordinal and Nominal variables that can be indicated when a variable is being defined (see Chapter 2). SPSS allows Ordinal or Nominal variables to be treated as Categorical variables within interactive charts. In addition, these categorical variables can be used as panel variables. A panel variable is used to create a group of multiple charts. Each chart in the group includes data from only one level of the panel variable. For example, if we were plotting the data from the three-way mixed ANOVA shown in Chapter 6, Section 5, then we might decide to produce two graphs showing the interaction of orientation by negation. One graph would display this interaction for the primed group and the other for the un-primed group. In this case group would be the panel variable.

Glossary and Index

Here we give a description of terms used in the book. In the descriptions, any term in italics has an entry in this glossary. Where appropriate, we have given an index to relevant Chapters and Sections. If you need further information about statistical or experimental design concepts then you should consult a statistics text.

ANOVA

Abbreviation of Analysis of Variance: an *inferential statistical test*   Chapter 6
that allows analysis of data from designs with more than two
experimental *conditions* and/or with more than one *factor*. The term
is often also used to refer to the *experimental design* used to obtain
the data. The statistical test is intended for analysis of *parametric*
data. The absence, however, of *nonparametric* equivalents for two-
or more-factor designs means that ANOVA is often used in such
circumstances. Fortunately, it is said to be robust to the
assumptions for parametric tests not being entirely met, provided
that the *cell* sizes are equal.

Introduction to ANOVA	Section 1
One-way *between-subjects* ANOVA (also see *Kruskal–Wallis*)	Section 2
One-way *within-subjects* ANOVA (also see *Friedman*)	Section 4
Multi-way between-subjects ANOVA	Section 3
Multi-way within-subjects ANOVA	Section 5
Multi-way *mixed* ANOVA	Section 6

Bar chart

A graph used to display summary statistics for a number of SPSS   Chapter 6
*variable*s: for example, the *mean* of data from two or more   Section 3
*condition*s. Also see *chart* and *interactive chart*.

Also available from the Charts button in the *Frequencies dialogue
box*: that version will plot the frequencies or percentages of values
in a single SPSS variable.

Between-subjects design

An *experimental design* in which all *factor*s are between-subjects   Chapter 6
factors; that is, when no *participant* takes part in more than one   Section 1
level of a factor. This term is part of *ANOVA* terminology. Also see
independent groups design.

Case

Normally, a single *participant* in an experiment. The main exception in psychology is for *matched subjects designs*, when the matched participants are the case. Each case should be entered into a separate row in the SPSS *data window*. For some studies, the case will not be people. For example, we may be interested in the average "A" level points for pupils from different schools: the cases would then be the schools.

Chapter 2
Section 1

Cell

An element in the *data window* table, into which a *value* is entered.

Chapter 2
Section 1

In *ANOVA* and *chi-square*, the combination of one *level* of one *factor* and one level of another factor. The cell size is the number of *case*s (normally *participant*s) that fall into that cell.

Chart

The name that SPSS gives to a graph. A wide range of graph types is available from the **Graphs** *menu item*. See also *interactive charts*.

Chapter 8
Section 6

Additionally, some graphs are available through the *Frequencies* command.

Chart editor window

The SPSS window which appears if you double click on a *chart* in the *output window*. *Interactive charts*, however, are edited in the output window.

Chapter 8
Section 6

The chart editor window has to be used to add a regression line to a *scattergram*.

Chapter 4
Section 2

Chi-square

An *inferential statistical test* that is used to analyse *frequencies* of nominal data (see *levels of measurement*). It allows comparison between the observed frequencies in the data and the frequencies that would be expected by chance. The chi-square most often used

Chapter 4
Section 1

in psychology is a test of association between two *variables*.

The chi-square tables are used to assess *significance* for some other statistical tests: for example, *Friedman* and *Kruskal–Wallis*.

Condition

See *Level*.

Compute

An SPSS procedure by which a new *variable* can be computed (calculated) from one or more old variables.

Chapter 5
Section 6

Confounding variable

Any *variable* which changes systematically over the *level*s of the *independent variable*. If there is a confounding variable, then you do not know whether the results of an experiment are due to the independent variable alone, to the confounding variable alone, or to some interaction between those two variables.

Chapter 1
Section 2

Correlation

A term used to describe a linear relationship, or association, between two *variables* (measured on ordinal, interval, or ratio *level of measurement*). *Pearson's r*, *Spearman's rho*, and *Kendall's tau* are *inferential statistical tests* of correlation. See also *scattergram*.

Chapter 4
Section 2

Count

An SPSS procedure by which the number of times that a particular value occurs, in one or more *variables* in the *data window,* can be counted.

Chapter 5
Section 7

Data handling

Manipulation of data after it has been entered into SPSS. The different types of data handling are accessed through the *menu items* **Data** and **Transform**. See also *compute, count, rank cases, recode, select cases, sort cases, split.*

Chapter 5
Section 1

Data editor window

The SPSS window in which data is entered and edited. It has the appearance of a spreadsheet window.

Chapter 1 Sections 4 and 5; Chapter 2 Section 1

Degrees of freedom

A number related to the number of *participant*s who took part in an experiment (*t-test*, *ANOVA*) or to the number of *factor*s (*independent variable*s) in an experiment (ANOVA, *chi-square*). The degrees of freedom are required when using statistical tables of *significance*. Although SPSS gives the exact *p* value, degrees of freedom should still be reported as shown on the annotated output pages of those *inferential statistical tests*.

Dependent variable

The *variable* that is measured in an experiment, and whose values are said to depend on those of the *independent variable* (or *factor*).

Chapter 1 Section 2

Descriptive statistics

Procedures that allow you to describe data by summarising it or displaying it. Often used as a general term for summary descriptive statistics: *measures of central tendency* and *measures of dispersion*.

Chapter 2 Section 8

Graphs (see *chart*) are also descriptive statistics.

Dialogue box

A box that appears on the screen, normally after you have clicked on a sequence of *menu items*. Windows computer packages use dialogue boxes to ask you for instructions. We show dialogue boxes in all the chapters, annotated to describe their use.

Error bar graph

A graph in which the *mean* of each *condition* is plotted with a vertical bar that denotes one *standard error* above the mean and

Chapter 6 Section 4

one standard error below the mean. SPSS allows you to alter what the vertical bars represent (for example, three *standard deviations* from the mean; the 90% confidence interval).

In SPSS it is available for plotting the means for *levels* of one *factor* only, although the *interactive chart* procedure allows you to plot a panel for each level of a second factor.

Experimental design

A term used to describe specific methods by which experiments are carried out and which are intended to prevent *participant irrelevant variables* from *confounding* the experiment: for example, *repeated measures design*; two-way between subjects *ANOVA*. Basic designs are described in Chapter 1, and other designs are described where relevant for particular statistical tests.
Chapter 1
Section 2

The term is also used in a more general sense to describe the way in which an experiment is to be carried out, including how *situational irrelevant variable*s are to be prevented from confounding the experiment.

Factor

Another term for *independent variable*. Factor is used particularly when discussing *ANOVA* statistical tests and designs. Also see *between-subjects design* and *within-subjects design*.
Chapter 6
Section 1

F-ratio

The statistic obtained in *ANOVA* calculations. It can be described as the variance due to manipulation of the *factor* divided by the variance due to error.
Chapter 6
Section 1

Friedman

A *nonparametric* equivalent of the one-way within-subjects *ANOVA*.
Chapter 6
Section 9

Frequency/ies

The number of times a particular event or value occurs. Also an
Chapter 2

SPSS command available from the *menu item* **Analyze** (Version 9) or **Statistics** (Version 8) that will produce tables of frequencies showing the number of times that a particular value occurs in each *variable*. Some *charts* are available through a button on the Frequencies dialogue box. See also *bar chart*.

Section 8

Graph

See *Chart*.

Chapter 8
Section 6

Grouping variable

An SPSS *variable* that specifies which *level* a participant carried out in an *independent groups design* or for a *between subjects* factor. Each level is given a number as a code. For example: 1 for male and 2 for female; or 1 for rehearsal condition, 2 for mnemonic condition and 3 for elaboration condition (in a memory experiment). *Value labels* should be used when defining a grouping variable.

Chapter 2
Section 2

Help

You can obtain help in a number of ways while using SPSS: for example, the Help button on dialogue boxes, right clicking, and the **Help** *menu item*.

Chapter 8
Section 3

Hypothesis

A prediction about the outcome of an experiment. The experimental hypothesis predicts that a difference between *condition*s will occur, that a relationship will be found, or that an *interaction* will occur. The null hypothesis predicts that there will be no difference between conditions, that a relationship will not be found, or that an interaction will not occur.

Chapter 1
Section 2

Independent groups design

An *experimental design* in which a *participant* takes part in only one *level* of the *independent variable*. This term is usually used for designs with two levels of one independent variable. See also *between-subjects design*s.

Chapter 1
Section 2

Independent variable

A *variable* either: that is systematically manipulated by the experimenter to have different values (true experiments); or, the values of which are chosen by the experimenter (natural independent groups designs). Each value of the independent variable is called a *level*. See also *factor*.

Chapter 1
Section 2

Inferential statistical tests

Procedures that allow you to draw inferences from the data collected. The outcome of an inferential statistical test gives you the probability of obtaining the results by chance if the *independent variable* had no effect. If that probability is low ($p \leq 0.05$ in psychology) then the experimental *hypothesis* is accepted; otherwise it is rejected. Various inferential statistics are covered in this book.

Chapter 1
Section 3

Interaction

An interaction is present in a two-or more-way *ANOVA* if each *level* of one *factor* has a different effect on each level of another factor.

Chapter 6
Section 1

Interaction graph

A *line graph* showing the effects of each *level* of two *factors*. The *dependent variable* is on the Y axis and the levels of one factor on the X axis; the levels of a second factor are indicated by individual lines drawn in the graph. See also *chart* and *interactive chart*.

Chapter 6
Section 5;
Chapter 8
Section 7

Interactive chart

A type of SPSS *chart* that allows you much greater flexibility in specifying the appearance of the chart, and allows some features not available in standard charts.

Chapter 8
Section 7

Irrelevant variable

Any *variable* other than the *independent variable* or *factor/s* and the *dependent variable/s*. Good *experimental design* should ensure

Chapter 1
Section 2

that no irrelevant variable becomes a *confounding variable*.

Kendall's tau

An *inferential statistical test* of *correlation* used to analyse *nonparametric* data.

Chapter 4
Section 2

Kruskal–Wallis

A *nonparametric* equivalent of the one-way *between-subjects ANOVA*.

Chapter 6
Section 9

Level

The term for each value of an *independent variable* or *factor*. There may be two or more levels of each factor. If there is only one factor, then its levels are equivalent to the conditions of the experiment. For two or more factors, the conditions may each be equal to one level of one factor (*between subjects designs*) or may be a combination of one level from each of two or more factors (*mixed designs* and *within-subjects designs*).

Chapter 1
Section 2

Levels of measurement

The type of scale used to measure *variables*. The four types are: nominal, ordinal, interval, and ratio. The first two are classified as *nonparametric* levels of measurement, and the last two as *parametric* levels of measurement.

Chapter 1
Section 2

Line graph

A graph in which the points plotted are joined by a line. The points could each represent the *mean* of one *sample*, or they could represent the *frequency* of particular values in an SPSS *variable*. See also *interaction graph*, *chart* and *interactive chart*.

Chapter 8
Section 6

Mann–Whitney

An *inferential statistical test* used to analyse *nonparametric* data from *two-sample independent groups designs*.

Chapter 3
Sections 4
and 5

Matched subjects design

An *experimental design* in which each *participant* is matched closely with another participant, to give a participant pair. Each member of the pair is then allocated, by a random process, to different *levels* of the *independent variable*. Also called matched pairs design. It is a type of *related design*.

Chapter 1
Section 2

Mean

A *measure of central tendency*: the scores are summed and the total is divided by the number of scores.

Chapter 2
Section 8

Measure of central tendency

The average or typical score for a sample. See *mean*, *median*, and *mode*.

Measure of dispersion

How variable the scores in a sample are. See *range*, *standard deviation*, *standard error*, and *variance*.

Median

A *measure of central tendency*: the scores are put into rank order and the middle score is the median

Chapter 2
Section 8

Menu items

The items (words) in the bar in Windows packages, normally across the top of the screen, that give you access to the drop-down menus. In SPSS the menu bar varies slightly between the different windows, and some of the drop-down menus may vary. For example, in the *viewer window* compare the **Help** menu before and after you have double clicked on one of the results tables.

Chapter 1
Section 5

Mixed subjects design

A design in which at least one *factor* is *between-subjects* and at least one is *within-subjects*. This term is part of *ANOVA*

Chapter 1
Section 2

terminology.

Mode

The most common value in a sample of scores: a *measure of central tendency*. If a sample of scores has more than one mode SPSS shows the lowest value only.

Chapter 2
Section 8

Multiple regression

An inferential statistical procedure used to investigate linear relationships between three or more *variables*. It indicates the extent to which one variable can be explained or predicted by one or more of the other variables. (See also *regression*.)

Chapter 7

Nonparametric

A term used to denote:
1. nominal and ordinal *levels of measurement*;
2. data that may be measured on ratio or interval scales but do not meet the other assumptions (equality of *variance* and normality of distribution) underlying *parametric* statistical tests;
3. the *inferential statistical tests* used to analyse nonparametric data. Nonparametric statistics make use of rank order, either of scores or of the differences between scores, unlike parametric statistical tests.

Chapter 1
Sections 2
and 3

Chapter 3
Section 4

Options

Options in *dialogue boxes* can be set to request additional statistics or to control the appearance of *charts*.

Additionally, selecting **Options** from the **Edit** *menu item* allows you to set options that will be applied more generally.

Chapter 8
Section 2

Output window

See *Viewer window*.

Parametric

A term used to denote:

Chapter 1

1. ratio and interval *levels of measurement*;
2. data that are measured on one of those scales and also meet the two other requirements (equality of *variance* and normality of distribution) for parametric statistical tests;
3. the *inferential statistical tests* used to analyse parametric data. Parametric statistics make use of the actual values of scores in each sample, unlike *nonparametric* statistical tests.

Sections 2 and 3

Participant

People who take part in an experiment. Previously the word "subject" was used, and still is in many statistics books. The word "subject" is, universally we believe, still used to describe *ANOVA* experimental designs and analyses (e.g. " 2*2 within-subjects").

Participant irrelevant variable

Any *irrelevant variable* that is a property of the *participants* in an experiment. In text books the term subject irrelevant variables is often still used.

Chapter 1 Section 2

Pearson's r

An *inferential statistical test* of *correlation* used to analyse *parametric* data.

Chapter 4 Section 2

Pivot table

The name that SPSS gives to a table of results displayed in the *output viewer window*. The appearance of a pivot table can be altered for the purposes of presentation in a report

Chapter 8 Section 4

Planned comparisons

A group of statistical tests used to compare *conditions* from *ANOVA* designs, when the comparisons to be made were decided upon before data is collected. If used inappropriately, then the frequency of *Type 1 error* will increase. See also *unplanned comparisons*.

Chapter 6 Section 8

Print

The content, or a selection, of all SPSS windows can be printed by selecting **Print** from the **File** *menu item* while the appropriate window is open.

Chapter 8
Section 4

Quantitative research

In psychology today this term is used to describe research that requires *variable*s to be measured on any of the four *levels of measurement*, in contrast to qualitative research (not covered in this book).

Chapter 1
Section 2

Note that the term quantitative data is sometimes used in the literature to describe data measured on ratio, interval or ordinal scales, and the term qualitative data is then used to describe data measured with nominal scales.

Range

A *measure of dispersion*: the scores are put into rank order and then the lowest score is subtracted from the highest score.

Chapter 2
Section 8

Rank cases

An SPSS procedure by which a new *variable* containing ranks for the values in an existing variable can be produced.

Chapter 5
Section 8

Recode

An SPSS procedure by which the value/s in a *variable* can be changed into different value/s.

Chapter 5
Section 5

Regression

If two *variables* have been measured, as in a *correlation* design, then regression can be used to allow prediction of a participant's score on one variable from his or her score on the other variable. If three or more variables have been measured, then *multiple regression* can be used to analyse the data.

A regression line is the line drawn using the regression formula, and represents the "best fit" to the data points in a *scattergram*.

Chapter 4
Section 2

Related designs

A term that includes both *repeated measures* and *matched subjects designs*. This term is usually used for designs with two *levels* of one *independent variable*. Also see *within-subjects designs*.

Chapter 1
Section 2

Repeated measures design

An *experimental design* in which every *participant* takes part in both *levels* of the *independent variable*. It is a type of *related design*.

Chapter 1
Section 2

Scattergram

Sometimes called a scattergraph, and in SPSS it is called a scatterplot. A graph in which one point is plotted for each *case*, used to display the data whenever a test of *correlation* is carried out. A single point represents the value of the X-axis *variable* and the value of the Y-axis variable for a single case. See also *chart* and *interactive chart*.

Chapter 4
Section 2

Select cases

An SPSS procedure by which certain *cases* can be selected on the basis of the *values* in a *variable*; subsequent analyses will only be performed on the selected cases.

Chapter 5
Section 4

Significance level

The level of probability (p) that the results are due to chance, at which we reject the null *hypothesis* and accept the experimental hypothesis. By convention in psychology, p must be less than or equal to 0.05.

Situational irrelevant variable

Any *irrelevant variable* that is to do with the situation in which an experiment is carried out or with the experimenter.

Chapter 1
Section 2

Skewed data

If a data sample is not normally distributed but instead has a "tail"

Chapter 1

of *cases* that are **either** particularly low **or** particularly high compared to most of the scores, then the sample is said to be skewed. Such a sample does not meet the assumption of normality of distribution (see *parametric*).

Section 3

Sort cases

An SPSS procedure by which the *cases* in the *data window* can be sorted into a desired order based on the values of one or more *variables*.

Chapter 5
Section 2

Spearman's rho

An *inferential statistical test* of *correlation* used to analyse *nonparametric* data.

Chapter 4
Section 2

Split

An SPSS procedure by which the *cases* in the *data window* are split into groups on the basis of the values in a *grouping variable*; subsequent analyses will be performed separately for each group.

Chapter 5
Section 3

Standard deviation

A *measure of dispersion*: it indicates the average, or standard, deviation of scores away from the *mean*. SPSS uses N-1, not N, as the denominator, giving the standard deviation for the sample rather than for the population.

Chapter 2
Section 8

Standard error

A *measure of dispersion*: its value is equal to the *standard deviation* divided by the square root of N. In this sense the full name is "standard error of the mean".

Chapter 2
Section 8

(The "standard error of differences between means" is obtained as part of calculations for the *t-test*; the "standard error of the estimate" is used in regression.)

Statistics

A general term for procedures for summarising or displaying data

Chapter 1

(*descriptive statistics*) and for analysing data (*inferential statistical tests*).

Section 3

Syntax

The programme language commands that underlie the instructions that, in Windows, you give to SPSS by means of the *dialogue boxes*. Only advanced users will need to use syntax. Syntax commands may appear in the *output window* (depending on the settings for SPSS on your PC). Syntax commands can be pasted into and edited in the *syntax window*.

Chapter 8
Section 1

Syntax window

The syntax editor window: a window in SPSS that shows *syntax*. This window does not normally appear. Only advanced users will ever need it.

Chapter 8
Section 1

t-test

An *inferential statistical test* used to analyse *parametric* data from *two-sample* designs. There are two versions: the independent *t*-test for *independent groups design*s, and the paired *t*-test for *related designs*.

Chapter 3
Sections
1 – 3

Two-sample designs

Experimental designs with two *level*s of one *independent variable*. Also see *independent groups design* and *related design*.

Chapter 3

Type 1 error

The situation in which the experimental *hypothesis* is accepted in error. If the *significance level* is set at 0.05 (as it is in Psychology), then even with an excellent experimental design, a Type 1 error will occur on one in 20 occasions, on average. If the significance level is reduced then the chance of Type 1 errors will fall, but the chance of *Type 2 errors* will rise. If more than one *inferential statistical test* is carried out on the data from one experiment, then the chance of Type 1 errors will increase. See also *planned* and *unplanned comparisons*.

Chapter 6
Section 8

Type 2 error

The situation in which the experimental *hypothesis* is rejected in error. The frequency of occurrence depends partly on the *significance level* and partly on the power of the *inferential statistical test*. (The concept of "power" is beyond the scope of this book, but it is briefly explained in Chapter 1 Section 3 and Chapter 3 Section 4.)

Unplanned comparisons

A group of *inferential statistical tests* that may be used to make all of the possible comparisons between *condition*s from *ANOVA* designs, as they control for the increased chance of obtaining *Type 1 errors*. See also *planned comparisons*.

Chapter 6
Section 8

Value label

The label that you can give to a value in an SPSS *variable* when you define the variable. It should always be used for nominal *level of measurement* (including values in a *grouping variable*). It can contain spaces, and can be up to 60 characters, although it is best to use a few words at most. Value labels are printed in *output*, and help you to interpret it.

Chapter 2
Section 2

Variable

In *experimental design*, anything that varies; that can have different values at different times or for different *cases*. See also *confounding variable*, *dependent variable*, *independent variable*, *irrelevant variable*.

Chapter 1
Section 2

In SPSS, the contents of a single column in the *data window*.

Chapter 2
Section 2

Variable label

The label that you can give to an SPSS *variable* when you define it. It can contain spaces, and can be very long, although a few words is best. When you put the cursor on the variable name in the data window, SPSS will show the variable label. Also, the variable label is printed in *output*, and often is shown in *dialogue boxes*.

Chapter 2
Section 2

Variable name

The name of eight or fewer characters that you give to an SPSS *variable* when you define it. It will appear at the top of the column in the *data window*, and may appear in the *output*.

Variance

A *measure of dispersion*: it is equal to the square of the *standard deviation*. Equality of variance between the samples is one of the requirements for using *parametric* statistical tests. SPSS will test for equality of variance (for example, when performing the independent *t-test*). A rule-of-thumb is that the larger variance should be no greater than three times the smaller variance.

Viewer window

The window in SPSS that displays the output from any statistical procedure that you have requested. Also referred to as the output window.

Wilcoxon matched-pairs signed-ranks test

An *inferential statistical test* used to analyse *nonparametric* data from *two-sample related designs*.

Within-subjects design

A design with one or more *factors* when every *participant* takes part in all *levels* of all factors (or when *matched subjects* take part in each level). This term is part of *ANOVA* terminology. Also see *repeated measures design* and *related designs*. If you have a design with two or more factors, each within–subjects, but each participant only takes part in the levels for one factor, then that cannot be analysed as a multi-way within-subjects ANOVA. It must be analysed as a series of one-way within-subjects ANOVAs or, if appropriate, as a mixed design counting the different factors as different levels of one factor.

References

Howell, D.C. (1987). *Statistical Methods for Psychology*, 2nd edition. Boston, Massachusetts: PWS-Kent.

Howell, D.C. (1992). *Statistical Methods for Psychology*, 3rd edition. Belmont, California: Duxbury Press.

Howell, D.C. (1997). *Statistical Methods for Psychology*, 4th edition. Belmont, California: Duxbury Press.

Kemp R.I., McManus, I. C. and Pigott, T. (1990). Sensitivity to the displacement of facial features in negative and inverted images. *Perception*, **19**, 531-543.

Mason, R.J., Snelgar, R.S., Foster, D.H., Heron, J.R. and Jones, R.E. (1982). Abnormalities of chromatic and luminance critical flicker frequency in multiple sclerosis. *Investigative Ophthalmology & Visual Science*, **23**, 246-252.

Newlands, P. (1997). *Eyewitness Interviewing: Does the cognitive interview fit the bill?* Unpublished PhD Thesis, University of Westminster, London.

Siegel, S. and Castellan, N.J. (1988). *Nonparametric Statistics for the Behavioral Sciences*, 2nd edition. New York: McGraw-Hill.

Tabachnick, B.G. and Fidell, L.S. (1989). *Using Multivariate Statistics*, 2nd edition. New York: HarperCollins.

Towell[*], N., Burton, A. and Burton, E. (1994). The effects of two matched memory tasks on concurrent finger tapping. *Neuropsychologia, **32**, 125-129.

Towell[*], N., Kemp, R. and Pike, G. (1996). The effects of witness identity masking on memory and person perception. *Psychology, Crime and Law*, **2**, 333-346.

[*] Nicola Brace was previously known as Nicoal Towell

Appendix: Data files

These data files are also available to download from the Internet (www.macmillan-press.co.uk/psychology/brace). We recommend you enter the first few data files to become skilled at entering data. You can then download the remaining files if you wish.

DATA FOR INDEPENDENT *T*-TEST

GROUP 1 = mnemonic condition 2 = no mnemonic condition	SCORE
1	11
1	14
1	17
1	18
1	18
1	18
1	19
1	20
1	20
1	20
1	20
2	9
2	10
2	12
2	12
2	14
2	14
2	15
2	16
2	19
2	20

DATA FOR PAIRED *T*-TEST

LARGE SIZE DIFFERENCE	SMALL SIZE DIFFERENCE
936	878
923	1005
896	1010
1241	1365
1278	1422
871	1198
1360	1576
733	896
941	1573
1077	1261
1438	2237
1099	1325
1253	1591
1930	2742
1260	1357
1271	1963

DATA FOR MANN–WHITNEY TEST

SEX 1 = male 2 = female	RATING
1	4
1	6
1	5
1	8
1	5
1	2
1	4
1	4
1	5
1	7
1	5
1	4
1	3
1	3
1	5
1	3
1	3
1	8
1	6
1	4
2	4
2	2
2	7
2	4
2	6
2	7
2	5
2	2
2	6
2	6
2	6
2	6
2	3
2	5
2	7

SEX 1 = male 2 = female	RATING
2	4
2	6
2	6
2	7
2	8

DATA FOR WILCOXON TEST

E-FIT RATING 1 (from memory)	E-FIT RATING 2 (from photograph)
3	6
3	4
3	5
5	6
2	3
4	3
5	3
5	3
4	3
3	3
2	3
6	6
5	3
4	3
3	3
3	5
4	5
3	2
4	5
3	5
3	2
5	6
3	4
4	3
4	4
4	2
4	5
3	3
5	3
4	3
3	2
3	3
6	4
3	3
3	2
3	3

E-FIT RATING 1 (from memory)	E-FIT RATING 2 (from photograph)
2	4
2	5
5	6
3	5
6	4
2	3
5	5
4	2
3	5
3	2
5	6
4	2

DATA FOR CHI-SQUARE

BACKGROUND 1 = Asian 2 = Caucasian 3 = other	MOTHER'S EMPLOYMENT 1 = full time 2 = none 3 = part time	SCHOOL 1 = comprehensive 2 = private	TENDENCY TO ANOREXIA 1 = high 2 = low
2	1	1	1
2	1	1	1
2	1	1	1
2	3	1	1
2	3	2	1
2	3	2	1
2	2	2	1
2	2	2	1
2	2	2	1
2	1	2	1
2	1	2	1
2	1	2	1
2	3	2	1
2	3	2	1
2	3	2	1
2	3	2	1
2	2	2	1
2	2	2	1
2	2	2	1
2	2	2	1
2	3	2	1
2	3	2	1
1	3	2	1
1	1	2	1
1	1	2	1
1	1	2	1
3	2	2	1
3	3	2	1
3	2	2	1
3	2	2	1
3	1	2	1
3	1	2	1
3	1	2	1
3	1	2	1
3	1	2	1

Table continued overleaf.

BACKGROUND	MOTHER'S EMPLOYMENT	SCHOOL	TENDENCY TO ANOREXIA
1 = Asian 2 = Caucasian 3 = other	1 = full time 2 = none 3 = part time	1 = comprehensive 2 = private	1 = high 2 = low
3	2	2	1
3	2	2	1
3	2	2	1
2	2	1	2
2	1	1	2
2	1	1	2
2	3	1	2
2	3	1	2
2	2	1	2
2	2	1	2
2	2	1	2
2	2	1	2
2	3	1	2
2	3	1	2
2	3	1	2
2	3	1	2
2	3	1	2
2	3	1	2
2	3	1	2
2	3	1	2
2	2	1	2
2	2	1	2
2	2	1	2
2	3	1	2
2	3	1	2
2	2	1	2
2	2	1	2
2	2	1	2
2	2	1	2
2	3	1	2
2	1	1	2
2	1	1	2
2	1	2	2
2	1	2	2
2	1	2	2
2	1	2	2

Table continued overleaf.

BACKGROUND 1 = Asian 2 = Caucasian 3 = other	MOTHER'S EMPLOYMENT 1 = full time 2 = none 3 = part time	SCHOOL 1 = comprehensive 2 = private	TENDENCY TO ANOREXIA 1 = high 2 = low
2	1	2	2
2	1	2	2
2	1	2	2
1	1	2	2
1	1	2	2
3	1	2	2
3	1	2	2
3	1	2	2
3	1	2	2

DATA FOR PEARSON'S CORRELATION

AGE (in years)	CFF
41	34.9
43	30.5
25	35.75
42	32.3
51	28.0
27	42.2
27	35.1
48	33.5
58	25.0
52	31.0
58	23.2
50	26.8
44	32.0
53	29.3
26	35.9
65	30.5
35	31.9
29	32.0
25	39.9
49	33.0

DATA FOR SPEARMAN'S CORRELATION

CONFI-DENCE	BELIEVA-BILITY	ATTRACT-IVENESS
4	4	2
4	3	3
4	6	4
4	6	4
4	4	3
4	4	4
4	3	2
5	5	4
4	4	3
6	5	4
4	6	4
4	5	5
4	4	3
6	5	4
5	5	4
4	5	3
2	4	3
6	4	4
3	5	3
3	3	3
2	5	5
5	5	4
5	6	4
5	4	4
4	5	4
5	5	4
5	5	4
4	4	5
4	4	4
3	5	4
5	6	4
5	5	4
1	5	3
5	5	4
5	5	4
5	6	4
5	5	5
4	5	4

CONFI-DENCE	BELIEVA-BILITY	ATTRACT-IVENESS
4	5	4
4	5	4
5	5	4
4	5	4
5	5	3
4	4	2
5	6	5
4	5	3
6	5	2
3	5	4
3	5	4
4	4	3
4	3	3
6	6	4
3	5	2
4	4	3
5	5	4
3	1	3
5	6	4
5	5	4
4	5	4
4	4	4
6	1	1
5	5	4
5	5	4
6	6	5
5	5	3
6	6	5
5	5	2
2	4	4
3	4	4
3	4	4
4	4	4
4	5	4
5	5	4
5	5	3
3	4	4

Data continued overleaf

CONFI-DENCE	BELIEVA-BILITY	ATTRACT-IVENESS
2	3	5
6	5	5
4	5	3
5	4	4
4	5	4
4	5	4
4	4	4
4	4	4
4	5	4
4	5	5
5	4	4
4	6	4
5	5	3
6	5	4

DATA FOR ONE-WAY BETWEEN-SUBJECTS ANOVA

PRESENTATION CONDITION 1 = unmasked 2 = greyblob 3 = pixelated 4 = negated.	MEMORY
1	68
1	75
1	65
1	69
1	70
1	72
1	65
1	66
1	58
1	59
2	56
2	58
2	59
2	54
2	61
2	54
2	57
2	58
2	48
2	52
3	58
3	59
3	62
3	63
3	52
3	53
3	55
3	56
3	68
3	51
4	69
4	70

PRESENTATION CONDITION 1 = unmasked 2 = greyblob 3 = pixelated 4 = negated.	MEMORY
4	67
4	65
4	72
4	74
4	68
4	63
4	66
4	58

DATA FOR TWO-WAY BETWEEN-SUBJECTS DESIGN

SEX DIFF. 1 = same sex as defendant 2 = opposite sex as defendant	ATTRAC-TIVENESS 1 = attractive 2= unattractive 3 = no picture	SEN-TENCE (in years)
1	1	6
1	1	8
1	1	7
1	1	9
1	1	5
1	1	7
1	1	10
1	1	9
1	1	9
1	1	5
2	1	5
2	1	11
2	1	7
2	1	5
2	1	8
2	1	5
2	1	9
2	1	10
2	1	10
2	1	5
1	2	7
1	2	9
1	2	12
1	2	14
1	2	11
1	2	11
1	2	9
1	2	12
1	2	13
1	2	14

SEX DIFF. 1 = same sex as defendant 2 = opposite sex as defendant	ATTRAC-TIVENESS 1 = attractive 2= unattractive 3 = no picture	SEN-TENCE (in years)
2	2	8
2	2	9
2	2	9
2	2	13
2	2	11
2	2	9
2	2	10
2	2	13
2	2	13
2	2	8
1	3	13
1	3	15
1	3	16
1	3	15
1	3	14
1	3	16
1	3	14
1	3	13
1	3	13
1	3	16
2	3	12
2	3	12
2	3	15
2	3	14
2	3	16
2	3	13
2	3	12
2	3	12
2	3	13
2	3	16

DATA FOR ONE-WAY WITHIN-SUBJECTS ANOVA

INCONGRUENT	CONGRUENT	NEUTRAL
13	9	11
13	10	12
16	9	13
13	8	9
14	9	10
15	10	11
14	8	12
13	9	10
16	8	12
17	9	11

DATA FOR TWO-WAY WITHIN-SUBJECTS ANOVA

h1s2 right hand/word	h1s1 right hand/position	h2s2 left hand/word	h2s1 left hand/position
-1.10	-5.52	1.66	0
11.11	1.48	22.96	4.10
-4.19	2.40	4.49	8.14
6.74	13.78	5.57	11.78
-4.91	-.61	-2.45	2.86
11.11	8.11	9.61	3.85
7.49	8.14	5.21	5.97
1.74	4.07	0	9.66
-3.47	-4.10	4.73	.34
6.04	7.09	1.84	1.66
6.51	9.47	6.21	7.58
7.02	19.06	12.04	17.27
5.91	15.68	.77	5.40
.57	1.15	4.31	3.64
.60	3.61	2.71	-2.07
.29	11.44	1.47	14.03
1.75	4.09	-.88	.35
9.87	9.87	14.4	17.82
1.02	3.73	3.73	-.36
8.27	4.53	10.93	2.05
.61	14.55	-6.06	7.95
2.84	-1.42	2.84	2.13
8.90	17.44	10.32	10.04
3.16	3.80	1.58	2.39

DATA FOR THREE-WAY MIXED ANOVA

GROUP 1 = unprimed 2 = primed	n1o1 normal/upright	n2o1 negative/upright	n1o2 normal/inverted	n2o2 negative/inverted
2	54.17	70.83	58.33	54.17
2	62.5	75	62.5	45.83
2	66.67	58.33	50	70.83
2	66.67	83.33	54.17	66.67
2	83.33	66.67	75	62.5
2	66.67	66.67	83.33	66.67
2	70.83	66.67	70.83	62.5
2	66.67	58.33	75	66.67
2	79.17	75	83.33	66.67
2	62.5	75	87.5	79.17
2	70.83	75	70.83	54.17
2	54.17	83.33	54.17	62.5
2	58.33	62.5	54.17	62.5
2	66.67	79.17	58.33	75
2	70.83	79.17	66.67	75
2	66.67	58.33	58.33	62.5
2	62.5	75	75	54.17
2	75	70.83	79.17	66.67
2	41.67	66.67	66.67	66.67
2	58.33	66.67	58.33	58.33
2	45.83	62.5	58.33	66.67
2	70.83	70.83	58.33	66.67
2	83.33	70.83	79.17	62.5
1	66.67	70.83	83.33	70.83
1	66.67	58.33	54.17	79.17
1	79.17	62.5	75	75
1	62.5	79.17	62.5	66.67
1	70.83	58.33	50	41.67
1	62.5	62.5	50	62.5
1	62.5	58.33	54.17	66.67
1	66.67	83.33	79.17	75
1	62.5	70.83	75	66.67

Table continued overleaf.

GROUP 1 = unprimed 2 = primed	n1o1 normal/upright	n2o1 negative/upright	n1o2 normal/inverted	n2o2 negative/inverted
1	70.83	66.67	58.33	58.33
1	54.17	62.5	70.83	70.83
1	58.33	79.17	70.83	58.33
1	62.5	66.67	58.33	66.67
1	62.5	66.67	70.83	62.5
1	66.67	66.67	79.17	75
1	50	62.5	54.17	75
1	79.17	75	75	79.17
1	58.33	45.83	54.17	70.83
1	45.83	41.67	58.33	50
1	83.33	79.17	79.17	79.17
1	54.17	58.33	54.17	62.5
1	70.83	66.67	66.67	70.83
1	58.33	70.83	83.33	58.33
1	66.67	45.83	50	62.5
1	62.5	62.5	54.17	54.17
1	66.67	45.83	58.33	50
1	66.67	75	75	58.33
1	75	79.17	66.67	62.5
1	58.33	58.33	37.5	70.83
1	54.17	54.17	75	75
1	66.67	58.33	75	70.83
1	66.67	58.33	75	58.33
1	70.83	62.5	70.83	50
1	75	70.83	62.5	70.83
1	62.5	70.83	79.17	66.67
1	70.83	62.5	75	70.83
1	58.33	58.33	50	54.17
1	58.33	66.67	62.5	58.33

DATA FOR KRUSKAL–WALLIS AND FRIEDMAN

CONDITION 1 = cognitive int. 2 = visualisation 3 = standard int.	BEFORE INTERVIEW CONFIDENCE	AFTER INTERVIEW CONFIDENCE	IDENTIFICATION CONFIDENCE
1	2	4	4
1	3	3	3
1	2	4	4
1	2	2	4
1	3	3	4
1	1	5	2
1	2	4	4
1	1	3	2
1	2	4	4
1	2	6	4
1	1	4	4
1	1	4	4
1	2	3	3
1	1	4	4
1	2	4	6
1	2	3	5
1	1	4	3
1	2	5	3
1	2	3	5
1	1	4	1
2	1	2	3
2	2	1	6
2	1	2	4
2	3	2	4
2	1	1	7
2	2	2	4
2	2	1	3
2	1	3	3
2	2	1	5
2	3	2	6
2	2	2	5
2	1	1	6
2	1	2	4
2	1	3	4
2	3	1	3
2	2	2	4

Table continued overleaf.

CONDITION 1 = cognitive int. 2 = visualisation 3 = standard int.	BEFORE INTERVIEW CONFIDENCE	AFTER INTERVIEW CONFIDENCE	IDENTIFICATION CONFIDENCE
2	1	1	6
2	3	2	4
2	1	1	1
2	3	1	4
3	1	3	5
3	2	3	5
3	1	4	3
3	2	3	4
3	2	2	3
3	1	4	1
3	2	3	5
3	2	4	2
3	1	3	3
3	3	3	5
3	1	3	4
3	1	2	3
3	2	4	6
3	2	4	2
3	1	6	6
3	2	2	1
3	2	4	5
3	2	4	4
3	3	5	5
3	3	4	6

DATA FOR MULTIPLE REGRESSION

AGE (in months)	READING AGE (in months)	STANDARDISED READING SCORE	STANDARDISED SPELLING SCORE	% CORRECT SPELLING
93	71	80	104	67
81	76	95		44
84	88	104	107	40
93	71	71	105	50
87	72	86	112	63
92	71	81	100	33
88	83	96	106	48
87	71	75	106	33
86	72	86	103	31
92	97	105	101	58
86	38	131	125	94
83	71	79	104	23
83	71	86	95	31
82	108	125	127	92
86	113	121	122	81
83	99	115		46
92	108	114	114	83
83	90	106	126	75
92	97	105	106	85
82	90	109	110	46
88	96	110	118	71
87	79	93		31
91	71	80		
92	95	102	119	79
85	114	125	120	75
92	72	82	96	44
81	84	103	120	67
97	127	119	118	90
100	95	95	107	77
96	71	79	101	29
95	147	127	141	96
94	114	117	126	92
95	71	71	85	23
96	76	83	109	77
100	87	88	118	83
102	71	69	81	38
93	98	105	104	63
95	114	114	127	94
95	71	79		31
99	83	84	94	52
97	71	79	100	44
100	71	74	75	25
93	77	85	92	42
95	95	99	123	83
101	147	121	128	98

Table continued overleaf.

AGE (in months)	READING AGE (in months)	STANDARDISED READING SCORE	STANDARDISED SPELLING SCORE	% CORRECT SPELLING
105	88	84	76	23
107	120	105	106	67
106	92	87	114	81
112	71	69	76	23
97	71	76	92	46
104	82	80	94	44
102	102	100	100	50